Olympics in Athens 1896

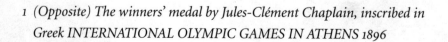

1 (Opposite) The winners' medal by Jules-Clément Chaplain, inscribed in Greek INTERNATIONAL OLYMPIC GAMES IN ATHENS 1896

Olympics in Athens 1896

The Invention of the Modern Olympic Games

Michael Llewellyn Smith

P

PROFILE BOOKS

First published in Great Britain in 2004 by
Profile Books Ltd
58A Hatton Garden
London ECIN 8LX
www.profilebooks.co.uk

1 3 5 7 9 10 8 6 4 2

Typeset in Minion by MacGuru Ltd
info@macguru.org.uk

Printed and bound in Great Britain by
Clays, Bungay, Suffolk

A CIP catalogue record for this book is available from the British Library.

ISBN 1 86197 342 X

CONTENTS

ILLUSTRATIONS

AUTHOR'S NOTE

This book presents the 1896 Olympic Games, the first of the modern era, in their Greek context, as an aspect of the 'Europeanization' of Greece.

I have had help from a number of people and institutions. Professors Roderick Beaton, Paul Cartledge, Richard Clogg and Peter Mackridge commented on parts of the typescript. Ann Eldridge discussed the Athens Olympics with me on a number of occasions, and made available her unpublished MA dissertation, *The Use of Classical Symbolism and Ritual in the Revival of the Olympic Games in Athens, 1896*. Stratis Stratigis, who for a time was President of the Athens Organizing Committee (ATHOC) for the 2004 games, lent me his father's copy of the special edition *Greece at the 1896 Olympic Games*, published in 1896 by Estia for the *Acropolis* newspaper. John Leatham, who died as this book was going to press, showed me various texts including his translation, and Richard Witt's, of Palamas's Olympic hymn. Eleana Yalouri showed me her forthcoming work on American and Greek approaches to the 1896 Games. Apostolos Doxiadis, great-grandson of Stathis Lampsas, owner of the Grande Bretagne Hotel, advised me on the involvement of the hotel in the 1896 events.

Princeton University's Program in Hellenic Studies offered me a visiting fellowship for three months in early 2002, and I am grateful to its

Director, Dimitri Gondicas. I found stimulation in the Program's weekly workshops on many aspects of Hellenism, and in the seminar of the King's College London Department of Byzantine and Modern Greek Studies.

I am grateful to the Directors, Archivists and Librarians of the British School at Athens, the Constantine G. Karamanlis Foundation, the Firestone Library at Princeton University, the Gennadius Library at Athens, the Greek Literary and Historical Archive (ELIA) in Athens, the Library at King's College London, the London Library and the National Library of Greece; and in particular to Manos Haritatos, Christina Varda and Maria Beneki at ELIA; Ekaterini Kordouli, Curator of the Department of Manuscripts of the National Library of Greece; Professor Constantine Svolopoulos, Director, and Marietta Minotos, Head of the Historical Archive of the Constantine G. Karamanlis Foundation. For advice and help with photographs of nineteenth-century Athens and the games I am grateful to Fani Constantinou, Director, and Aliki Tsirgialou of the Photographic Archive of the Banaki Museum; to Ioannnis Mazarakis-Ainian, General Secretary of the Historical and Ethnological Society of Greece, and Niki Markasiotou of the Photographic Archive of the National Historical Museum; and to Manos Haritatos, Director of ELIA. Ioannnis Lambakis kindly allowed me to reproduce his fine photograph of the picnic at Daphni. Helen Cromarty of the Wenlock Olympian Society gave helpful advice and provided the photograph of William Penny Brookes and the Wenlock Games.

I am grateful to Professors John Koumoulides, Harry J. Psomiades, and Tom Gallant for invitations to lecture on the Olympics at Ball State University, Muncie Indiana, Queens University New York, and in Toronto at the 2003 symposium of the Modern Greek Studies Association; and also to Durham University Hellenic Society, Swan Hellenic, and the Anglo-Hellenic League, for which I have lectured.

A number of friends in Greece have helped me to complete this book by putting me up at various times, and in other ways. They include Paul and Ariane Condellis, George and Kaity David, Costas Petropoulos and

Anthy Doxiades, Peter and Aline Haritatos, and James and Christina Whitley. I thank them all. I thank also Peter Carson and his colleagues at Profile Books for their enthusiasm and help.

My system of transliteration of Greek words is a mixed one, designed to make the book easy to read. I use Latinised forms of well-known ancient Greek names (Thucydides not Thoukydides) where they seem easier to western European and American readers. In transliterating modern Greek I compromise between the phonetic and the customary (so Eleftherios, not Eleutherios, but Dimitrios not Dhimitrios).

Greece followed the so-called Old Style, Gregorian calendar, twelve days ahead of the western calendar, in 1896. I have normally given dates in the new western style, and designated the Old Style 'o.s.' where I have used it. But I am bound to have made some mistakes.

Michael Llewellyn Smith
Childrey

INTRODUCTION

On 5 April 1896, James B. Connolly of the Suffolk Athletic Club, Boston, projected himself 13 metres and 71 centimetres through the Attic air in the newly restored Panathenaic Stadium of Athens, in the hop, step and jump or triple jump, and became the first Olympic victor for more than 1,500 years; the first in fact since a boy called Zopyros from Athens, who won the boys' boxing and *pankration* (a kind of mixed boxing and all-in wrestling) at one of the last recorded games at Olympia, in 385 AD. These were the 291st games of the four-year cycle which began in 776 BC. The dream of Pierre Frédy, Baron de Coubertin, had come true. The revival of the Olympic Games was under way.

The way in which Connolly won charmingly illustrates the unformed state of international athletics at the time. There were no fixed rules on the required style. Connolly made two hops on his right foot and then jumped. The French runner-up, Alexandre Tufferi, made a hop, step and jump. The Greek third, Ioannis Persakis, apparently took two steps and a jump. But the rule-makers were waiting in the wings, to standardise sport.

On 13 August 2004, doves will be released to mark the 28th Olympiad of the modern era. In fact these will be the 25th summer Olympic Games of our era – 26th if you include Athens 1906, which officially but unfairly does not count, for reasons which will become clear. It will be a climactic moment, for which the Greek government and the Greek Olympic Committee have been preparing for seven years. With the exception of the settlement of one and a half million refugees from Asia Minor in the 1920s, the games are the largest peacetime national effort of planning, construction, preparation and execution which Greece has ever undertaken. The efforts of the organisers are regarded by the Greek people with a blend of patriotic sentiment, sceptical amusement, and an eye for the money-making opportunity. We shall know after August 2004 how well they have succeeded.

Greece has been through it twice before: in 1896, at the first Olympic Games of the modern era, and in 1906. The Olympic Games, and Greece, and Athens, have changed too much for there to be many practical lessons from those earlier games which are relevant today. But the story of 1896 is still illuminating, both of the state of Greek society at the close of the nineteenth century, and of the phenomenal growth of sport as a leisure pursuit and mass spectacle in the twentieth. Besides, the origins of a great institution such as the modern Olympics are always interesting, and (as with the ancient Olympics) always liable to generate myths which need untangling.

This story moves from Athens, the young capital of the new Greek state, to Much Wenlock in Shropshire, the Rugby School of Dr Arnold, Paris of the second Empire, Olympia in the Peloponnese, Princeton University, and back to Athens of the 1890s. Though Greece was viewed by some western Europeans as a comic Ruritania or toy kingdom, Athens in 1896 was a young capital city of charm, developing a European identity and a modernised economy. The Greeks were busily recreating their own culture, social arrangements and political presence, of limited independence because of the dominant position of the Great Powers which had presided over the birth of the independent

Greek state. One of the motors driving Greek politics was the 'national question' of extending the frontiers of the Greek kingdom. From time to time Britain and France would intervene and blockade Greek ports. From time to time the state was threatened with bankruptcy. It actually went bankrupt in 1893, a development which almost scuppered the Olympic Games.

The story brings together a French aristocrat fascinated by the British public school system and British notions of amateurism and fair play; a German scholar who revealed to the world what lay under the silt at ancient Olympia; a Greek translator of Shakespeare and best-selling novelist who became the first President of the International Olympic Committee; a Greek King who was assassinated by a madman in Salonica in 1913; a Crown Prince who led his country's armies to humiliating defeat by the Turks in 1897 and then to brilliant victory over the Turkish armies in the Balkan Wars, and was later, as King, forced into exile by Britain and France during the Great War; a great Greek statesman who disapproved of the games as an expensive frippery, was out-manoeuvred, and died in exile while the games were taking place; a farmer who won the first Olympic marathon and subsequently acquired a monopoly on the supply of fresh water from the springs of Maroussi to the thirsty citizens of downtown Athens. Among the spectators was the observant young French author, monarchist and anti-democrat Charles Maurras, who went on to found l'Action française.

The modern Olympic Games have accumulated so much by way of ritual, history, commercial interest and national involvement that it is refreshing to look back to a time when everything was new and most issues were still to be decided. In the games of 1896 we can trace the origins of some of today's rituals but we find little of today's commercial interest, nor the technical proficiency and dedicated mental and physical preparation of today's athletes. This was a different and more casual world, where an English visitor holidaying in Athens could enter the lawn tennis competition just for the sport, and win it, and an American student could pick up a discarded discus in the stadium the day before the games, throw it a few times, decide to enter for the discus on the morrow; and defeat his practised Greek opponents.

Then as now, the games were seen as an instrument of national propaganda, and were therefore an object of politics. The 1896 games were to be the means both of impressing the outside world and of raising national morale. Then as now, the games were seen as a national challenge, a test of the maturity and efficiency of the Hellenic state. The perception of challenge was an effect of the relationship of dependency between Greece and the Great Powers of nineteenth-century Europe. In the changed circumstances of today, the sense among Greeks that the country has to prove itself still remains strong. That is why the Greeks themselves will scrutinise the performance of the Greek state and its organs so closely at the 2004 games.

The 1896 games were a sign of the growing 'Europeanness' of Greek society and institutions. They were an aspect of modernity, though closely related to antiquity and dependent on it for most of their allure. There are ironies in these conjunctions. Athletics were a modern cult. They grew in the nineteenth century, especially in Britain, the nurse of modern sports, in a complex relationship to industrial society, the desire of individuals to control their use of leisure, and a growing demand for mass entertainment.[1] The growth of sports was not a simple product of greater leisure opportunities: the big reductions in the working week came later, in the twentieth century.

In taking to sports ahead of her Balkan neighbours and Ottoman Turkey, Greece was borrowing one more feature of the industrialised west. In her own terms, she was joining the 'civilised world' in this pursuit. Athens would not have been chosen – or if chosen would have failed in the task – if Greece had not been developing rapidly as a European nation state, with accommodation, transport, the appurtenances of civilisation and a rudimentary infrastructure for athletic sports. But at the same time Greece was drawing on the stock of antiquarian lore in hosting the revived Olympics. They would not have taken place at

Athens but for the fact that the ancient games had taken place in Greece, and were a part of the classical heritage which inspired western European and North American education, and had now become an important part of the identity of the Greek nation and state. The fascination of the revived Olympic Games lies in the unique blend of ancient and modern and the tensions between them, which were resolved mainly in favour of the modern.

It was ironic that Harilaos Tricoupis, the Greek Prime Minister of the 1880s and 90s, who was the great moderniser and European of the second half of the nineteenth century, regarded the Olympic project as a frivolity which Greece could not afford; whereas the man subsequently reviled as a reactionary in liberal western Europe, Crown Prince, later King, Constantine, through his enthusiasm and his perseverance made the games happen. Constantine was thus one of the founders of the modern Olympic movement. The European network of contacts of the Greek royal family helped, not least in attracting Coubertin, who was a snob as well as an aristocrat.

The nature and outcome of the games were contested. For the Greeks they were a national project. Constantine and his father King George saw them through the eyes of Greek nationalists and members of the club of European royalty. They wanted Greece to have the games and the international contacts and respectability that came with them. They wanted to show that Greece held her place among the civilised nations, and that the Greeks of 1896 were worthy of their illustrious 'ancestors'. They wanted a share in the glory of the games, which were popular. Constantine may also have seen in the development of Greek sports a benefit for the armed forces, with which, as a trained professional officer, he was closely identified. Seeing these Olympic Games through Greek eyes, he and his father wanted the games to be permanently located in Greece. The Greek roots of the Glucksberg dynasty, which had come to Greece only in 1863, were shallow; but of the Greek monarchs of this dynasty it was Constantine who was seen by his people as being most closely identified with his country. He was a charismatic figure who commanded the devotion of a large part of the population.

Pierre de Coubertin, on the other hand, had no particular interest in the modern Greek state and its progress. He cultivated a philhellenism rooted in admiration for ancient Greece and what he took to be its values. But these values, and the lure of Olympia and the Greek ideal, were instruments in Coubertin's purpose of establishing a modern international sporting festival of youth, named after Olympia, a travelling circus that would move from one great city of the world to another. His internationalist vision was idealistic; but he knew exactly what he wanted and was formidably effective at getting it. In the Olympic documents associated with Coubertin you find the phrase 'in conformity with modern conditions' constantly attached as the necessary condition of the revival of the Olympic Games. Coubertin was a modernist, not an antiquarian, so far as the sporting content of the games went. Yet he was also a master of the use of antiquarian rhetoric and symbol to mobilise support for his ideas.

Given their different assumptions about the nature of the games, it is not surprising that Coubertin's vision clashed with that of Constantine and the Greeks.

But what were Coubertin's modern sporting requirements for the games? There were divergent traditions of sport in different countries, some hostile to others. There were nationalist rivalries between countries, in particular Germany and France. And there were disputes and struggles for turf within countries between the proliferating clubs and federations. Coubertin had his own, strong, views as to the relative merits of particular sporting traditions. He favoured Anglo-Saxon track and field athletics, English ball games, and a mixture of other sports such as fencing and wrestling. He was suspicious of gymnastics, particularly when they were carried out with an excess of militaristic discipline and over-complicated apparatus. But he was ready to suppress these views, or prejudices, in the interests of a general agreement on the contents of the new Olympic institution. The result was an international mixture of sports capable of enlisting Germans and Swedes as well as Americans, British and French.

The 1896 games were a success. They helped to present Greece and Greek achievement to Europe and to America in a favourable light. They encouraged, in a modest way, the newish practice of tourism. But they were followed within a year by a disastrous war against Turkey which led to the demoralisation of the Greek nation and its armed forces. A number of those who organised the 1896 Olympics had their share in the responsibility for this war.

The 1906 games, also held in Athens, were again a success, and a bigger and better show than the games of 1896. Whether or not they should be termed Olympic Games – the title was refused them by Coubertin and the International Olympic Committee – they are widely held to have saved the young and fragile Olympic movement after the disappointing Games of Paris (1900) and St Louis (1904), which suffered from being associated with world exhibitions. The 1906 games were the nearest Greece came to making good the claim that the games should have a permanent Greek home. If Greece had succeeded in holding another round of games in 1910, her four-yearly cycle might have been established and resumed after the Great War. But the turbulent times of 1910 did not allow for games in Athens and the chance was lost. Constantine Karamanlis's tenacious attempts to put forward Olympia as a permanent home for the Olympics in the 1970s and 80s were not successful because by then the momentum of the four-year cycle from country to country was unstoppable. But, for once at least, the games will return to Athens in 2004.

The 2004 games are altogether a bigger challenge for Greece, economic, organisational, and in security matters, than the early games of 1896 and 1906. The contrast shows us how far the games have come, developing from an idealistic late nineteenth-century internationalist movement into a global event, mixing sport, big business, politics, marketing and mass ritual for spectators and the global audience of television. And yet, as we shall see in Athens, this unique medley is still tenuously connected to the Olympic Games sung by Pindar and recorded by Pausanias.

The 1896 games quickly acquired their own myths of origin and legendary apparatus, reflecting the interests of different parties: Greek nationalists and Greek romantics looking for proofs of continuity and heroes in the archaic mould, historians and bureaucrats of the Olympic movement in search of an authorised version, American myth-makers looking for a mass audience. The most extravagant example is an NBC television mini-series, *The First Olympics: Athens 1896*, which incorporates a mythical account of the games in an American vision of the world. It has Louis Jourdan as Coubertin without the moustache; a Princeton team of athletes who learn to run and jump solely in order to take part in this distant festival of sport; open, fresh-faced American boys beating stuck-up imperialist British; Spyros Louis spending the night before the marathon in prayer. Jayne Mansfield, surprisingly, also played in a Hollywood film about the 1896 Olympics. Such mythical accretions have their own interest. They are part of the story, just as, more seriously, the invented traditions and rituals of the Olympics, which started in 1896, are part of the story. Nevertheless, the main point of this book is more down to earth: to explain how and why the games began in Athens in 1896, and what the games meant for Greece then and mean now.

Should the Olympic Games have found a permanent home in the land of their origins? Some politicians, notably President Jimmy Carter, mounted the platform erected by Karamanlis for their own political purposes in prosecuting the boycott of the Moscow 1980 Olympics. But not many people have taken the Greek claim seriously. The Greeks themselves tacitly abandoned it, in bidding for the 1996 and then the 2004 games. The truth is that Coubertin's conception prevailed. The games are an international festival reflecting twentieth- and twenty-first-century realities. They have little to do with their origins, despite the adoption of some of the symbolic and historical features of the ancient games. In creating and developing their own ritual and proto-

2 *Athens and the Acropolis: a lush romantic view by Fred Boissonas of the city landscape in the early twentieth century, taken from near the Stadium: the columns of the temple of Olympian Zeus in the middle ground, the Ilissos river in the foreground.*

col, a subject of absorbing, even obsessive interest to Olympic followers and historians, the pioneers of the Olympic movement drew on imagined ancient ritual (such as the torch relay, invented for the 1936 Berlin games) but much more on modern nationalism, with flags, national anthems, and the apparatus of the modern world. Athens 2004 will not reverse this, though no doubt it will give rhetoric and images of ancient Greece a good run. But perhaps those who attend and who watch on TV will catch a glimpse, behind the modern razzmatazz, of the beauty of Greek lands and the enduring fascination of those distant struggles in the plain of the Alpheios river at Olympia.

1

A LITTLE KINGDOM

It is in and by freedom only, that adequate preparation for fuller freedom can be made.

W.E. Gladstone, writing of Greece

The kingdom of Greece took formal shape in 1832 when the three Great European Powers, Britain, France and Russia, selected Otho, the seventeen-year-old second son of the philhellenic King Ludwig of Bavaria, to be King of the fledgling state of Greece, or Hellas. No one expected his task to be an easy one. The new state had emerged from the struggle against their Ottoman Turkish rulers of Greek 'notables', prelates, captains and assorted freedom fighters assisted by foreign philhellenes, which forced the then Great Powers of Europe to take Greek claims seriously and eventually to agree to the establishment of a new state. It was small, weak and poor, with a population of about 800,000 and revenues of less than £400,000. Its frontiers were set on a line between the gulf of Arta in the west and a point near Volos on the Pagasitic gulf on the eastern seaboard. This secured for Greece the Peloponnese, which was the heart of old Greece and of the insurrection which turned into the war of independence; a strip of land north of the gulf of Corinth including the fever-ridden town of Missolonghi, hallowed by Byron's death in 1824; Attica and Athens; and the islands of the Saronic gulf and the Cyclades.

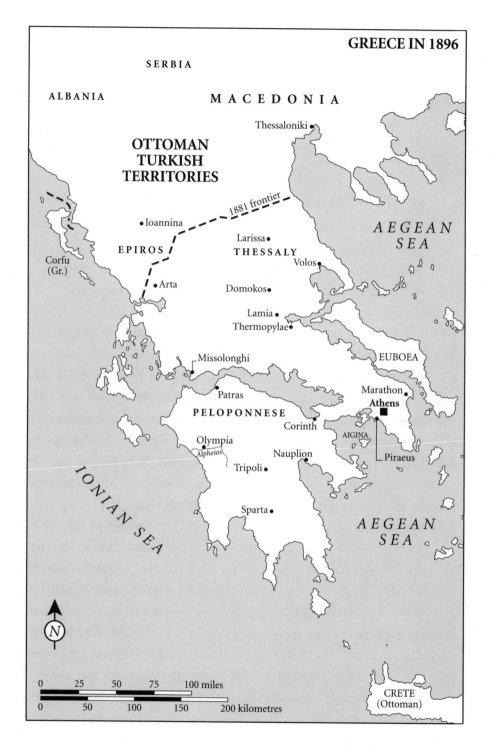

GREECE IN 1896

SERBIA

ALBANIA

MACEDONIA

Thessaloniki•

OTTOMAN
TURKISH
TERRITORIES

1881 frontier

•Ioannina

EPIROS

Larissa•

THESSALY

Volos•

*AEGEAN
SEA*

Corfu
(Gr.)

•Arta

Domokos•

Lamia•
Thermopylae•

•Missolonghi

EUBOEA

Patras•

PELOPONNESE

Marathon•
Athens■

Corinth•

AIGINA

Olympia•
Alpheios

Nauplion•

Piraeus

Tripoli•

IONIAN SEA

Sparta•

*AEGEAN
SEA*

N

| 0 | 25 | 50 | 75 | 100 miles |

| 0 | 50 | 100 | 150 | 200 kilometres |

CRETE
(Ottoman)

Measured against the territories where Greek communities clustered, in Macedonia, Thrace, Asia Minor, Crete and the Aegean islands, this was not much. But it was enough. There was now an independent Hellenic kingdom, a source of pride and a focus of high ambitions. It included most of the sites made famous by antiquity: Athens with its monuments and its glorious history, Thebes, renowned in mythology, Sparta and Olympia. The latter, tucked away in the hilly country of the western Peloponnese, consisted of a few ancient stones protruding from the silt of the river Alpheios, indicating the ancient site.

With the establishment of the new kingdom, it might be thought that the work of Byron and the other philhellenes who had taken part in the struggle was accomplished. Byron was dead, posthumously justified. So were hundreds of others, of wounds or sickness. Some survivors retired to their farms, metaphorically or literally. They were commemorated in 1841 by a dark, lettered wooden arch erected across the door of the Roman Catholic church at Nauplion, carrying the names of 278 philhellenes who had been killed, or died, in the war in Greece. The inscription in French reads, 'To the Memory of the Phil-hellenes who died for Independence. Hellenes, we were and are with you.' This modest duty of gratitude accomplished, the Greeks could look forward to running their own show. They had indeed already started doing so, and were on the point of launching the first revolution against their duly constituted but heavy-handed king.

In 1833 the omens for Otho seemed bright. He travelled to Greece in a British ship, HMS *Madagascar*, under the command of Captain Edmund Lyons. He was accompanied by a suite of ships containing Bavarian troops, and by the three Bavarian Regents selected by his father, who quickly started to boss the Greeks about and make themselves unpopular. He disembarked on 6 February 1833, to an enthusiastic welcome from the priests, politicians, officers and people at Nauplion, previously known as Napoli di Romania, on the gulf of Argos in the eastern Peloponnese. This attractive little town, a few miles down the coast from Argos with its Homeric associations, was to be the capital of the new kingdom. Dominated by a mighty fortress, it was the scene of one of the insurgents' triumphs during the war of independence. It had survived the war battered but unruined. But it lacked weight and renown, and was badly placed for communications with those parts of Greece north of the gulf of Corinth.

A debate ensued on the proper site for a permanent capital. Some argued for Corinth, superbly placed on the isthmus, with access westward to Europe through the gulf of Corinth and eastward to Athens, the islands and Turkey (the Corinth canal did not yet exist). Others spoke for Tripolis, bang in the middle of the Peloponnese, or Argos near Nauplion, or the island of Syra, or Megara, on the route from Athens to the Peloponnese. Others argued for Athens, with its classical, Periclean associations and its fine Acropolis, also sanctified by blood shed during the battles of the recent war. Yet others preferred the concept of a rotating seat of government, so that no one city should acquire dominance, pending the acquisition by Greece of Constantinople, former capital of the Byzantine empire, as a permanent capital city. This, the *Megali Idea* or Great Idea, became the aspiration of the new political nation, expressed in January 1844 by the Prime Minister, John Kolettis, in a famous speech to the Greek National Assembly:

> *The Kingdom of Greece is not Greece; it is merely a part, the smallest, poorest part of Greece. The Greek is not only he who inhabits the Kingdom, but also he who inhabits Ioannina or Salonika or Serres or Adrianoupolis or Constantinople or Trebizond or Crete or Samos or any other region belonging to Greek history or the Greek race … There are two great centres of Hellenism. Athens is the capital of the Kingdom. Constantinople is the great capital, the City, the dream and hope of all Greeks.*

The choice fell on Athens, and on 28 August 1834 Otho made his official entry into the new capital. Once again he travelled on the *Madagascar*. He was greeted at Piraeus by delegates who presented him with

3 *View of Athens c. 1870 from near the Acropolis, showing the unrestored Panathenaic stadium in the middle distance on the left. The arch of Hadrian is in the foreground, with the temple of Olympian Zeus behind it. There were summer theatres and cafes in the greenery between the temple precinct and the stadium. On the far left is the Protestant Cemetery, later moved to become a part of the Athens First Cemetery, where it still is. Mount Hymettus is in the background.*

a live owl, the symbol of Athens, and an olive branch. ('Owls to Athens' is the proverbial equivalent of coals to Newcastle.) Proceeding up from Piraeus to the city of Athens, Otho passed under the arch of the Roman Emperor Hadrian, an earlier philhellenic ruler, near the modern Constitution Square. It was festooned with a large wreath of laurel with the inscription: 'This is Athens which was the city of Theseus and Hadrian, and is now the city of Otho.'

City of Theseus, Hadrian, and now Otho it may have been, but reduced to a pitiful state. Athens had been the site of fierce fighting during the Greek war of independence. The Acropolis had twice been besieged and taken, by the Greek chieftain Odysseus in 1822, and by the Turkish general Reshid Pasha in 1827. In the early 1830s travellers' accounts describe a battered village, or small town, of mud huts without windows. Disraeli visited Athens in November 1830 and described every house as roofless. Two years later the headmaster of Harrow School and future Bishop of Lincoln, the Revd Christopher Wordsworth, found the town lying in ruins:

> *The streets are almost deserted: nearly all the houses are without roofs. The churches are reduced to bare walls and heaps of stone and mortar. There is but one church in which the service is performed. A few new wooden houses, one or two of more solid structure, and the two lines of planked sheds which form the bazar, are all the inhabited dwellings that Athens now can boast. So slowly does it recover from the effects of the late war.*[1]

No lamps, no windows, no newspapers, no books, fewer than 300 houses, the streets between Athens and the outlying villages rife with robbers. It was to this depressed capital that Otho's court, his ministers, and the diplomatic representatives of the Powers, moved from Nauplion in the winter of 1834. There is a surviving paper recording this wholesale removal which shows which houses were taken over in the new capital and at what rent. The relatively grandiose house of the Negrepontis family taken by the British Legation was valued at 42,000 gold drachmas and rented for 6,300 gold drachmas, a rental higher than that of any other building listed, including the house occupied by King Otho as his first palace. This was a fair reflection of the relative influence of the ambassadors of the Great Powers compared with government ministers or even the King. The move to Athens gave a sharp boost to the housing market as Greek ministers, war heroes and foreign diplomats competed for the few desirable properties.

'Ancestor worship' was an important part of the formation of the Greek nation. A direct line from ancient to modern was part of the rationale of the new state developed by Greek enlightenment thinkers. Ancient Greece was the new Greece's unique asset. The early years of the new state therefore witnessed a purging of Ottoman and other non-Greek aspects of history and architecture and a blossoming of antiquarianism. The ancient Olympic Games were a part of this. As early as 1835 the romantic poet Panayiotis Soutsos proposed to the Greek minister Kolettis that they should be revived, rotating every four years from Athens, to Tripoli, Missolonghi and Hydra.[2] Nothing was to come of this for many years.

Otho eagerly embraced his new country's history and the irredentist dreams of his Greek subjects, though he refused to adopt the Orthodox religion. Athens began to grow into a handsome city, distinguished by the neo-classical architecture introduced mainly by foreigners and Greek architects trained abroad. (It was a paradox of the new state and culture that much of Hellenism was reimported.) Otho's wife Amalia took solace in the National Gardens which she laid out and carefully tended. But Otho – advised by his father to rule his subjects with a firm hand and have no truck with new-fangled ideas such as constitutions – fell foul of the quick-blooded former chieftains who were now turned politicians. They extracted a constitution from him in 1844 following a bloodless coup. But that was not enough. In 1862 there was another uprising by the officer corps. Otho gave up the struggle and abdicated. He left Greece in October 1862 on a British frigate, the first example of how difficult it has been to be King of the Greeks.

There were virtually no republicans in Greece. The departure of Otho meant not the end of the monarchy, but a request to the Great Powers to find a new King. To guide them in their search, the government gave notice on 1 December to Greeks at home and abroad that there would be a referendum on the matter. Greeks aged twenty or more therefore proceeded to the polls in the hope and expectation that they were helping to elect a new monarch.

The results indicated where Greek voters expected to gain the greatest accretion of power and influence to their state. Prince Alfred, Duke of Edinburgh, the second son of Queen Victoria, topped the poll with 230,066 votes. He was followed by the Duke of Leuchtenberg, a Romanov, with only 2,400. Votes were also cast for, among others, 'an Orthodox king' (1,917); the Czar (1,841); 'a king' (1,763); 'long live the three powers' (482); Prince Napoleon (245); 'A French Imperial prince' (246); a republic (93); Prince Amadeo of Italy (15); the Count of Flanders (7); Prince William of Denmark (6); Prince Ypsilanti (6); Garibaldi (3); King Otho (1). Apart from the obvious predominance of the British faction, the main interest here lies in the sensible preference expressed for an Orthodox monarch, the very slender support for the republican idea, and the prescience of the six who voted for Prince Willy of Denmark. For it was he who became King, as King George I.[3]

Why not Alfred? The rules of the game which governed this search excluded candidates from any of the Great Powers themselves. Greek supporters called him 'our Alfred', 'Alfredaki' (a diminutive term of endearment) and 'son of the widow'. But the widow was not having it. She made her views clear: 'upon no earthly account and under no circumstances would she ever consent to it'. Alfred, thus debarred, was nevertheless to visit Greece at least twice during his career in the Royal Navy, and even to take part in one of the Powers' blockades of Greek ports. As a midshipman serving on HMS *Euryalus* he attended a glittering ball at the British Legation in 1859, and watched the chariot race at one of the early 'Olympic' meetings in Athens. Some years later he took his ship to the Holy Mountain of Mount Athos and visited the Holy Monastery of Vatopedi, establishing a royal link which has been revived in recent years by Prince Charles.

The choice of the Powers finally fell on the seventeen-year-old Prince Willy of Denmark, full name Christian William Ferdinand Adolphus George, a young shoot of the Glucksberg dynasty, the son of Crown Prince, later King, Christian. Willy was a tall, fair-haired naval cadet with an equable temperament and simple tastes. When the summons came, probably originating with Queen Victoria, he accepted without demur. He took the throne in 1863, accompanied by Count

Sponneck, a kind of Danish 'minder' who made himself so unpopular with the Greeks that he was soon forced out. As a dowry, Britain handed over to Greece the seven Ionian islands: Corfu, Paxos, Cephalonia, Zakynthos, Ithaca, Lefkas and Venus's island, Kythera. These had been a British protectorate since 1815, the remaining traces of which in the year 2004 include the metalled roads and bridges of Cephalonia, and cricket and ginger beer on Corfu. This was the best possible start for King George, who took the throne under the title King of the Hellenes, to show that his moral jurisdiction went wider than the relatively narrow bounds of the present Greek kingdom, encompassing the entire nation in the diaspora.

The diarist Henry Greville reported an illuminating story about George's first round of foreign visits, which he got from Freddy Leveson, who got it from the Duchess of Cambridge, who presumably got it from George himself:

> *When the young king went to St Petersburg the Emperor received him with great ceremony and courtesy, and before taking leave of him, His Imperial Majesty said to the King he had only one piece of advice to give him, which was, to beware of the intrigues of France and England in Greece. From St Petersburg he proceeded to London, where he remained six days without any one of the Ministers calling upon him. At last Palmerston paid him a visit, and the King expressed his surprise that John Russell should have taken no notice of him. However, before he left London John Russell called on him, and before leaving him said the only advice he would offer his Majesty was to be on his guard against the intrigues of Russia. On arriving in Paris he was lodged at the Tuileries, and treated with great cordiality by the Emperor, who on taking leave of him said the only advice he had to give him was to beware of the intrigues of Russia and England.*[4]

Early in his reign George confided to the British diplomat Horace

4 *The Greek Royal Family in the 1890s. King George and Queen Olga are sitting; Crown Prince Constantine, President of the Olympic Games, standing centre; Prince George, senior judge at the Games, later High Commissioner of Crete, seated on the right; Prince Nicholas standing left.*

Rumbold that he had a horror of 'vice' and felt impelled to get married so as to put himself beyond temptation. He therefore accepted an invitation from the Czar to make an extended visit to Russia in 1867, the subtext of this visit being the search for a wife. His uncle John, brother of the Danish Crown Prince, stood in for him as Regent. George found Olga, the fifteen-year-old daughter of Grand Duke Constantine, and married her in St Petersburg in October. Though he was moderately uxorious, this marriage scheme seems not to have been 100 per cent effective in the respect mentioned to Rumbold. Prince von Bülow recorded that there were occasional episodes with other women during the annual visits to Aix-les-Bains.

George was prolific. Nine months after his wedding to Olga a son was born. At the urging of the crowds who gathered outside the royal palace, the boy was named Constantine, recalling the name of the last Emperor of Byzantium, and looking forward to the recovery of that historic capital. Constantine was given the title Duke of Sparta, although the constitution made no room for titles of honour. Further children followed: George, known as 'Big George', in 1869, Alexandra in 1870, Nicholas in 1872, Marie in 1876, Olga (who died as a baby) in 1881, Andrew (father of the Duke of Edinburgh) in 1882, Christopher in 1888. They were brought up as Greek and not Greek. They spoke the language; they were raised, as the constitution prescribed, in the Orthodox faith; but they also spoke English, French, German and Danish, and were educated by foreign governesses and tutors. The boys had a Prussian tutor on whom they played pranks. English was the main language spoken at home. The childhood of the royal princes and princesses was probably the happiest and certainly the most tranquil time in what was to prove for most of them a life turbulent though less tragic than that of their Russian cousins. The family would gather around the paterfamilias at contented Sunday lunches at the palace or at his country estate at Tatoi, north of Athens in the foothills of Mount Parnes.

George proved a more subtle, amenable and worldly ruler than Otho. His approach to his duties was shrewd and relatively laid back. After a few rounds of the country on horseback, he settled for a placid existence between his palace in Athens, his country house at Tatoi, and western Europe. His critics said that he was idle. William Miller, the most experienced foreign observer in Greece and a distinguished historian of the medieval and modern Hellenic worlds, wrote in 1905 that apart from his Peloponnesian progress in the year after the 1897 war he had hardly ever travelled in the country. 'Again and again I have been told in important provincial centres that the King has never been there.'[5] But by following Talleyrand's principle of 'surtout, pas trop de zèle', and by observing carefully the Greek constitution, he hoped to avoid the fate of his two predecessors, assassination in the case of Capodistria, the first President of Greece, expulsion in the case of Otho.

King George struck a skilful balance between the nationalist pressures of Greek public opinion and the veto of the Great Powers, which were continually telling Greece not to make trouble with Turkey. He exploited a wide network of royal contacts. George spent some four months of the year in western Europe. He went to take the waters every year at Aix-les-Bains. His annual visit to Denmark enabled him to keep up with his royal relatives, who included his father King Christian, the 'father-in-law of Europe', his brothers-in-law the Prince of Wales and the Czar, and all the other monarchs, princes and grand dukes who congregated every Christmas at Fredensborg. They in their turn visited Greece. E.F. Benson ('Freddy'), a young archaeologist working in the 1890s at the British School in Athens, later a successful society novelist, described the pattern:

> *To all of them Athens was a sort of holiday home, the Empress Frederick came to be with her daughter, the Czarina came to see her brother, the Princess of Wales to see her sister, the Czarevitch to see his uncle and his cousins, and all the Greeks thought they had come to render homage to the land of Hellenic culture. They could relax at Athens, and forget about their crowns.*[6]

Sophia, the daughter of the Emperor Frederick II of Prussia, brother of the future Kaiser Wilhelm II, and (of course) granddaughter of Queen Victoria, married Constantine in great splendour in the Metropolitan Cathedral of Athens on 27 October 1889.

George tried to moderate the wilder policies of some of his ministers. As a monarch bound by a constitution which placed the source of power firmly in the hands of the people, he preferred to stay out of the political arena whenever he could. But he had much scope for influencing events by appointment of his Prime Ministers, dissolution of parliament, and informal advice. In the 1870s he accepted a limitation on his powers in internal affairs, whereby he would be obliged to appoint as Prime Minister the chief of the party which had a clear majority in the parliament; and this led to a period of two-party rule in which power alternated between two dominant political figures. But foreign affairs were accepted as different. In the course of time the King established a pre-dominance in the field of foreign policy which was unchallenged until the first decade of the twentieth century, when a new force entered Greek politics in the person of the Cretan revolutionary Eleftherios Venizelos.

Making due allowances for the hagiographic nature of most biographies of royalty, one gets the impression that George was a nice, sensible, if rather lazy, man. As a young man he was full of boyish spirits and fond of practical jokes, as were his sons, particularly his second, 'Big George'. In fact practical jokes and horsing around seem to be a common trait of the British, Danish and Greek royal families of the period. The eminent Lord Granville, a raconteur, used to say that when Minister in Waiting at Balmoral, he never bothered to tell Queen Victoria and the Prince of Wales his best stories, because he found that if he pretended to pinch his finger in the door he roused a far more heartfelt mirth.[7]

The nearest Freddy Benson came to witnessing royal horsing around in Athens was when, relaxing in the royal gardens, he heard the sound of tripping feet and male laughter and female cries of dismay, and round the corner of the rose-pergola where he sat came King George, kicking in front of him what had once been a hat. Behind him tripped the Princess of Wales, shrilly protesting.

> *'I beg you not to, George,' she cried; 'it is my hat: so rude of you!'*
> *'But she had an ugly hat,' pleaded the King, 'and I did not like it.*
> *So I took it off and I kicked it.'[8]*

Another royal trait was attraction to animals, including the exotic. George's son Prince Andrew was a case in point, the owner of a cockatoo as well as a number of dogs. George's grandson Alexander, who became King in 1917 when his father Constantine was forced into exile, had a German shepherd dog which caused his untimely death. When he heard the dog scrapping with a tame monkey, Alexander moved to separate them. He was bitten and the wound turned septic. He died in November 1920, precipitating a political crisis.

George was tall and fair, and grew long moustaches. He settled into a routine, rising early, taking his walk, reading his daily selection of newspapers (English, French, German, Russian, Greek), family lunch, walk again or ride down to the beach at Phaleron by horse-drawn tram or carriage, quiet evening varied by the occasional soirée, dinner or ball. The US Consul George Horton sketched this routine in the late nineteenth century:

> *From Athens to Phaleron is the favourite carriage promenade, and when His or Her majesty sets forth, all the fashion of the city is not far behind. Arrived at the beach the King and Queen or the King and his daughter walk up and down in the most democratic manner possible, usually followed by a fat dachshund.'[9]*

Benson recorded how often on a Sunday afternoon a small compartment was reserved on the steam tram from Athens to Phaleron, which stopped outside the palace. There was a prodigious tootling from the palace bugler, and the King and several of his family came out and walked briskly towards the tram, so as not to keep the others waiting. 'This royal simplicity pleased the Greeks; that was what a king should be.'[10] Returning from one such excursion to the seaside King George narrowly escaped assassination by two desperadoes with rifles. They paid the penalty of execution.

If there was a 'problem' of the royal family, it was indeed their lack of roots in Greece. King George made a point of telling all and sundry that his bags were always packed in readiness for departure should the Greeks tire of him as King. He is reported as telling his sons, 'Never forget that you are foreigners among the Greeks, and never let them remember it,'[11] a shrewd remark, but double-edged, suggesting both a realistic assessment of the Glucksberg relationship with the Greeks but also a determination to remain semi-detached, as if the monarchy was

5 *King George I (1845–1913) who funded the excavation of the stadium, opened
the Games, and tried to secure them permanently for Greece. He was
assassinated by a madman in Thessaloniki in 1913.*

a contractual relationship between King and people which could be terminated by either party. It was no doubt the determination to avoid being associated with any Greek clique that gave some people the impression that he was flighty. The multi-millionaire financier Andreas Syngros summed him up as 'sharp-witted, charming, ironical, very good, but not very solid in his likes and dislikes, and wholly opportunist in his doings and attitude to persons.'[12]

The problems with which King George and the Greek political world had to grapple were truly formidable. On the internal front they consisted of no less than the construction of a viable, modern state with a functioning economy, educational system and decent infrastructure. A condition for this was law and order in the country, and a working political system free of the grosser forms of corruption. On the external front there remained the great tracts of territory with as yet unredeemed populations to which Greece might lay claim on the grounds of history, culture, religion or language. The way to make good such claims was by effective armed forces, which Greece did not have.

A further issue was Greece's unequal relationship with the Great Powers, or to put it more bluntly, Greece's limited sovereignty. Even sympathetic westerners often had difficulty getting their minds around the idea that Greece was an independent state. Back in 1811 Byron, the most clear-sighted of observers, had concluded during his visit to Greece that there seemed to be no very great obstacle, except in the apathy of the 'Franks' – the western Europeans – to Greece becoming 'a useful dependency, or even a free state with the proper guarantee', though he conceded that many well-informed people doubted the practicability even of this.[13] As late as 1841 the same naval officer who had brought out Otho to Greece, Edmund Lyons, having become British Minister (i.e. Ambassador), wrote that a truly independent Greece was an absurdity: 'Greece can either be English or Russian, and since she must not be Russian, it is necessary that she be English.'[14]

The Powers were both a problem and a solution. Greece could not prosper or achieve her foreign policy ends without them. But apparently she could not achieve her ends with them either, for the Powers were conservative and tended not to approve of any radical shifting of the balance of power in Europe. Conservative Britain under Disraeli stood for the maintenance of the integrity of the Ottoman empire, and any wild attempt by Greece to assert herself against the Ottoman state could be frustrated by the intervention of the Powers. Britain, France and Russia could find a specious justification for intervention in the guarantee which they had given to the fledgling kingdom, as an independent and constitutional state, though how that justified flagrant intervention in matters of Greek foreign policy was not clear.

Such intervention took place with distressing frequency. It happened in 1850, in Otho's time, in the affair of Don Pacifico. Don Pacifico was a British subject, a Jew born in Gibraltar who had served as Portuguese Consul in Athens. At Easter 1847 in the course of an anti-semitic disturbance his house was ransacked by a rioting crowd of Athenians, and his furniture and effects were destroyed or damaged. He put in a claim for compensation against the Greek government, and asked for the consular support of the British. The Greek government disputed the claim. This was the period of Palmerston in his fullest vigour as Foreign Secretary. After the affair of Don Pacifico's claims had dragged on for months without resolution, Palmerston sent the British Mediterranean fleet to blockade Greek ports and exact satisfaction.

Palmerston was not anti-Greek. He had spoken vigorously for Greece and for constitutionalism earlier in his career. In fact he was neither anti-Greek nor pro-Greek: he famously pronounced that Britain has no eternal allies and no perpetual enemies, only eternal and perpetual interests.

But Palmerston believed in wielding a big stick in foreign policy in defence of what he saw as these perpetual British interests, which included the rights of British subjects, even Don Pacifico. Especially if the country in question was too weak to oppose his will. The Don Pacifico affair made Palmerston very popular in England. His speech in the famous debate in parliament in June 1850 was a rhetorical triumph. He asserted the right and duty of British governments to protect the interests of British citizens overseas. He challenged the House of Commons for its verdict; 'whether, as the Roman, in days of old, held himself free from indignity, when he could say *civis Romanus sum,* so also a British subject, in whatever land he may be, shall feel confident that the watchful eye and the strong arm of England will protect him against injustice and wrong'.[15]

The debate of June 1850 was a classic instance of British parliamentary life, presenting two opposed and coherent views of foreign policy, embodied by Palmerston and his great opponent Gladstone. They still have resonance today. Gladstone denounced Palmerston's insular temper and spirit of interference. He spoke of a 'mania and an itch for managing the affairs of other nations'. He commended the idea of 'non-interference or non-intervention' in the affairs of other countries as a principle of policy. Interference in foreign countries, if it took place at all, should be rare, deliberate, decisive in character, and effective. Ill-judged meddling would isolate Britain from the Concert of Europe. It would go against the common sentiment of the civilised world. This conception of a moral order in international affairs, embodied in the general sentiment of the civilised world, or the Concert of Europe, was at the heart of Gladstone's thinking.

Gladstone asked whether Palmerston wished to claim that Britain occupied a platform high above all other nations. Were we to be the universal schoolmasters? Palmerston's duty was to observe that great code of principles which is termed the law of nations:

> *Let us recognise, and recognise with frankness, the equality of the weak with the strong; the principles of brotherhood among nations, and of their sacred independence. When we are asking for the maintenance of the rights that belong to our fellow-subjects resident in Greece … let us do as we would be done by, let us pay all respect to a feeble state and to the infancy of free institutions.*

Gladstone had the opportunity to put these principles into practice in relation to Greece twenty years later. But in the bellicose climate of 1850 he was spitting into the wind. Palmerston was saying what parliament and public wanted to hear. The fleet proceeded to press the Greeks into submission and reparation.

The Great Powers bullied Greece again in 1854, when Britain and France joined Turkey in the Crimean War against Russia. The Russian, or rather the anti-Turkish cause, aroused enthusiasm in Greece. With the encouragement of King Otho, Greek bands of irregulars, some professional bandits, some idealistic young men, crossed the border into Ottoman territory in support of Greek aspirations. The Powers were not going to stand for this. The British and French fleets blockaded the port of Piraeus again, strangling Greece's trade until she came to heel.

In 1881, thanks largely to the persistence of Gladstone in supporting their claims, Greece acquired from Ottoman Turkey the rich agricultural province of Thessaly, and part of Epirus. This was a major acquisition and seemed to confirm that an assertive foreign policy was right. The main focus of irredentist activity was now Crete, which had risen in revolt in 1866, winning the sympathy of radicals and poets including Victor Hugo and Algernon Charles Swinburne. After Crete, the next focus was to be Macedonia, a cockpit of competing ethnic, religious and national claims.

The internal state of the country was insecure and this too was a concern to the Great Powers. Brigandage was rife. It had become a way of life for many of the rural population who had fallen foul of the law or for whom there was no current employment in the service of the state. The boundaries between the band of brigands and the posse of gendarmes or platoon of soldiers were fluid. According to circumstances, a man would move from one to the other. There were recurrent border skirmishes with Turkish forces. In 1878, the London *Times* correspondent Charles Challoner Ogle unwisely intervened on behalf of Greek Christian villagers in the Volos-Mount Pelion region and was found killed by the Turks. Greek brigands with a price on their heads might retire behind the Turkish–Greek frontier for refuge, or make their homes in the Greek mountains, preying on local villages for supplies. The capture of the occasional group of hostages provided richer, but also riskier pickings.

An incident of hostage-taking in 1870 became an international scandal, with embarrassing consequences for Greece's reputation for civilisation, law and order and her relations with Britain. A well-connected group of British tourists, including Lord and Lady Muncaster and the deputy head of the British Legation, the saintly Edward Herbert, was abducted by brigands while returning from a tourist excursion to the battlefield at Marathon, east of Athens. For the next ten days four of the hostages were moved around the mountainous Greek countryside by their captors, never stopping for long in any one place, while negotiations for ransom were put in train between the brigand chieftain and the Greek government and British Legation. The story ended in tragedy when the bandits were provoked by the intervention of Greek forces into murdering their hostages near Dilessi in Attica. This intervention broke the unwritten rule of hostage dealings, that hostages' lives were immediately forfeit if the authorities used force to resolve the situation. British feelings were outraged. The Greek government sought to shift the blame for the tragic outcome on to other shoulders, including those of Frank Noel, the head of the Noel family, related to Lady Byron, which had settled on the former Turkish estate of Achmetaga in Euboea. Noel had allowed himself to become involved in the negotiations.[16]

One can imagine what Palmerston might have done. But Britain's Prime Minister at the time was Gladstone, who opposed punitive intervention, on the grounds that the Greeks themselves must find the answers to their own problems of lawlessness. He stood firm in the view that improvements in government and the growth of what today would be called civil society come about through the efforts of indigenous governments and societies. The episode ended with the arrest, a public inquiry and the judicial execution of the brigands. Gradually the situation in the countryside improved.

The young state was riven by political, social and economic problems which struck foreigners and Greeks alike. One was the instability of political life. Ministry succeeded ministry with disturbing, comic frequency. The reasons were easier to identify than to correct. Greek politics were highly personalised. The state was the main source of employment. Parliamentary deputies and voters were mutually implicated in a spoils system for which the Greek word, taken from Turkish, is *rousfeti* (favours). Prime Ministers could deliver their programmes only so long as they mustered majority support in parliament. But groups of deputies had no compunction in deserting the government party for the opposition if they felt inadequately rewarded by jobs for their clients.

The public token of this client–patron system was the binding of party leaders to voters through the relationship of godfather to godson. An experienced observer looking back from the first decade of the twentieth century noted that one political grandee, Dimitrios Rallis, was said to have 1,000 godchildren in Attica. Not surprisingly, he was immensely popular in Attica. Each godchild was calculated to cost him more than one pound sterling, at 32 drachmas to the pound (£1 in 1900 equalling approximately £100 in 2000).[17] *Rousfeti* is still an issue in Greece. The great barons of politics still have personal ties with hundreds of their constituents, and are expected to deliver concrete benefits.

Political instability gave easy targets to foreign and domestic critics, who were quick to point out that the real problems of the country were neglected. Nevertheless, in the first thirty years of King George's reign, the country made progress in building its infrastructure, and in developing a fairer and more effective political culture. This halting progress was defined by the struggle and alternation of two politicians who came to symbolise the opposing priorities of internal reconstruction and of foreign expansion. The first, Harilaos Tricoupis, was known familiarly as the Englishman on account of his phlegmatic character. The second was Theodoros Deliyiannis. The emblems of their parties were the olive-leaf of Tricoupis, and the piece of rope of Deliyiannis.

Harilaos Tricoupis was the son of a distinguished Greek fighter in the war of independence who had pronounced the funeral oration over Byron at Missolonghi and went on to become the historian of the revolution, and Greek Minister (Ambassador) in London. Harilaos was brought up there, and became the model of the 'westernising' Greek, of enlightened, progressive ideas. He believed in responsible government, good administration, the development of Greece's infrastructure, roads and canals, and in education. To finance all this he relied on foreign loans. In foreign policy he flirted with the idea, premature as it proved, of a Balkan alliance of Greece, Bulgaria and Serbia. But his instinct was that domestic reform and consolidation must take precedence over foreign affairs. The Great Idea, of incorporating the unredeemed Greeks of the Aegean rim into the Greek Kingdom, remained his ideal, but it required a mature, developed state. Greece should not embark on adventures in pursuit of expansion into Ottoman territory before she was stronger. She did not have the resources to beat the Turks or to defy the Powers.

Deliyiannis was the opposite, an old-style gentleman of perfect courtesy in private and aggressively nationalist rabble-rousing views in public – a combination foreshadowing the supreme populist Andreas Papandreou in the later twentieth century. He combined energy and force of character with ceaseless activity. He was a consummate parliamentary fixer, dedicated to the day-to-day arts of politics, working the crowds. Elegantly dressed, he wore a flower in his buttonhole and a top hat on his head. He commanded enthusiastic support in Old Greece, the Peloponnese, and among the bootblacks of Athens, who traditionally came from Arcadia. William Miller wrote that 'no one can help admiring the physical and mental powers of this veteran politician', who walked younger men off their feet in his rambles about Kifissia, never missed a public function, sat up all night for budget debates in the parliament, and would cover all Greece in his political tours in search of support. By the 1890s he had already been in public life for fifty years and was probably about seventy-five years of age.

These two men alternated in a sort of biparty system, Tricoupis advancing his reforming programme until the high taxes it entailed, or the emotion of some foreign policy crisis, broke his hold on power. Then Deliyiannis would take over for a short time, until his profligacy or nationalist excess led to his fall. Meanwhile the country gradually progressed. The railway system was developed. The Corinth canal was opened in 1893, slicing through the isthmus and cutting forty-eight hours off the journey time from Marseilles to Piraeus. But in the same year, while Tricoupis was Prime Minister, the Peloponnesian currant trade collapsed. It was the backbone of Greece's commerce, essential to the servicing of the foreign debt. Greece defaulted. In December 1893 Tricoupis went before parliament with the laconic announcement, 'Unfortunately we are bankrupt.'[18]

In 1852 a young French scholar named Edmond About had travelled to Athens to take up a position as a fellow at the newly established French School. The French were first in the field in 1846 with their own institute, to be followed in 1882 by the Germans and in 1883 by the Americans. The British were last of the big powers to enter the field, establishing the British School at Athens only in 1886. The French School extended wider than archaeology, into philology, architecture, classical studies and the modern Greek language, which About took the trouble to learn. A mordant and ironic observer, sympathetic to the Greek people but critical of their rulers, he described the absurdities, the corruption and the occasional brutalities of the Greek mini-state, in a book published in 1854, *La Grèce Contemporaine*. Later, in his best-selling book *Le Roi des Montagnes*, he depicted the life of brigandage in the Greek mountains and the interconnections of brigands with the political world. Both books achieved a scandalous success.

Before he even reaches Greece it is clear that About is going to puncture the balloon of received opinion. The companions he meets on his ship on the way to Piraeus start to disabuse him in advance:

'Ah!' said they, 'so you are going to Greece without being

*compelled; you go the right way to work to look for amusement!
Imagine mountains without trees, plains without grass, rivers
without water, a sun without pity, dust without mercy, fine
weather a thousand times more tiresome than rain, a country
where the vegetables grow ready cooked, where the hens lay eggs
hard-boiled, where the gardens have no leaves, where the colour
green has been effaced even in the rainbow, where your weary eyes
will look for verdure, and not find even a salad to repose upon!'*[19]

About's light-hearted approach concealed a sharp and ironic critical
scalpel. He accused the Greek state of ingratitude to the gallant philhellenes who had fought for the existence of that very state and promptly
been forgotten, so that the word 'philhellene' already required a glos-
sary. His main target was the state itself, burdened with maladministra-
tion and corruption, extortion, brigandage, suppression of freedom.

About's strictures greatly irritated the Greeks, who tried to laugh
them off. But other observers were equally caustic about the the state of
the nation, or more accurately the state of the state. The Scottish historian George Finlay, who did good service to Greece in the war of independence and then settled in Athens, was one such critic whose faith in
the Greek people could not be doubted. Finlay saw that the problem
was Greece's mixed relationship of dependence, subservience and defiance in relation to the Great Powers. He reflected sombrely during the
sea passage back to Greece in October 1868:

*Greece ought to look to Switzerland and Holland for lessons but she
looks to France, England and Russia. France has robbed her of her
institutions and given her fashions and centralisation. England has
given her a King and Russia a Queen and Russia has done her least
harm. Making due allowance for the Greeks and pardoning their
presumption it must be said that they have not done their duty.
They have sold their future prosperity for present salary. Passed
Modon at ½ past 11 ...*[20]

33

The problem was the contrast between the high expectations of free Greece after the war of independence and the realities of an inefficient state machine and primitive physical and social infrastructure; between rhetoric and reality. But those who came to know Greece well also came to see that behind the continual political crises, the country was making progress, forging an identity and laying the foundations of a western-ised, modern state.

About's book continued to sell throughout the nineteenth century. His charges acquired their force from the background of romantic phil-hellenism in which his readers were brought up. Much has changed in Greece, and most of his specific accusations are outdated. But a preoc-cupation with the state, bordering on hostility, remains strong. In the face of one of the recurrent failures owing to natural disaster or human inefficiency or both, such as forest fires and disasters at sea, where others might blame bad luck or the weather, Greeks tend to shake their head and say, '*We have no state here!*'

Charles Tuckerman was the first Minister/Ambassador, at the United States mission in Athens. A more sympathetic observer than About, he diagnosed no less acutely the problems with which the new state and its politicians had to grapple. In his book *The Greeks of Today*, published in 1878, he concentrated mainly on the external factors hindering the development of the new state. Tuckerman attributed the bad name which Greece had acquired among foreigners to the effects of the East-ern Question, and specifically to the deliberate choice by the Powers to favour Turkey over Greece for commercial as well as political reasons. He blamed England for this state of affairs:

> *England has been disappointed in Greece from the day she assisted to save her at the battle of Navarino* … When the Greeks boast of*

---

*Navarino was the naval battle at which, in 1827, the combined British, French and Russian fleets under Admiral Codrington destroyed the Turkish-Egyptian fleet in Navarino bay near Pylos in the south-west Peloponnese. The victory led to Greek independence. Wellington called the affair an 'untoward event' in the British parliamentary debate.

*their independence, England does not fail to remind them that they
are indebted to her for that independence … The kingdom has not
been as grateful to the Powers for that 'untoward event' as they
would have wished.*[21]

Byron had asked sixty-six years earlier what reason the Greeks had to be
grateful to the Powers. Now Tuckerman repeated the question.

The attitude of Greek politicians and public to the Powers, in so far as
it can be summed up in a generalisation, was of respect for their superior strength, admiration for their advanced 'civilisation', willingness to
borrow techniques and processes, readiness to show deference where
that was necessary for short-term reasons, but also a sense of injustice
and a determination to exploit the Powers where that was possible so as
to entrench Greek independence and enlarge the degree of freedom of
Greeks to run their own affairs.

It was not only foreign policy which led to the denigration of Greece
by western Europeans. It was also pique at disappointed hopes, the
obverse of philhellenism. One who saw this was the philhellene historian E.A. Freeman, a substantial figure in Victorian intellectual life,
though not much read today. Freeman was a bearded liberal of large
private means, who became father-in-law to Arthur Evans, the excavator of Knossos in Crete. He ended up as Regius Professor at Oxford. He
led a life somewhere between scholarship and politics, corresponding
with the leading figures of his day, including Gladstone in Britain and
Harilaos Tricoupis in Greece.

Freeman wrote in 1880 that the different feelings with which public
opinion in England had at different times looked on the affairs of
Greece formed a curious chapter in the history of the fluctuations of
the popular mind:

*Five and fifty years ago philhellenism was one of the most
prominent and distinctive signs of liberal sentiment ... The cause
of Greece was in truth a noble and a righteous one ... Among their
western friends again, many expected far too much; they expected
to see all the virtues and all the wisdom of the brightest days of
Greece spring up at once among men just delivered from Turkish
bondage. The expectation was utterly unreasonable; an
unreasonable expectation was in a great measure disappointed;
and this disappointment led to a tone of depreciation towards
everything Greek, which was quite as unreasonable as the
exaggerated expectations of the old philhellenes. Those who,
because of the greatness of ancient Greece, expected impossible
wonders from a regenerate Greece, did their favourites endless
damage in the long run.*[22]

Anyone who has lived long in Greece knows what Freeman meant by
that 'tone of depreciation towards everything Greek' which sometimes
succeeds the rosy first expectations of the philhellene.

Thus by the closing decade of the nineteenth century, Greece's
national ambitions were still only partially satisfied, its economy was
weak, its system of law and order and criminal justice deficient, its
infrastructure and commerce largely undeveloped; but still this was a
lively country with an increasingly educated population and a clear
sense of direction. The direction was western, towards European
institutions, towards what the Greeks called 'civilisation'. Mediators
who played an important role in this orientation were the prosperous liberal Greeks of the commercial diaspora in London, Liverpool,
Marseilles, Livorno, Odessa, Constantinople and Smyrna. A good
example of this type was a writer named Dimitrios Vikelas, who
spent more than twenty years in London working in the shipping
office of his two uncles and then moved to Paris, before settling
finally in Athens. Caught up in the Olympic movement almost by
accident, he played a significant part in the revival of the Olympic

Games as the first President of the International Olympic Committee (IOC).

In the sixty years of its existence, the Greek state, much reviled by critics including Greeks, had established itself, had created a worthy capital city, and had forged a sense of national identity. Greece's nationalism, like all nationalisms, was both unique and similar to others. It appealed to the Byzantine imperial past in its expansionist aspirations, and to the classical Greek heritage in the face it presented to Europe. It had yoked the Captains of the war of independence to the harness of a Greek state through what was in essence a modern European policy issuing from the ideas of the enlightenment.[23]

Competitive sports, a famous feature of the ancient Greek world, played little part in the social life of the new state. That was to change.

2

THE RISE OF SPORT

When Greece frequented active Sport and Playes,
From other men they bore away the Prayse;
Their common-Wealths did flourish; and their Men
Unmatched were for worth and Honour then:
But when they once those pastimes did forsake,
And unto drinking did themselves betake,
So base they grew, that at this present day
They are not men, but moving lumps of Clay.

Robert Dover, from *Annalia Dubrensia. Upon the Yeerely Celebration of*
Mr Robert Dover's Olympick Games upon the Cotswold Hills, London, 1636:
an early example of the cliche of the degeneration of the Greek people

The ancient Olympic Games were a feature of the history of antiquity familiar to the western European mind since the renaissance.
Shakespeare, Milton and Voltaire all referred to them. Attaching the
name Olympic to some sporting festival was a natural thing to do and
became fashionable in the nineteenth century. How close a connection
such events had with the ancient world is another question. So-called
Olympic, Olympick or Olympian Games were many, French, English,
Scandinavian, and Greek.[1] Most of them amounted to little more than
local country festivals dressed up in romantic Hellenic fancy and an
antique name.

Robert Dover's Cotswold Olympics of the early seventeenth century are a case in point. A wealthy Catholic lawyer who settled at Winchcombe in the Cotswolds, Dover instituted 'Olympick Games' to be held annually on the Thursday and Friday of Whitsun week, with feasting and prizes. They took place on a field between Evesham and Stow-on-the-Wold. Dover was to be seen directing the proceedings himself, mounted on a white horse. His games included cudgel playing, wrestling, the quintain (a device for practising tilting or jousting, which would smartly knock you off your horse if you moved too slowly), leaping, 'pitching the bar and hammer', handling the pike, playing at balloon or handball, leapfrog, walking on the hands, a dance of virgins, men hunting the hare (which, by Dover's orders, was not to be killed) and horse racing. The Dover games, a demonstration against the rise of puritanism in English life, represented the typical pursuits of an English country festival. This did not stop Dover's fans, who included the poets Michael Drayton and Ben Jonson, from commending him on a jolly and timely classical revival.[2]

Drayton congratulated Dover that in 'these dull yron times' he had revived the Olympic Games, the glory of the Golden Age. He painted an agreeable picture of Greek youths leaping, wrestling, running, riding and throwing the javelin, but placed the event on Mount Olympus, initiating a confusion between Olympus and Olympia which is still prevalent. Dover's Cotswold Games, which lasted nearly forty years, were an example of Hellenic antiquarianism grafted on to country jollification. He died in 1641 and his games did not long survive him.

The Olympic-inspired manifestations of revolutionary France had a greater influence on the modern imagination of Europe. The Paris salon of 1791 showed a vast academic painting by Jean-Pierre Saint-Ours, entitled *99e Olympiade – Combat de la lutte aux Jeux Olympiques, les juges se disposent à proclamer vainqueur un jeune athlète qui vient de défaire le dernier de ses rivaux.* The Revolution introduced four-yearly 'Olympiads' in 1796. Massive '*fêtes*' were held on the Champs de Mars to celebrate the foundation of the Republic. These grand spectacles, containing ingredients such as a footrace matching seven brigades of fifty runners each, had little to do with competitive sport and nothing to do with internationalism. They reflected the belief that enlightened revolutionary France had become the repository of ancient Greek values of liberty and free thinking.[3]

What is lacking in all the early 'Olympic' events is what we would recognise as serious, competitive sport open to athletes from a wider than local background. The watershed was the mid-nineteenth century, when suddenly sports in their modern shape – football, rugby football, cricket, track and field athletics – began to develop in England, spreading rapidly to the United States and to the British colonies, and more gradually infiltrating the continent of Europe.

The start of this process can be dated with some precision to the 1840s and 1850s. The old universities, Oxford and Cambridge, played a key part, particularly in rowing and athletics. The major public schools helped to 'refine', civilize and regulate what had been rough, disorganised communal sports such as football. Variants developed, some of which remained localised, while others, notably football, spread and took root in other countries. Clubs sprang up devoted to all kinds of sports. The first Oxford and Cambridge boat race took place in 1829 at Henley, moved to the Thames in London and was put on an annual basis in 1856. Within a few years the event had become wildly popular. Following a challenge by Cambridge, the first athletics contest between the two universities took place at Christchurch in Oxford in March 1864, with eight events – recognisably a modern track and field meeting.

The gradual regulation of the various sports reinforced the growing taste for physical exercise. Records of times and distances began to be kept, and to be broken, the universities showing the way. The modern stop watch permitted accurate measurement. Codification and measurement allowed sportsmen to face each other on equal terms and with known rules, and match each other's records at a distance. The new sports clubs and their federations helped to draft rules and to enforce them. The Amateur Athletic Club was established in 1866. In its later manifestation as the Amateur Athletic Association (AAA) this became the controlling body for track and field. It was founded in 1880 at the initiative of a group of Oxford men, bringing together regional federations and clubs. Its charter included a definition of amateurism.

England was followed closely by the United States. The phenomenal growth of sports in the United States in the last three decades of the nineteenth century included the development of baseball and football as sports with a mass following, and the rise of track and field athletics in the 1870s in the Ivy League universities and the new athletic clubs of New York, Boston and other east coast cities. Princeton claimed primacy in track and field with the first organised contest in June 1873, a Caledonian Games meeting under the direction of their Scottish director of athletics, George Goldie. The formation of the National Association of Amateur Athletes of America in 1880 was a landmark. It became the Amateur Athletic Union (AAU), the controlling body, in 1888.

The American universities provided a relaxed curriculum with plenty of time available for extracurricular activities. Football became a passion, the American version soon displacing British models. The so-called Princeton rules were adopted in 1867, with twenty-five players on each side, and the Princeton–Rutgers match of 1869 marked the beginning of intercollegiate football. Big intercollegiate matches attracted national interest in the 1880s and 1890s. The universities built large stadiums. Entrance tickets were expensive. Gambling proliferated. The new wire services enabled the exploits of sportsmen to be transmitted swiftly to bars, saloons and clubs. They were magnified and diffused by the sporting press. The era of the sporting hero had arrived.

Despite the lack of regular international sporting meetings before 1896, there were attempts to match teams and individuals of one country against another. Professional athletes on the lookout for new sources of income were ready to travel. The English runner W.G. George and the New York runner L.E. Myers, both amateurs, competed against each other in England and in the US in 1881 and 1882;

the American Myers went on to win most of the British records for middle distance running. Individuals were followed by whole teams. The Manhattan Athletic Club of New York competed in England in 1888 and in England and Paris in 1891. The London Athletic Club took a team to New York in 1895, the year before the Olympics, and lost all eleven events in a match against the New York Athletic Club.

The universities also were beginning to compete across the Atlantic. In 1894 Oxford beat Yale at the Queen's Club in London. In 1895 Yale beat Cambridge 8–3 in the US. In 1899, 1901 and 1904 combined teams of Harvard and Yale competed against Oxford and Cambridge combined.

A pattern of transatlantic competitions between British and American clubs and universities was therefore emerging in the late nineteenth century. The contestants were evenly matched and competed in broadly the same track and field events, without major problems of standardisation. It is difficult to say why this did not develop into some regular institutionalised international event. Because of the advanced evolution of sports in Britain and the US, an Anglo-American basis for international sports events would have seemed just as plausible as an open, global basis. In fact it was only Coubertin's stubbornness and imagination that caused the wider format to prevail. As late as 1911 the entry on athletic sports in the *Encyclopedia Britannica* recorded that 'International athletics contests of any importance have, with the exception of the Olympic games, invariably taken place between Britons, Americans and Canadians, the continental European countries having as yet produced few track or field athletes of the first class, although the interest in sports in general has greatly increased in Europe during the last ten years.'

There was at least one attempt to bring together American, British and British colonial athletes in an international sporting festival. This was a sustained campaign by a British imperialist named J. Astley Cooper to promote what he first called an 'Anglo-Saxon Olympiad' and later called 'Pan-Britannic Games', an inaccurate description since his proposals all envisaged athletes from both the Empire and the United

States taking part. Despite the obstacles, financial and other, this scheme in the hands of a more effective propagandist might have succeeded. Cooper lined up some heavyweight supporters among bishops, headmasters and sportsmen, including C.B. Fry. But Cooper was too ambitious, and ensured failure by loading down his athletics with proposals for conferences, scholarships, exhibitions and the rest. His plan never took wing.[4]

Perhaps the American and British athletes felt happy to continue to compete for their clubs and universities. They had no particular incentive to invite teams from other countries, which with the possible exception of Australians would be unlikely to meet their standards in track and field. Paradoxically therefore the impetus for internationalisation or globalisation of athletics came not from the 'advanced' Anglo-Saxons but from another source altogether.

In continental Europe, the story was different from England and the US, and varied from country to country. The common factor was that in virtually every country there was an explosion of physical activity and sport in the last quarter of the nineteenth century. Each country developed its own variety of physical education, and there were sharp philosophical debates over which was the best. In the early nineteenth century Germany and the Scandinavian countries established a tradition of mass gymnastics rooted in their own social customs and carrying their own political overtones. Germany adopted 'turning', the form of gymnastics created in the early nineteenth century by the '*turnvater*', the nationalist Friedrich Ludwig Jahn (1778–1852). The German gymnastic clubs, deriving their membership mainly from artisans, functionaries and skilled workers, became a political force favouring the unified state and its imperial expansion. Until late in the day the Germans resisted the growing Anglo-Saxon fashion for track and field, and the ball games which originated in England. The Swedes, following the philosophy of Pehr Henrick Ling (1776–1839), developed their own brand of gymnastics, more flexible and less reliant than the Germans on apparatus.

France was different – traditionally strong in the aristocratic and military sports of riding, shooting and fencing, and an early adept at the new sport of cycling, which became massively popular after the invention in the late 1880s of the modern bicycle.[5] This helped to launch in France the new phenomenon of the professional sports hero. It spawned also, in the big towns, the 'velodromes' or cycling stadiums which contained track races, from sprints to marathons. These were eventually displaced by the road races for which France is famous, of which the Tour de France is pre-eminent.

A turning point for France was the defeat of the French army by the Prussians at Sedan in 1870. This disaster led to widespread fears among the intellectuals of the degeneration of the French nation in comparison with the victorious Germans, and to a national debate about the place of physical education in the life of the country, a debate which was the starting point for Coubertin's own quest. It was largely in response to these fears that the state supported the growth of gymnastics, which spread rapidly among the lower middle classes in the last quarter of the century. The sport was encouraged by moralising educationalists and social Darwinists. The motives of the young participants who flocked to village halls and improvised gymnasia were more varied and less elevated: they sought opportunities for physical exercise in the evenings, and to meet and socialise in their spare time. Towards the end of the century the newer sports of the English type, especially football in its two varieties, began to make serious inroads in France. Eventually they infiltrated the gymnastic clubs.

Athletics including track and field events on broadly Anglo-Saxon lines developed in France in the late 1880s and 1890s. The kernels of innovation were some Catholic private schools, and some of the élite French *lycées*, state secondary schools whose alumni founded the Racing Club de France in 1882 and the Stade Français in 1883. These élitist and highly selective associations promoted rugby football in the winter and athletics in the summer. They came together to create the Union des Societés de Course à Pied de France in 1887.

One European country which lagged behind in sporting developments was Greece. Given the connection between organised modern sport and the development of industrial society, this was hardly surprising. Travelling troupes of athletes including exotically costumed strongmen had performed in village festivals (weightlifting is still a sport in which Greece excels). Legendary athletic feats, of running and stone-throwing, featured in Greek popular song. But except in Athens and to a lesser degree Patras, the conditions for organised sport on any significant scale hardly existed before the last quarter of the nineteenth century. The early attempts at organising sporting events were an illustration of this rather than the reverse. There were other priorities for the young and undeveloped state.

While Greece could not expect to be among the leaders in what was a product of advanced industrial societies, there were channels through which the new ideas were diffused in Greece. The Ionian islands were a British protectorate from 1815 until 1864, and among the legacies of this period were flourishing cricketing clubs and a lawn tennis club established in Corfu in 1888. Immigrants from Bavaria and Switzerland had brought with them some of the Germanic traditions of gymnastics. Gymnasia were set up in Athens and provincial cities. Greek officers learned to ride, fence and shoot. Just as Greeks were determined to imitate and incorporate the achievements of western Europe in the economic and cultural spheres, so it was to be expected that they would follow in sport where England and others led.[6]

By the late nineteenth century the Olympic Games were an event waiting to happen. They were a part of the common European stock of imagery about ancient Greece. But they could have remained there, in the realm of the imagination, or at most of pastiche and play on a local scale, but for social and political developments in Europe and America in the second half of the nineteenth century which prepared the ground. The first of these was the rise of organised sport as a leisure pursuit. The second was the development of a western-looking Greek state in pursuit of European 'civilisation' and values.

The 1870s and 1880s were decades of change in Greece. The chief agent of this change, representing a new force in politics, was Harilaos Tricoupis, who achieved power in 1875.

Tricoupis had a high reputation as the diplomatist who had negotiated with Britain the transfer of the Ionian islands to Greece. His prestige and popularity were enhanced in 1874 when he published, anonymously, an article in a Greek newspaper criticising the Crown for systematic intervention in politics through the practice of appointing minority governments. The publisher of the newspaper was arraigned and thrown into jail. Tricoupis came forward to accept full responsibility for the article and was himself imprisoned for four days before being released with an unstained reputation. His fearless intervention led to the adoption of the constitutional principle whereby the King accepted the obligation to send for the leader of the party which enjoyed a declared majority in parliament, a significant advance in the practice of Greek democracy.

From 1882 to 1895 Tricoupis governed Greece almost without interruption, an unprecedented feat of continuity in Greek experience. He stood for economic reconstruction and expansion and the creation of a modern infrastructure. His policy depended on foreign loans and, as it turned out, on the profitability of the currant trade, which enjoyed large profits in the 1870s owing to the collapse of French production following the impact of phylloxera on the French vines.

In external affairs, Tricoupis stood for a close alignment with England. There were political, economic and cultural reasons for this. Britain exerted the greatest influence and was the great maritime power in the Eastern Mediterranean. No other power could be so helpful to Greek interests. British imperial policy created opportunities for Greek enterprise. The obvious case of this was Egypt, where under the wing of

6 *Harilaos Tricoupis (1832–96), the modernising Prime Minister who declared*
   Greece bankrupt in 1893 and considered the Olympic Games an unnecessary
   frivolity at a time of national austerity. He fell from power in early 1895,
   retired to the south of France, and died there while the Games were in
   progress. The photograph, annotated by his sister Sophia 'photograph of my
   brother in 1891' was later dedicated by her to his private secretary.

the British government Greek businessmen in the cotton and tobacco
trades flourished. One of them, George Averoff, was to be one of
Greece's greatest private benefactors and to endow the ancient stadium
of Athens with marble for the Olympic Games.

Tricoupis represented a new political and economic world. Out of
a society where virtually all forms of economic activity except peasant farming depended on the state, a new middle class was gradually
emerging, creating new forms of commerce and industry. Piraeus
was developing into a serious commercial port, to rival Syra. In
Patras the currant trade was creating new wealth. Greek finances and

banking were being transformed by a new class of immigrants, successful commercial figures from the Greek diaspora. Several of them came in the 1870s, from Constantinople, Alexandria and other centres of Greek commerce, deciding to take up residence in Athens even though Constantinople would still have provided a larger field for their ambitions.

One of these immigrants, not himself one of the super-rich though very comfortably off, was the writer Dimitrios Vikelas. He built himself a house in Athens in the 1880s, out of a mixture of patriotic sentiment and the feeling that his place as a Greek writer in search of a Greek readership was at the capital and heart of the independent state. An equally interesting case was that of Andreas Syngros, a banker and financier from Syra who came to Athens from Constantinople in the 1870s, already a very rich man. He established a close connection with Tricoupis, and played a major part in Greek finances thereafter, leaving the bulk of his fortune after his death in 1898 to fund public works, which included the Evangelismos hospital and the broad Syngrou Avenue which leads from the city to the sea front at Neo Phaleron.

These changes in Greece's social mix included an increasing interest in sport. This came about rather suddenly in the 1890s. There existed already a minority, most of them officers in the armed forces, in touch with western European ideas, who took an interest in fencing, shooting and riding horses. The Athens Club, a social club which still exists, introduced fencing in 1875. Gymnastics made some headway in the 1880s: it was introduced as an element in the primary schools curriculum in 1889. These were early indications. Then in 1891 the Panhellenic Gymnastic Association (PGA) was founded in Athens, closely followed in 1893 by the National Gymnastic Association (NGA), a breakaway from the Panhellenic. The Lawn Tennis Club was founded in 1895. The floodgates then opened: some sixty athletic bodies were set up in the three years 1894–6, many of them not to survive for more than a few months or years. The administration of athletics was put on a coordinated national basis with the establishment of a national federation of athletic clubs in 1897.[7]

We should not take this proliferation of clubs and acronyms as evidence of well-established athletic practices or standards. Many of them were founded because of the imminence of the Olympic Games. But it was a start. The fashion for sport was taking hold, and the Greeks were and are quick to respond to fashions. The author of the Acts of the Apostles observed that the Athenians of his day spent their time in nothing else, but either to tell, or to hear, some new thing. In this respect not much had changed.

Another new element in the 1890s was the increasingly assertive nationalism of the Greek armed forces, and especially the junior officers. Tricoupis's record in government included a wide-ranging reform of the officer corps, the expansion of its numbers, the establishment of new training facilities, new schools for reserve officers and non-commissioned officers, and professional exchanges with France. One effect of this was that the officer corps became increasingly aware of its professional interests and its privileged place in society. Junior officers began to see themselves as guardians of the nation's interests, with a right and duty to bring to book those who were regarded as promoting 'anti-national' or defeatist policies. On 20 August 1894 a large group of young officers from the Athens garrison invaded the offices of the newspaper *Acropolis* and broke them up, as a sanction for what they considered to be the unpatriotic views of its editor. The editor, Vlasis Gavrielides, was a sharp critic of the arrogance of the officer corps, the obscurantism of the Orthodox Church of Greece, and the excesses of nationalist rhetoric of those whom he called 'neurotic pseudopatriots'.[8] Eighty-six young officers were arraigned before the Athens Court Martial, only to be found innocent three years later.

In November 1894 a much smaller group of officers founded in Athens a secret society called the National Society (Ethniki Etaireia), with the declared aims of raising national morale, watching over the interests of the enslaved Greeks, and preparing at any cost in sacrifice for their liberation. It had fourteen founding members, all but one of them lieutenants. Its rules authorised members and associates to take 'the most severe and drastic measures' against those who were guilty of 'crimes' against the interests of the nation.

There was a tradition of secret associations in Greece. Indeed the so-called Friendly Society (Philiki Etaireia) was a leading instigator of the movement which led to the Greek war of independence. But the National Society was different. For the first time members of the officer corps of a professional army were setting themselves up, secretly, as the unique interpreters and protectors of the interests of the nation, in distinction from the lawfully elected government.[9] As well as acting as a ginger group exhorting government to aggressively nationalist policies in Macedonia and Crete, the Society acted as a professional interest group lobbying for more resources and jobs for the officer corps. From this point on the National Society, which in 1895 expanded its membership to include civilians, developed its nationalist mission in a sinister counterpoint to the western-looking policies of Tricoupis and his followers. As the Society expanded its membership, it took in several of those who were to play a role in the Olympic movement.

3

FORERUNNERS:
BROOKES AND ZAPPAS

In what way can it be possible, that the inhabitants of a small town like Wenlock, can contribute to the national welfare? In this way – drop a stone in the middle of the lake, and the little ring first formed will go on gradually increasing in circumference till, at length, the distant shores are reached.

William Penny Brookes, 1867

Two institutions have the strongest claims to be regarded as forerunners, in some sense, of the modern Olympic Games: the Wenlock Olympics of William Penny Brookes, and the Zappas Olympics in Athens. The inspirers of these events, Brookes and Zappas, could hardly have been more unlike, the one an English doctor and philanthropist, the other an adventurer who made millions in trade and property speculation in Romania. But both had a romantic leaning towards ancient Greece.

Much Wenlock is an attractive market town in Shropshire, the hilly county of middle England which marches with Wales. This is the area celebrated in A.E. Housman's cycle of poems *A Shropshire Lad*, which was, coincidentally, published in 1896, the year of the first Olympic Games, and influenced a whole generation of English young men.

Much as one would like to find a direct connection between Housman and Brookes, there is none; though the Shropshire lad might have benefited by the brisk sporting remedies for morbid adolescent thoughts prescribed by Charles Kingsley and later by Pierre de Coubertin. That Housman was aware of country athletic sports, as he was aware of football, is clear from his poem 'To an Athlete Dying Young' (*A Shropshire Lad* No. XIX), but there is no suggestion that he took much interest in them, nor that he knew Brookes.

> *The time you won your town the race*
> *We chaired you through the market-place;*
> *Man and boy stood cheering by,*
> *And home we brought you shoulder-high.*

> *Today, the road all runners come,*
> *Shoulder-high we bring you home,*
> *And set you at your threshold down,*
> *Townsman of a stiller town.*

> *Smart lad, to slip betimes away*
> *From fields where glory does not stay*
> *And early though the laurel grows*
> *It withers quicker than the rose.*[1]

In the pastoral setting of the real Shropshire, a young man named William Penny Brookes established a unique institution in the 1840s. Brookes was born in Wenlock in 1809, the son of a local doctor. After studying in London, he travelled to Paris and Padua to further his education before returning to Wenlock on his father's death to take over the practice. A local figure of substance, benevolent, idealistic, philhellenic, a knowledgeable botanist, perhaps a bit of a bore, he threw his energy into improving the lot of the working men. He became a Justice of the Peace and Commissioner for Roads and Taxes, a pillar of the community with

7 *The Wenlock Olympics of the Shropshire doctor William Penny Brookes (1809–95), which influenced Coubertin. They continue to this day. The champion at 'tilting the ring' is crowned with an olive wreath by the daughter of the Rector of a nearby village. Brookes, with chestful of medals, is on the right, flanked by a herald.*

a hand in many local enterprises. In 1840 Brookes founded the Much Wenlock Agricultural Reading Society, with a public reading room 'for the promotion and diffusion of useful information' among local farmers and agricultural labourers. He wanted to do for the people of Shropshire what Dimitrios Vikelas was later to do for the people of Greece, when he devoted the final years of his life to bringing books to a wider readership through the Society for the Distribution of Useful Books.

In 1850 Brookes added to the Reading Society a 'Wenlock Olympian Class', established for the 'moral and physical improvement of the Inhabitants of the Town and Neighbourhood of Wenlock and especially of the Working Classes, by the encouragement of out-door recreation, and by the award of prizes annually at public Meetings for skill in Athletic exercises and proficiency in intellectual and industrial attainments'.[2] Later, in 1860, the Olympian Class became the Wenlock

Olympian Society. Brookes held the first of what became annual Olympian Games Meetings in October 1850. They still take place today.

Brookes's annual sports festival was a success at a local, and regional, level. But it never took off as a national, still less international, event. What distinguished Brookes from other wealthy philanthropic Victorians was his peculiar fascination with the symbols and history of the ancient Olympic Games. However he was no dogmatic revivalist. The Wenlock Games were syncretic, a mix of ancient imagery (laurel wreaths and rhetoric), medieval pageantry (jousting and tilting, processions in fancy dress, announcements by a herald), brass bands and bell-ringing, glee singing, odes to the victors, traditional English country sports, and modern athletics. There were football and cricket, running, jumping and quoits, cash prizes for the winners, feasting and drinking. There were children's events, including reading, spelling, history, art and knitting. The fun is best illustrated by the programmes, which also show the not insignificant prize moneys to be won.

The event in which Brookes took greatest pride was the medieval sport of 'tilting at the ring'. A mounted horseman charging down the lists had to spear with his lance a narrow ring, hanging from a frame. The winner of this event was crowned with laurel by a smartly dressed young lady of Wenlock. There is a well-known photograph of this coronation taking place, with Brookes standing nearby, a corpulent gentleman with a top hat and white whiskers, an air of benevolence, and a chestful of medals most of which no doubt came from his own Wenlock Society.

In October 1858 a Shrewsbury journal reported that 'Olympic Games', funded by a wealthy Greek named Evangelis Zappas, were to take place in October every fourth year in the ancient stadium of Athens, starting in 1859. The games were to include horse-races, wrestling, quoits and other athletic sports. This news, correct in its essentials, greatly interested Brookes. From this moment his efforts were entwined with the history of Olympic sports in Greece.

Brookes was a wordy correspondent, tenacious in riding his hobby horses, and undaunted in addressing Kings and Foreign Ministers. Through the unpopular British Minister in Athens, Sir Thomas Wyse, he sent suggestions for the Olympic programme based on his Wenlock experience. He followed up in February 1859 with a gift of ten pounds for a prize for the winner of the tilting event which he had naïvely suggested should be held at Athens. There was to be no such event. But the ten pounds prize was not wasted.

Evangelis Zappas was a wealthy Greek from Epirus, the mountainous region in north-west Greece and southern Albania which at this period was still under Ottoman Turkish rule. Zappas had an adventurous early career first in the service of Ali Pasha, the governor of the region, and later with the forces of Greek chieftains in the war of independence. In the 1830s Zappas made a fortune in Romania as a trader, landowner and financier of Greek shipping. Like other successful entrepreneurs, he looked for a national cause for his money. This was the period of the great benefactors from the Greek diaspora who helped to adorn the modern city of Athens with many of its finest buildings. Zappas found his cause in the idea of an Olympic revival, which he had picked up from the works of the poet Panayiotis Soutsos, who had proposed in 1835 that the Olympic Games should be revived. He had been banging the same drum in the press ever since. One of its beats had reached Zappas in Romania, and excited him.

Inspired by Soutsos, Zappas wrote to King Otho in early 1856, offering to fund a revival of the Olympic Games, on a three-yearly basis, with prizes for the victors. The King asked his Foreign Minister to deal with what seemed to him a highly unpractical proposal. The Foreign Minister, Alexander Rizos-Rangavis, was a sophisticated 'westernising' Greek with a Scottish wife. He was also a poet, and he had little time for athletics. Like most of the Athenian intellectual and political establishment of his generation, he believed that national progress would come about through economic and scientific rather than physical activity.

But Zappas was offering a large sum of money: to wit, 400 shares of the Greek Steamship Company, the interest on which was to fund the Olympic events, and the sum of 3,000 imperial florins. With the King's approval therefore, Rangavis responded warmly with a counter-proposal for a quadriennial exhibition of Greek industrial, agricultural and artistic products, to be housed in a new exhibition hall which could serve in between the Olympiads as a technical school. Thus was born the idea of the present Zappeion building in central Athens. Rangavis argued that in the present period of history 'nations and peoples are not distinguished to the same degree as in the past by superiority in bodily strength and skill, but much more by intellectual energy and development'.[3] This was the age of the Exhibition, pioneered by France and Britain. The Great Exhibition at the Crystal Palace in 1851, inspired by Prince Albert, showed the way. Greece had been represented by a very modest stand, provoking sententious comments that Commerce had upped sticks and moved from the Mediterranean to northern climes, along with the arts, inventions and comforts.

As a sop to Zappas, Rangavis proposed that the Sundays during the four-week period of the agro-industrial exhibition should be devoted to popular amusements including athletic sports and artistic contests. Zappas accepted these amendments. But he was not willing to abandon the idea of games, which he wanted to take place in Athens's ancient stadium, restored and remarbled. This stadium had been built in the fourth century BC outside the main city, on the south side of the Ilissos river, within the natural horseshoe formed by two hills. Up to that time the athletic games which were part of the annual Panathenaic festival, and an important element in the social and religious life of the city, seem to have taken place in the agora, the city's meeting and market place. The stadium was gloriously restored by the super-rich Athenian Herod Atticus in 143–4 AD. The travel writer Pausanias reported, wrongly, that he had used up most of the marble from the quarries on Mount Pendeli in this operation. The restored stadium was linked to Athens by a bridge over the Ilissos river which survived until the late eighteenth century.

Though by then the stadium had fallen into disrepair and decay, its physical outline was still visible in the nineteenth century and its history well known.

Zappas's proposals finally obtained official sanction in a Royal Decree of 19 August 1858, announcing the establishment of 'National Contests to be held every four years and called "Olympics", which have as their purpose to exhibit the products of the activities of Greece, especially, industry, agriculture and animal husbandry'. The first competitions were to be held in October 1859. On the third Sunday during the period of the exhibition there would be 'solemn, public athletic games' in the stadium, with cash prizes and olive wreaths. An Olympic organizing committee was established, known as the Committee for the Encouragement of National Industry, chaired by a university professor. It became a formidable bureaucratic organisation, issuing a plethora of circulars and proclamations about events, rules and prizes in successive Olympic festivals.[4]

Reading between the lines, this was a victory for Rangavis. The athletic sports were to be a footnote to the agro-industrial exhibitions, and to the accompanying contests for works of art and drama. And so it proved. The athletic sports took place on 15 November, not in the stadium but in what was known, after Otho's father, as Ludwig Square, the present day Koumoundourou Square near Piraeus Street. Competitors came from all parts of the Greek world including Turkish territories. There were three track races which took their names from their ancient Olympic prototypes, the single length of the stadium (one 'stade') of about 200 metres, a two-lap race, the *diaulos*, of about 400 metres, and the *dolichos*, nearly a mile. The winner of this last, Petros Velissariou from Smyrna, was awarded the ten pounds prize, equalling 281 drachmas, which Brookes of the 'Olympic committee of the city of Moudenlok in England' had offered for the winner of the tilting event which never happened. (Moudenlok for Wenlock is not so surprising a mistake in the transliteration of Brookes's handwriting into Greek.) There were also discus and javelin contests, long jump, and climbing a greasy pole.

These games were a combination of antiquarianism and traditional sports. By all accounts, including that of Rangavis, who himself took part in the horse race, they were badly organised and not much fun for the spectators. The square lacked the advantages of a proper stadium. The underlying reason for the failure was the lack of experience in sports.

This ramshackle Olympic festival led the enthusiastic Brookes to incorporate further Greek elements in his Wenlock festival. He expanded the Wenlock programme, accommodating for example the javelin, thrown as in the Greek games at a target. His interest in the Greek model led him to absurd lengths, such as calling a public meeting at which Sir Thomas Wyse's letter and the summary results of the Athens games were read out. Every communication from Greece was translated and pasted into Brookes's scrapbook, where they can be seen today in the Wenlock Olympian archive.

In 1860 Brookes expanded from a local to a regional basis, initiating Shropshire Olympian Games, to be held in rotation in the large towns of Shropshire. At the combined Shropshire and Wenlock Games in 1860 Greek slogans were displayed on banners. A medal was struck showing the Greek goddess of victory, Nike, with a quotation from Pindar, the ancient poet who made a special corner in odes to Olympic and other sporting victors. Brookes offered a prize for the best ode to the victor of the tilting event.

Brookes was not the only Olympic player in England. A Liverpool Athletic Club, founded in 1862 with the motto '*Mens sana in corpore sano*', held Olympic games in 1862, 1863 and 1864, open only to 'gentlemen amateurs'. As well as track and field, the organisers were enthusiasts for German-style turner exercises in the gymnasium.

In 1865 Brookes and a few other enthusiasts founded a National Olympian Association (NOA), intended to bring together the various regional organisations which had sprung up. Its articles excluded professional athletes (but without defining 'professional' by social class) and provided for open competitions on an international basis. The

Association planned its first national meeting in London in 1866. Brookes enthusiasts have claimed plausibly that it was this which spurred the fledgling London sporting establishment into forming the Amateur Athletic Club (later the AAA), which organised its own counter-attraction in March 1866 at Beaufort House.

The NOA games, held in July and August at the Crystal Palace (with swimming events in the Thames and gymnastics in the German gym at King's Cross), were boycotted by most of the members of the London athletic clubs, but still were judged a success. They included a wide selection of track and field events, including for the first time a steeplechase, wrestling, boxing, fencing, gymnastics, swimming, multiple events on the lines of the pentathlon, and, in an echo of the ancient Olympic race in which the contestants had to run in full hoplite armour, an event run in full battle kit. W.G. Grace, the great cricketer, then eighteen years old, won the 440 yards hurdles in 1 minute 10 seconds. In a premonition of troubles to come, the winner of the mile and two mile races was disqualified for not being an amateur.

This was the pinnacle of Brookes's efforts to establish his Olympic festival on a national basis. His Shropshire Olympics, like the Liverpool Olympics, ceased in 1864–5, leaving only the Wenlock Games. The national Olympic festival also soon died out. The AAC, which drew from the London athletic clubs and from Oxford and Cambridge, established control over British athletics. It had not the least interest in what was going on in Greece.

Brookes's Wenlock Games reverted to a local festival of sports and pageantry incapable of attracting top athletes from the south of England.

Evangelis Zappas died in 1865. He left a detailed will, drawn up at Brosteni in Romania in 1860, which opened with the traditional words,

'Since man is mortal, and the grace has not been given to him by Divine Providence to know the hour of his death, which threatens him at every moment, he is therefore obliged to put his affairs in order before this hour arrives, so that after his departure from this life there shall not follow dissensions among his relatives.' The will, which was in fact to be the cause of much dissension since he did his best to tie the hands of his legatees in every particular, left most of his property to his cousin Constantine Zappas, who had 'worked faithfully' with him. Following Constantine's death it was to go to the Olympic Committee, to be named the 'Committee for the Bequests', which in the meantime got the revenue from 400 shares in Zappas's shipping company for the expenses of the four-yearly Olympic exhibitions. Zappas instructed that a 'worthy and spacious building for the Olympia with its stadium' should be built, according to the plan which he had sent to Mr Rangavis, and provided verbal elucidation of what the building – today's Zappeion – should consist of. The will confirms that the Rangavis conception of the Olympics had prevailed. It is virtually silent on the sporting component of the four-yearly festivals. The bizarre antiquarianism of Zappas's approach emerged in the provision that whenever a Greek should be found making some great achievement or invention, the entire income of the estate after paying for the Olympic festival should be devoted to making a golden crown with which to crown him (or her).

The foundation stone of the Olympia hall, to be called the Zappeion, was laid on 20 January 1874. It took nearly fifteen years to complete.

A second Zappas Olympic festival was held in November 1870. By now King Otho had been driven into exile and replaced by George I, the new nominee of the Great Powers. The main emphasis was again on the industrial and agricultural competitions. But the athletic events were held, for the first time, in the ancient Panathenaic stadium, according to Zappas's wishes. The German archaeologist Ernst Ziller had carried out the first phase of an excavation at the personal expense of King George. The spectators watched from wooden benches and from the grassy hillside surrounding the stadium.

Athletes again came from all parts of the Greek world, including Greek communities within the Ottoman empire, in Constantinople and Smyrna. They competed in a limited programme of track and field and gymnastic events: 400 metres, triple jump, long jump, wrestling, discus, javelin (thrown at a target), pole vault (for distance), pole climb, rope climb, and tug of war. No records were kept of times or distances. As in 1859 the organisers drew on various aspects of the ancient Olympic Games, including this time an oath for the competitors, and a nationalist hymn written by Professor Orphanides of Athens University.

This fairly rudimentary athletic festival attracted a large crowd, estimated at 20–30,000, and was generally judged a success. Yet after the event something went wrong. The next Olympic athletic events, in 1875, were a flop. Again they took place in the ancient stadium with the Athenian spectators lounging on its grassy banks, the elite paying 3 drachmas to sit on wooden benches at the upper end. The ebullient Anglo-Irish classical scholar J.P. Mahaffy, whom we shall meet again, happened to be present. He left a light-hearted but critical account of the games, poking fun at the pretension of 'transferring Olympia to Athens' and resuscitating the ancient names for the judges and contestants. Part of the track was in ridges like a potato field. The Athenian dogs were everywhere. The runners, in grey check shirts and grey trousers, with tight spring-sided boots, had to thread their way past a fat old lady walking her two dogs on the course. 'The King's absence,' wrote Mahaffy, 'was pointedly regretted.'[5]

The shambolic nature of the 1875 games can be attributed partly to the lack of enthusiasm and investment by the committee in track and spectator facilities. The main organiser of the 1875 games was Ioannis Phokianos, a professor of maths and physics and the director of a gymnasium, one of the pioneers of Greek sports. Under his influence the games seem to have shifted from being a traditional festival open to all to being largely drawn from high school and university students.

The Zappeion building was inaugurated on 20 October 1888. This

8 *The Zappeion exhibition hall, designed by Boulanger, in a modern photograph. The late nineteenth-century 'Olympia' industrial and agricultural shows, and the 1896 Olympic fencing events, were held here. It is still used for European summits.*

was the occasion of the repatriation of Evangelis Zappas's head, which he had instructed should be sent to Athens and interred in the building he had funded. The head was duly bricked into a wall of the building, where a plaque recording this can still be seen. A further, fourth Olympic festival was held, the agro-industrial show taking place in the newly commissioned exhibition hall. Rangavis was disgusted by the way this had turned out. The athletic contests which had been announced to take place in the stadium as part of the festival did not happen. And that was the end of the Zappas Olympics, though the Zappeion hall built to encompass them has proved a prominent and agreeable feature of the Athenian city-scape, surrounded by cool wooded gardens where Athenians can stroll in the evenings and nurses pushed their prams between the wars. The 'Committee for the

Olympia' continued both to manage the Zappas bequest and the agro-industrial exhibitions and to show minimal interest in sport.

Paradoxically it was at this time that sport really started to take off in Athens. In 1891 Phokianos formed the Panhellenic Gymnastic Association (PGA), with the revival of the ancient Olympics one of its charter aims. The PGA held a first meeting in May 1891, and held games in May 1893 under the patronage of Crown Prince Constantine. Among those who took part were the weightlifter Miltiades Gouskos and the gymnast and discus-thrower Soterios Versis, both of whom went on to perform well in the 1896 Olympic Games. A visit by German gymnasts in July 1893 impressed the spectators. The newspaper *Acropolis* speculated on the connection between bodily strength and fighting ability. Somehow, despite all the problems and earlier failures, sport was beginning to catch on.

Throughout these years Brookes remained in touch with events in Greece. In 1877 he requested through John Gennadius, the Minister at the Greek Embassy in London, that the King of Greece should give a prize for the victor in the pentathlon in the '5th national Olympian Games', due to be held at Shrewsbury in August 1877. King George agreed, and donated a silver cup to a value of ten pounds sterling, the exact equivalent of Brookes's own gift to the Zappas games in 1859.

The decline of the Wenlock Games seems to have spurred Brookes to wider ambitions. Some time in 1880 he wrote to Gennadius proposing that some form of international Olympic festival should take place in Athens.[6] Gennadius replied on 8 November 1880 thanking Brookes for his 'most excellent proposal', but regretting deeply that 'in the present troubled and critical circumstances of the kingdom it would not be possible to carry out in a befitting manner the theme of your proposal. If, as we must hope, later on a more settled and satisfactory state of affairs be established ... I have every reason to believe that such a proposal would meet with a ready and cheerful response.'

This was enough encouragement for Brookes, who wrote back looking forward to the day when British athletes would have the opportunity of 'visiting the classic land ... and of contending in a generous rivalry with the Athletes of other nations, in the time-consecrated stadium at Athens'. He continued to pursue Gennadius, writing at least once a year. Gennadius continued to put him off.

It appears from this correspondence that Brookes conceived some form of international, or at least Anglo-Greek, Olympic games taking place regularly at Athens, in the ancient stadium, under the auspices of an international Olympic association based in Athens. It is possible, as the Olympic historian David Young does, to see in this the seeds of Coubertin's later Olympic Games and IOC, but the crucial conditions for implementation were lacking. Brookes had no international network of contacts through which to engineer such a festival. Nor did he have the resources. He was reliant on the Greeks to do what he wanted, and on his pen to persuade them; and at this period the Greeks were not interested. No one in the official Greek world was likely to pay much attention to an elderly, eccentric Englishman with no official position.

Brookes and his ideas might at this point have faded from the scene, and remained only an agreeable Shropshire country diversion, but for a visit to Wenlock by the French Baron Pierre de Coubertin. This was to ensure Brookes a place among the founding fathers of the Olympic revival.

4

PIERRE DE COUBERTIN

'You are a stranger in Cambridge?
– Not only in Cambridge but in England.
– German, perhaps?
– Frenchman.
– Frenchman, oh!'
Et, levant son chapeau avec un demi-sourire de courtoisie, il me
dit:
'Vive la république!'
Je réponds:
'God save the Queen!'
Et nous nous séparons.

Pierre de Coubertin, *L'Education en Angleterre*

Human imperfection tends always to transform the Olympian
athlete into a circus gladiator. One must choose between two
athletic methods which are not compatible ... The re-
establishment of the Olympic Games on a basis and in the
conditions in keeping with the needs of modern life would bring
together, every four years, representatives of the nations of the
world face-to-face, and one is permitted to think that these

*peaceful, courteous contests constitute the best form of
internationalism.*

Extract from Coubertin's 15 January 1894 circular invitation
to the Sorbonne Congress of June 1894

I n photographs, Coubertin looks out at the spectator with the melan-
choly eyes of a visionary. His enormous moustaches conceal the set
of the mouth. The portrait photo does not show that he was a short
man.

Pierre de Coubertin, full name Charles-Pierre Frédy de Coubertin,
was born in Paris on 1 January 1863, the fourth child of parents both
descended from noble families. His father Charles-Louis was a moderately talented artist, who exhibited genre and historical paintings at the
Paris Salons from 1846 to 1887. At the moment of Pierre's Olympic triumph he produced an allegorical painting, *The Restoration of the
Olympic Games*, which appeared on the cover of successive issues of
Pierre's *Revue Olympique*. Pierre's mother was a pious Catholic lady, a
musician, devoted to good works. Both parents were patriotic Royalists
and legitimists, mourning the departure of the Bourbons, dismayed by
the national shock of defeat in the Franco-Prussian war and the insurrection of the Paris Commune.

Pierre was educated at the Collège Saint-Ignace in Paris, where he
learned from one Father Carron the Jesuits' ideas about the ancient
world, and the balance of body and mind which Greece of the classical
period was held to represent. He learned fencing, riding, boxing and
rowing. Pierre went on from school to study law, as his parents wished,
but with no enthusiasm. He was drawn to the study of current affairs at
a time of profound changes in society. Reacting against his parents'
views, he came to identify himself with the Republicanism of Léon
Gambetta, Jules Ferry and Sadi Carnot, and to believe that the answer
to France's national decline lay in education for democracy and republicanism.

By 1883 the twenty-year-old Coubertin was well read in educational

9 *Baron Pierre de Coubertin (1863–1937), the man who revived the Olympic Games, made them international, and insisted that they move from city to city rather than staying in Greece (IOC/Olympic Museum Collections).*

and social theory, from John Locke, Spencer, Mill and Darwin to Rousseau, Montaigne and the egregious nineteenth-century educationalist Bishop Dupanloup. He absorbed the writings of contemporary educational reformers such as Jules Simon and Michel Bréal, later the architect of the modern marathon. He was drawn towards England by the influential *Notes sur l'Angleterre*, published in 1872 by the philosopher and historian Hippolyte Taine. From Taine he learned about Dr Arnold and Rugby School, Charles Kingsley and muscular Christianity. He was intrigued by the concept of the British gentleman and by stories about the Englishman's attitude to sport. Britain seemed to be an enviably successful imperial society. In 1883 he went to England to see for himself.

Coubertin travelled round the great public schools and visited Oxford and Cambridge. Always an effective networker, he had the help and advice of a number of schoolmasters and dons. He described Eton, Harrow, Rugby, Wellington, Charterhouse, Westminster, Marlborough, Christ's Hospital, not all of which he visited, and also Toynbee Hall in the East End of London, where a great social experiment was taking place.

He described the results in a book, *L'Education en Angleterre*, which was published in Paris in 1888. It is a mixture of anecdote, statistics and moral reflections, a sort of educational ethnography and travel book. Coubertin's English was fluent and he spoke with staff and pupils at a wide variety of schools. He did not always get the right end of the stick, but he saw enough to fall in love with the vigour and independence which he found in the system by contrast with the 'boredom and weakness, those purveyors of immorality' of the French state schools.[1]

Coubertin was an enthusiast, a man who needed a cause and found it in England. His book was carelessly argued, snobbish, but weirdly readable. The main conclusion which he took away was that there was something here for the French to learn, in the striving of British education to develop the free and autonomous character of the schoolboy – what Arnold called 'sovereignty'. He liked to cite the story in Taine in which a child astride his pony, entering a field near a threatening bull, calls back down the line of horses to his big sisters, 'Hey, girls, don't be afraid, I'll lead the way.' He quoted Arnold's credo, the antithesis of autocracy: 'I wish to form Christian Gentlemen; my goal is to teach children to govern themselves, which is far better than governing them myself.'

Coubertin was well aware that this was a difficult message to put across to French people. He begged his readers not to label him an 'Anglomaniac'. ('Well then, we are agreed!' he wrote. 'We hate the English, and they hate us.') It was still useful to study the English neighbour, so as to imitate what he did well and try to do even better. He rebutted also, in advance, the objection that there was no use in studying the English because 'our characters are too different'. Nevertheless, Coubertin does come across at this period as an Anglomaniac, trying to graft on to a very different French system elements from England which he did not fully understand.

The hero of his book is Dr Arnold of Rugby, long gone by the time of Coubertin's visit, but still presiding in a ghostly form over Rugby School and, in a wider sense, over English public school education. On his second visit to England, in 1886, he reflected on Arnold's spirit in the chapel of the school. Meditating at twilight before Arnold's tombstone, he dreamed that he saw before him 'the cornerstone of the British Empire'.[2]

Arnold was the right figure to serve as symbolic representative of British education in its character-forming mode. He was less right as a representative of the healthy and character-forming influences of sport. In fact he seems to have had little interest in sport at all. He was too busy wrestling with the moral, political and intellectual problems of the age, as in his tortured sermons in Rugby chapel on the problem of evil. Coubertin, undeterred, tried to enlist him by describing his jolly games of snowballing with his children. 'He would not have been an Englishman if he had not loved sport; at Laleham, where he had first founded a private school, he played at snowballing with his "pupils" and took part in all sorts of gymnastic exercises, swimming and rowing with them. Once he got to Rugby, he continued to encourage games and athletic sports. One can see the role that he attributed to sport from the question which he put to himself: "Can one," he asked, "hasten the transformation which turns a child into a man without running the risk of crushing his physical and intellectual faculties?"'[3]

Actually Arnold thought that boyhood was an awkward but unavoidable phase of transition to manhood and was keen to shorten the period as much as possible. Coubertin's Arnold was largely a figure of Coubertin's imagination, conceived through the medium of Thomas Hughes's vastly influential *Tom Brown's Schooldays*, published in 1857, a book which Coubertin had read in France and which largely informed his view of England, Rugby, Dr Arnold and sport.

Arnold's period at Rugby was the 1830s, the period of the ideal of 'godliness and good learning' represented by such figures as Arnold himself and later by Edward White Benson, the first headmaster of Wellington College, who was father of the young archaeologist Freddy Benson, and who was to become Archbishop of Canterbury.[4]

These were men whose passion was the spiritual and moral development of their charges. Sport was of marginal interest to them. 'Free time' was more profitably spent rambling in the countryside observing the manifold works of God than in organised competition. In so far as sport featured at the mid-nineteenth-century schools, it did so typically in forms organised by the boys themselves, with minimal involvement of the masters. This was to change, radically, in the 1870s and 1880s, under the influence of Thomas Hughes's ideas about boyhood and sport. *Tom Brown's Schooldays* put forward the ideal of the plucky, God-fearing, honest schoolboy. The England that Coubertin encountered in 1883 was the England of Kingsley's 'muscular christianity', Thomas Hughes's manliness, and a rapidly growing cult of sport, though he did not appreciate how recent was the change in ethos at the schools.

Coubertin's conclusion was that the English public schools provided the very element that was lacking in French education. This was not surprising, for though he claimed to have gone to England an anglophobe, he probably went there looking for this element. The problem of French education was what he called '*surmenage*' or overwork. The *lycée* school day lasted twelve hours. French schools were forcing houses of oppressive discipline and stultifying routine, concentrating on the mind to the exclusion of the body. A national debate was in course in

France on what should be done to remedy this, provoked in part by the defeat of 1870.

Coubertin was convinced that a simple reform of the curriculum designed to create more free time was not the answer. Free time in itself was an invitation to waste time, or worse, to indulge in corrupt and louche practices. He gave a vivid picture of the degeneration of French students and the grim surroundings of their schools. What was needed was to inject into the system healthy pursuits which would balance the intellectual content of the curriculum. The English schools provided a model of such pursuits. 'I am convinced that experience will quickly show, better than any arguments, that the true remedy for overwork or rather the effects which we attribute to it does not lie in the weakening and slowing down of studies, but in the counterweight which sport can provide for intellectual fatigue. It is sport which will re-establish the broken equilibrium; it should have a place marked out for it in every educational system …'[5]

Gymnasiums (then becoming popular) and fencing schools were not enough. Every school should have its playing-field, along with changing-rooms and covered playground. In most cases these would be out of town, so transport would have to be provided. If necessary, the state should facilitate all this. The French pupils should be offered a variety of sports, including team games. He mentioned football, lawn tennis, chases such as hare and hounds. Coubertin did not shrink from offering his French readers the option of cricket: 'Why has cricket always been despised by us? It is a superb game, of the greatest interest, demanding discipline and fostering esprit de corps.'

In Coubertin's view, sport would not only produce in France a more rounded people, holding mind and body in equilibrium, it would help to suppress vice. But sport must be distinguished from militarism (a Prussian attribute) and military training. 'It is not militarism that our education needs, it is freedom.' Only this would contribute to the 'moral unity' of the country.

A preoccupation with vice was a well-known Victorian concern. Its part in Coubertin's thinking emerges in his fascination with the sleeping arrangements at various schools, such as the individual cubicles at Wellington College, which could not be locked on the inside. This arrangement had been devised by Benson, who mused on the possibility of nailing a wire lattice flat over the top of each cubicle but concluded sensibly that a system of perfect surveillance 'sufficient to prevent evils of a gross nature' was next to impossible to achieve, and that the best inspection would be the 'introspection of leading boys of high tone and character'.[6]

In his book Coubertin described the problem of vice as 'extremely serious'. He quoted with approval the saying that 'every collectivity of men constitutes a collection of vices and corruptions, and children are men in the making'. Once again he found the right approach in England. The English knew that evil was transmitted from one to another, and had found ways of stamping it out. One of these was expulsion, Dr Arnold's device for preventing the bad apples from corrupting the good. Coubertin did not visit Uppingham, where another influential headmaster, Edward Thring, took the opposite view, believing that expulsion represented a failure on the part of the school.

The report which Coubertin took back to France on the character-forming benefits of team sports and the virtues of democracy and self-government in schools was addressed to the perceived failures of French education. Its object was to improve the moral character of the French schoolboy. The insight which later led him to imagine the revival of the Olympic Games had no part in it. Clearly his English journey was crucial in forming his views. It convinced him of the moral dimension of sports, an idea which he was to transplant into his conception of international athletics. It also helped to confirm his views on the necessity of amateurism. At the same time the journey had something of a youthful romantic fling about it. The spell of Anglomania wore off in time. It did not make Coubertin any more inclined to seek to give the English any particular role in the Olympics, as we shall see. If anything, the contrary.

Coubertin's reforming efforts paid off with his appointment in 1888 as Secretary General of the new Committee for the Propagation of Physical Exercise in Education, of which Jules Simon was the President. The position gave Coubertin the platform he needed. For a few years he threw himself into the practical problems of persuading the educational establishment that his reformist ideas were right. He found one or two enlightened schools and teachers to serve as models. Among them was the private Catholic school L'Arceuil, where the radical Dominican priest Père Henri Didon inculcated his ideas. Another, praised by Coubertin, was the Ecole Monge. He was right in looking to the *lycées*, French public secondary schools, to lead the revolution. But it is not easy to assess how much real progress he made in introducing not only sports, but also the sporting ethos he had found in Britain. There was a great inertia among the teachers in the French public system. As with any radical movement of true believers, there were factions; and there was opposition, from the radical deputy Pascal Grousset, to the wholesale importation of British sports and habits.

Coubertin was a doughty scrapper on the metaphorical playing fields of French educational bureaucracy and debate. And he was active at exactly the right time, when sports were beginning to take off. We have seen the growth of gymnastics and cycling, followed by the English sports, football, rugby football and athletics, which began to invade France in the 1880s, under the influence partly of expatriate Britons, partly of the propaganda of Coubertin and his friends.

In 1889 the Minister of Public Instruction sent Coubertin to North America to study how athletics were organised at US and Canadian universities. He read Tocqueville before embarking. The result of his extensive three-month journey around New England, Canada, the Mid-West, Florida, Louisiana and Virginia was his long book *Universités Transatlantiques*. Like his work on English education, it is a travelogue full of anecdote and analysis of the American way of life. He described his method of judging how adolescents had been raised: 'just watch them play, listen to them talk to their teachers, and find out how they wash themselves'. He found that this threefold criterion was never wrong, but for the older boys of university age more detailed inquiry was needed.

Coubertin reported his conclusions to the minister on his return in what he conceded was an unusual report by academic standards. He found that American universities were worthy of Europe's attention: their efforts were not always well thought out ('in their zeal, they are mixing the wheat with the chaff'), but their 'perseverance and hard work overcome all difficulties, and their progress must prove a stimulus for fruitful competition on our part'.[7]

Once again he found evidence of the superiority of Anglo-Saxon models. He saw in US universities a battleground between two extremes in systems of physical education, free games from England, and scientific gymnastics from Germany. The German method was based on intolerance, allowing only 'group movements, rigid discipline, and perpetual regulation'. Coubertin disliked the 'incredible power' of gymnasium directors, the 'bizarre apparatus' they sometimes used, and the excessive zeal which he thought that the American universities had brought to team sports. He watched the way ('pseudo-scientific') in which élite athletes were picked out, on the basis of anthropometric tests, and formed into élite teams of champions, to the neglect of the other students. It seemed to him like animal husbandry.

However, there was much more to admire than to deplore. The university debating societies and in-house journals showed that the Americans were serious and dedicated to freedom, which for Coubertin was the essential moral ingredient. Outside the universities and colleges, there were numerous well-organised athletic associations. He noted the advanced state of track and field, and the popularity of baseball and football. ('Baseball is extremely simple in terms of its rules, but it is quite difficult to play.') He observed that after any rather taxing exercise, Americans young and old would take a shower bath. He recommended the absolute necessity of providing French students with showers.

The freedom which Coubertin approved was not discriminatory. He was shocked by the racial segregation he encountered in the south, where he saw a well-dressed black lady forced to vacate his carriage in the train to Jacksonville and move to the dirty and uncomfortable 'Negro car'. He mocked a mischievous Senator whose proposed solution to the 'negro question' was repatriation to Africa: 'It is their native country,' he said. 'What a glorious mission for them to bring the civilisation they have gotten from us to their brothers who remained barbarians!' He noted that in a dispute, the black man was always wrong. 'People speak to him as they would to a dog, and everyone does his best to give him a clear idea of his inferiority. Yet that inferiority is far from proven. After so many years of servitude, it is not surprising that the intelligence is slow to open up. In the schools, the little Negroes learn wonderfully, and show great aptitude for work. Then it all comes to a sudden stop. They never get past a certain limit, but that limit is always being pushed back.'

In the course of his travels Coubertin was entertained at Princeton University by a historian of France, Professor William Milligan Sloane. The son of a pastor and theologian of Scottish origin, Sloane was a brilliant scholar with a knowledge of European affairs acquired during a spell in Berlin as private secretary to the diplomat and historian George Bancroft, who was Minister at the US Embassy. Sloane became Professor of the Philosophy of History at Princeton in 1883. During the 1880s he entered the world of inter-collegiate athletics. He became chairman of the university's athletic advisory committee at a time when students and faculty were disputing the control of college sports. Coubertin and Sloane found an immediate rapport. Coubertin later recalled the night air at Princeton, the atmosphere at Sloane's home, and the warm discussions far into the night. There is no evidence that on this occasion they discussed a revival of the Olympic Games.

Coubertin's visit to America taught him that the US could not be ignored as a coming force. He referred in his report to the high degree of civilisation achieved by this great country, with its short but glorious past, and with a future that seemed so brilliant. 'Therefore let us pursue our reforms,' he wrote, 'strengthened by the example of England and America. Let us attempt to implement the program summed up in these words: sports and freedom.'

A year after his American tour, in late October 1890, Coubertin visited Much Wenlock. There he discovered Brookes's Olympian experiment, which he called 'one of the most curious in the annals of athletics', and enjoyed the pageantry and the Hellenic and medieval associations with which Brookes had invested his Wenlock Games. Brookes was, he noted, the one who began the games forty years ago, and at age eighty-two, still alert and vigorous, he was still organising and running them. 'The fact that the Olympic Games, which modern Greece has been unable to restore, are being revived today is due not to a Hellene, but to Dr W.P. Brookes.'

Coubertin's article on his Wenlock visit is a panegyric to the man Brookes, 'whose activity and energy are equaled only by the clarity of his vision and the uprightness of his approach', and to his Olympic vision. Brookes spoke with 'that simple and intelligent eloquence that, when placed at the service of a fixed, authoritative idea, is irresistible to his listeners'. The idea of the Olympics fixed itself in Coubertin's mind, but this was the only occasion on which he acknowledged the authority and the authorship of Brookes.

He described the scene:

*On festival days, long processions wound through the streets of the
small town. School children sang hymns and strew flowers.
Banners were carried aloft. Green garlands adorned the houses. At
the head of the procession, riding on horseback, came the tilters
who competed for rings, a very popular exercise at Wenlock. For*

the most part, the athletes were young farmers from the neighboring area, people who did not always have the most delicate touch, but solid fearless riders nonetheless. Wenlock is located at the bottom of a valley … Pastures and hills dotted with woods lie all around. The playing field for the Olympian Society includes a track for foot races, areas for cricket and lawn tennis, a track for equestrian exercises, great stands for the spectators, a pool used in good weather, and finally, a carefully manicured lawn where open-air dances are held. But what contributes most to the beauty of the site are the skilful plantings that surround the place with a wreath of green. An exceptional variety of precious species is represented there. All these trees commemorate some significant event, a victory, or a visit.[8]

Coubertin was invited to plant an oak tree, which joined trees named after Queen Victoria, King George of Greece, the Prince of Wales and other dignitaries. He was welcomed by a triumphal arch of flowers at the entrance of the field, with a banner wishing him and France well. He was particularly attracted by the pageantry of the medieval 'tilting'. His day at Wenlock ended with a banquet in the reading room attached to the public library, at which the assembled company sang 'For he's a jolly good fellow'.

Coubertin published his Much Wenlock article on Christmas Day 1890. He included in it an account of Brookes's correspondence with King George, as a result of which the King 'donated a magnificent cup for the competitions at Wenlock, and supported the restoration of the Olympic Games at Athens', a remark that suggests that Coubertin's mind had started to bring together the ideas of an Olympic revival and of Greece. His enthusiasm for the Wenlock Games was clear but in his article he drew no practical conclusion from them. When he did finally engage with the revival of the Olympic Games, Brookes dropped out of the picture entirely, a good illustration of the absorbing egotism of Coubertin. The credit assigned in 1890 to Brookes as a pioneer

Olympian was forgotten, or suppressed, and no further reference to Brookes appears in Coubertin's published writings.

Some time between Coubertin's visits to the US in 1889 and to Much Wenlock in 1890, and the autumn of 1892, he committed himself to the idea of a revival of the Olympic Games. Exactly how and when this happened we do not know. It is clear that he had been impressed and influenced by Brookes, though after his one article about Wenlock he was not going to admit as much again. It is less likely that the Zappas games had any effect on him. Whatever the reasons, the weight of his attention now shifted from the internal French educational debate to the wider issues of international sport, the question of amateurism, and the Olympics. From this time on, the Olympics were the ruling idea of his life.

He first spoke publicly about an Olympic revival in November 1892, at a sporting congress in Paris marking the fifth anniversary of the founding of the Union des Sociétés Françaises de Sports Athlétiques (USFSA), the federation of which he was Secretary General. Here he put to an uncomprehending audience his proposal for the restoration of the Olympic Games.

The manuscript draft of his speech encapsulates Coubertin's naïve, progressive philosophy. He described athletics as democratic and international, two vital features of the modern age:

> *It is clear that the telegraph, railways, the telephone, the passionate research in science, congresses and exhibitions have done more for peace than any treaty or diplomatic convention. Well, I hope that athletics will do even more ... Let us export runners and fencers; there is the free trade of the future, and on the day when it is introduced within the walls of old Europe the cause of peace will have received a new and mighty stay.*

This is enough to encourage your servant to dream now about the second part of this programme; he hopes that you will help him as you helped him hitherto, and that with you he will be able to continue and complete, on a basis suited to the conditions of modern life, this grandiose and salutary task, the restoration of the Olympic Games.[9]

He wrote later, 'Naturally I had foreseen every eventuality except what actually happened. Opposition? Objections, irony? Or even indifference? Not at all. Everyone applauded, everyone approved, everyone wished me great success but no one had really understood. It was a period of total, absolute lack of comprehension that was about to start.'

This was hardly surprising. The idea came more or less out of the blue. People missed the 'modern' in his formulation, and thought he had in mind pageantry or some re-enactment of the ancient world. The joke was to inquire whether the men would have to perform naked and whether women would be allowed as spectators.

Coubertin was not dismayed. He set out to gather support. He determined to use a further USFSA congress in 1894, planned to deal with the contentious question of amateurism in sport, as a screen for his Olympic revival. In his memoirs, written thirty-seven years later, which are the main evidence for his intentions at his period, he refers to amateurism as 'an admirable mummy that could be presented ... as a specimen of the modern art of embalming'.[10] That was hindsight. It was a real issue, which was to plague Coubertin and his successors. But it was also an issue on which he could get round a table a varied group of sporting officials from different countries to discuss the Olympics.

In autumn 1893 Coubertin set off on his second trip to the United States, aiming to renew acquaintances and to proselytise for the Olympic idea. He visited the Chicago Exhibition, stayed in California, and returned to Washington and New York via Texas and Louisiana. He met a warm welcome at the universities he had visited before, despite the fact that his new book had ruffled some feathers there. But he found no enthusiasm for the Olympic idea apart from Sloane, with whom he stayed for three weeks. On the eve of his departure for Europe Sloane gave a dinner at the University Club in New York, for carefully selected guests. Coubertin noted, 'Very warm conversation, sincere interest, but an obvious feeling of inevitable failure.' He had the same impression, only stronger, at a dinner in London at the Sports Club in February 1894.

Coubertin had additional problems. Universities, on which he relied to bolster the 'classical' credentials of the plan, were showing little interest. Nor were the Germans, whom he regarded as indispensable participants. And politics were creeping in: the Belgian Gymnastic Federation took the view that gymnastics and other sports were diametrically opposed, and the French federation threatened to withdraw if the Germans took part. As the congress approached, everything seemed, in Coubertin's words, 'streaked with light on a grey background'.[11]

Undeterred, Coubertin got on with the preparation of the congress. He used his position as Secretary General to do everything possible to fix matters in advance. His main weapons were the membership of the executive board, and the agenda which he prepared. 'At the head, an immovable trinity: C. Herbert, Secretary of the Amateur Athletic Association (London), for Great Britain and the British Empire; W. M. Sloane, professor at Princeton University, for the American continent; and myself, for France and continental Europe. This unusual geography was intended to simplify propaganda for me. My two colleagues had accepted mainly in order to please me.' Herbert, taciturn but understanding, had an organised infrastructure at his disposal (which, ironically, Coubertin in the end failed to exploit). Sloane had access to the transatlantic university circles which he saw as dominating American athletics.

The circular letter which Coubertin sent out to athletic bodies abroad on 15 January 1894 announced that the International Congress would open in Paris on 17 June, with the twofold objects of defining and debating amateurism, and re-establishing the Olympic Games 'on a basis and in conditions in keeping with the needs of modern life'. The preliminary programme set out seven points for discussion on amateurism, ranging from its definition to practical questions concerning suspension, disqualification, betting, prizes and distinctions between sports in their attitude to amateurism. There followed one clause on the possibility of restoring the Olympic Games.

Coubertin worked hard at stage management and at attracting the great and the good. He was always good at exploiting aristocratic networks. The chairman of the congress was Baron de Courcel, a Senator and former Ambassador to Berlin. There were royal patrons – Honorary Members – including the King of the Belgians, the Prince of Wales, the Crown Prince of Sweden, Grand Duke Wladimir of Russia and Crown Prince Constantine of Greece. The long list of Honorary Members also included the politician A.J. Balfour, the British Ambassador, Charles Waldstein, Director of the American School at Athens, Ioannis Phokianos and William Penny Brookes.

5

THE PARIS CONGRESS

Let us export runners and fencers; there is the free trade of the future, and on the day when it is introduced within the walls of old Europe the cause of peace will have received a new and mighty stay.

Coubertin, speech of 25 November 1892

The congress opened in the impressive main amphitheatre of the Sorbonne in the presence of 2,000 people, with seventy-eight delegates from forty-nine societies in Australia, Belgium, Bohemia, France, Great Britain, Greece, Italy, New Zealand, Russia, Spain, Sweden and the United States. After considerable diplomatic toing and froing, Germany, with which Coubertin always had difficult relations, was represented by an unofficial observer.

The highlight of the opening session was the first choral performance of a newly discovered Hymn to Apollo. The words of this, with what appeared to be musical notation, had been discovered inscribed on tablets during excavations at Delphi by the French School of Archaeology. It was translated by the French Hellenist Théodore Reinach, and set to music for choir and orchestra by Gabriel Fauré. Coubertin detected a subtle feeling of emotion spreading through the auditorium as if the sound came from the distant past: 'Hellenism infiltrated the whole hall.' It was a master stroke to allow the Greeks themselves to speak across the ages. He claimed later to have known from this moment that the congress would succeed.

One of the delegates at the Paris congress, who was catapulted into the Olympic movement seemingly by accident, was the Greek writer Dimitrios Vikelas.

Vikelas combined the commercial enterprise and mobility of the Hellenic world of the nineteenth century with the reflective temperament of the scholar. He was born in 1832 in Syros, the island centre of shipping and commerce in the Cyclades that for long outranked Piraeus as a commercial port. His father was a merchant and his mother, who taught him to love books and educated him at home, a member of the prosperous commercial family Melas. When he was six the family moved to Constantinople, and ten years later to Odessa, where he started work in his father's office.

At the age of seventeen Dimitrios showed his literary precocity by translating Racine's tragedy *Esther* into Greek fifteen-syllable verses. Then in 1852 he took the step that was to change his life. He travelled across Europe to England and started work as a bookkeeper in his uncles' shipping office in the City, Melas Bros. He lived with his uncles Leon and Vasileios Melas at their house near the British Museum, and walked to work every day. Vikelas now began the regular weekly correspondence with his mother which lasted forty-nine years, until her death in 1901. He opened up to her his inner as well as his outer life; she was his 'pole star, guiding my steps in the path of life: the centre around which turned my very existence'.

Business never satisfied Vikelas; but he set out to master it, and eventually became an equal partner in the Melas firm, and thus a member of the extraordinarily successful community of Greek traders and shippers in the City of London which rapidly grew in the first half of the nineteenth century. His life is mapped out for the reader in his published works and private papers, especially the correspondence with his mother. He kept a diary in London and at other stages in his life. At his uncle Leon's suggestion he also noted all the books he had read, with comments. He wrote an attractive memoir, *My Life*, describing these years in London, in which he combined evening study at University College London with the hard work of the shipping office, a strenuous reading programme, and the social life of the Greek community.[1] He married Kalliope, the younger sister of his uncle's wife Ekaterini and the fifth daughter of a prosperous family of the London Greek community.

By the time of his marriage Vikelas was formidably well read, having devoured most of the great writers of the century in English, French and German, as well as Greek. He began to publish: a collection of poetry in 1862, articles in periodicals about the British press and the cultivation of cotton in Greece. In 1865 he started a correspondence with Harilaos Tricoupis, who had served as an attaché and later Chargé d'Affaires at the Greek Embassy in London, and was embarking on his career in politics.

Vikelas used his position in the world of letters to intervene with British writers and scholars in support of the Cretans who rose in rebellion against their Ottoman Turkish rulers in 1866. The Cretan insurgence was like a wind fanning the embers of philhellenism, arousing the sympathy of British and French liberals including Victor Hugo and Algernon Charles Swinburne, who wrote a long ode on the siege of Candia. Vikelas had turned himself into an interpreter of Greece to the British (as later in Paris he was to the French) and of Britain to the Greeks. But though he straddled the worlds of western Europe and of Greece, his heart lay in his home country.

Disaster struck the Vikelas couple in 1874. Following the death of her father, Kalliope began to show symptoms of severe disturbance, with irrational feelings of guilt and inadequacy. She made a number of attempts on her own life. Vikelas took her abroad in the hope of finding a cure. They ended up in Paris, where doctors pronounced that she was mad. His mother Smaragda arrived from Constantinople to give help. On the doctors' advice they kept a detailed day-to-day record of Kalliope's illness. It is a harrowing document. She spent seven and a half months in the clinic of the psychiatrist Jules Luys at Ivry-sur-Seine. From then until her death twenty years later her life was a hell of melancholia, delusion and horror, in alternating periods of relapse and recovery. There were times when she could not bear the presence of Vikelas, whom the doctors advised to keep away from her.

In the face of this disaster, Vikelas turned to Shakespeare as a distraction. In rapid succession he translated *King Lear*, *Romeo and Juliet* and *Othello*. They were published in Athens in 1876, and extracts were read at the Parnassus literary society. The evening was a success. Though these translations seem pedestrian today, they helped to introduce Shakespeare to a new audience in Greece.

Vikelas had written in 1872 that his burning wish was to establish his household in Athens, but he was waiting for his purse to be filled. By now he had put away a tidy sum. In one remission of Kalliope's illness they decided to make the move to Athens, arriving there in January 1877 and starting to build a house at the corner of Panepistimiou and Academias Streets. But soon Kalliope suffered another relapse. Vikelas decided that she must return to Dr Luys's clinic at Ivry, and accompanied her there. During her confinement he translated *Macbeth* and set to work on a new book, *Loukis Laras*, a novel set in Smyrna, Chios, Syros and the islands in the time of the Greek war of independence. The hero Loukis, a grandfather, looks back in prosperity from London on the trials and desperate adventures of his youth. It was patriotic, moralistic, but also an adventure story written in an accessible language. Vikelas submitted the book to the prestigious periodical *Estia*, where it languished in a drawer for some time. It was eventually serialised in 1879, narrowly escaping being dropped in the wastepaper basket as being too different from *Estia*'s normal fare of foreign stories. When printed it ran quickly to several editions. A French translation appeared, followed by German, Italian and Danish: in all eleven foreign language editions. It is for this book, a kind of national monument and in its time a European best-seller, that Vikelas is mainly remembered today.[2]

Over the next fifteen years, living in Paris where his wife was in and out of the clinic, Vikelas consolidated his links with the French literary and scholarly world and continued to pour out articles, travel books and stories. He became more involved in the political affairs of Greece, publishing a long article in 1885 on the role and aspirations of Greece in the Eastern Question. In 1887 he published a collection of stories in both Greek and French. He continued to travel, within Greece, in Scotland, to Constantinople, in Spain and Switzerland. In 1892 he bought a plot of land on the corner of Kriezotou and Valaoriti Streets in Kolonaki, where eventually he built a house and settled, selling the old house.

By 1894 Vikelas was sixty-two years of age, a substantial figure in the worlds of literature and scholarship in Greece, France and Britain, and a respected commentator on Byzantine history, the affairs of Greece and the Eastern Question. Distressed by his wife's condition, he nevertheless found no difficulty in leaving her for his frequent excursions and travels all over the European continent. He was in the process of putting down roots in Athens and looked forward to the opportunity to settle there permanently.

In 1894 Vikelas's life was to change dramatically. He told the story himself in an address to the Greek students of Paris a year later.

> *One evening around the beginning of last June, the postman*
> *brought me a package from which I extracted a diploma in my*
> *name, as member of the Panhellenic Gymnastic Association*

*[hereafter PGA] of Athens. This club and its affairs were wholly
unknown to me – I had not sought the honour of becoming a
member, nor had I the qualifications for this. The mystery was
solved the next morning by the postman again. He delivered an
enormous envelope containing a letter from the Association,
inviting me to represent it at the International Athletic Congress.
This official document was accompanied by letters from friends of
mine, members of the Association, begging me to agree – and
indeed by telegram, since the congress was to meet in a few days'
time. I had not even been aware that an international athletic
congress was to meet in Paris. What did I have in common with
athletics? But how could I say no to well loved friends? Besides, I
had been present on other occasions at congresses, without having
the requisite qualifications justifying my presence, and I had not
only concealed my ignorance, maintaining a salutory silence, but I
had taken advantage of the opportunities presented by such
meetings for agreeable contacts and entertainment. In the hope
that I would find a similar harmless entertainment at the Athletic
Congress, and wishing not to displease my friends, I accepted the
mandate.*[3]

One may wonder whether Vikelas was quite as reluctant as he made
out.

In considering whom to invite from Greece to his congress, Coubertin
must have taken advice. It was probably the archaeologist Charles
Waldstein who suggested the name Phokianos and the PGA. Waldstein
had an unusually international profile for a scholar of the nineteenth
century. Trained in Germany, he became the first lecturer in classical
archaeology at Cambridge University in the early 1880s; a founder of

the Museum of Classical Archaeology, later Director of the Fitzwilliam Museum, and then Director of the American School of Classical Studies at Athens, from which he directed the excavations at the sanctuary of Hera at Argos. According to the Cambridge scholar Jane Harrison, he was an 'ugly little man'.[4] He cultivated contacts in good society as well as in archaeological circles.

On receipt of Coubertin's invitation, Phokianos sent his regrets. He could not afford to be away at a time of intensive preparations for the opening of his new gymnasium. But he wrote to Coubertin welcoming the Olympic aspects of the proposed congress and saying disingenuously that the Association had invited one of its most suitable members, who lived in Paris, to attend as their representative. Phokianos then sat down to write a long memo on the questions of Olympism and amateurism raised by Coubertin.

The 'friends' who incited Vikelas may have included Phokianos himself, whom he knew already from the literary circles of which they were both members. But the letter he received was from Alexis Rangavis, another friend, writing on behalf of Phokianos. Rangavis was a son of the scholar, poet and Minister Alexander Rizos-Rangavis, who had dealt with Zappas over his generous donation. There have been suggestions that the 'friends' included Crown Prince Constantine, and that the choice of Vikelas had been arranged in advance by Coubertin and the Crown Prince. There is no evidence for this, though Constantine was already aware of Coubertin's plans. Waldstein had lobbied him during a visit by the Royal Princes to his excavation at Argos in April 1894. It was then that Constantine allowed his name to be used as a patron of the Paris congress.[5]

Vikelas wrote back to Rangavis that he could not refuse, though he felt his 'extreme unsuitability ... I hope this does not entail my taking part in athletic sports, heaven forbid!' He reported that he had tried to visit Coubertin to find out what he would have to do, but the Baron was not at home. Ten days later he received a further large envelope from the PGA. It contained Phokianos's paper and a request that Vikelas translate it and communicate it to the congress. Given the length of the paper, this was no joke – but he knuckled down to the task, and passed the paper to the Secretary General of the congress.

The Secretary General was of course Coubertin, whom Vikelas now met for the first time. The Secretary General invited him to chair the Committee of the Congress which was to deal with the revival of the Olympic Games.

Why Vikelas as chairman? And why Athens? Coubertin's invitation is difficult to explain unless he was already considering Athens as a possible host city. There was no other reason for choosing an elderly, inexperienced Greek author, unless Coubertin thought that it would be good to have a Greek as chairman to bring out the ancient Greek associations of the proposed new institution.

The question of where and when the games should take place was clearly crucial. The accounts by Coubertin and Vikelas are incomplete and in some respects contradictory.[6] Coubertin claimed to have changed his mind about the venue. He had originally envisaged that the first games should take place in Paris in 1900. He had not thought Greece capable of coping. Conversations with Vikelas, whom he immediately liked, led him to change his mind. According to Coubertin, Vikelas wanted the games to take place in Athens, but hesitated at the responsibility of involving his country. The two men encouraged each other, and Athens was finally accepted to the accompaniment of wild applause.

For his part, at the start of the congress Vikelas did not expect Athens to be chosen as the first host city, and probably did not seriously consider proposing Athens. He reported to the PGA merely that at the appropriate moment he would propose that Athens be included in the list of capital cities where the International Olympic Games would take place. But the issue came up at a meeting of his Olympic committee on 19 June. The minutes of the congress, deciphered and analysed by the historian David Young, show that at this meeting there was a discussion of the relative merits of London and Athens. Most delegates, including two of the French, took the view that the first games should take place in London. Coubertin blocked this, helped by the fact that Herbert, the British delegate, was absent. The issue was put off, for later discussion in plenary. Later that same day Vikelas wrote a note to Coubertin: 'I have not seen you since the congress meeting to tell you how moved I was by your proposal that the Olympics should start with Athens. I am sorry that I could not support you enthusiastically at that moment.'[7] It is clear from this that by 19 June Coubertin was actively working to block London and to promote Athens, or at the very least to keep Athens in the ring as potential host.

Vikelas told the Greek students that he was in doubt until the eve of the last day of the congress, 22 June. On the one hand he felt obliged to take advantage of this unique opportunity, and argue the claims of Athens to be the host city. On the other, he was inhibited by the fact that he had no mandate from the Greek state, or indeed the PGA, to propose Athens. He was inhibited also by the fact of Greece's bankruptcy, which Tricoupis had declared the previous year. But on the evening of 22 June he received a visit from a Greek friend, 'known for the generous and patriotic way he used his wealth', who was passing through Paris. Vikelas let his hair down and told him everything. The friend, whom he never named, enthusiastically approved his aims, and assured him that somehow the money would be found. That was enough for Vikelas to make up his mind. He decided to propose Athens on his own authority. He wrote to Phokianos saying that he would support Athens, believing that in doing so he was interpreting the desire not only of the Association but of every Greek, but that he foresaw difficulties owing to the distance of Athens. (Distance had been one of the objections raised against Athens at the 19 June meeting.)

When the congress met the next day, it first endorsed the decisions of the committee on amateurism. Then it was the turn of Vikelas's committee. He made his case for Athens, stressing that he was speaking without a mandate from the government. A Greek institution was being revived, for which a Greek city was the appropriate host. He warned the delegates that they should not expect an imposing festival; the warmth of their reception and the ruins of antiquity would have to make up for the many deficiencies. He invited the congress to formulate the wish, without committing anybody, that the games should be celebrated in Athens.

Vikelas sat down, expected to hear objections. Instead, Coubertin, the President of the Amateurism Committee, Professor Sloane and others warmly supported his proposal, which was adopted unanimously. Clearly Coubertin had prepared the ground.

In his brilliant analysis of what happened in Paris, and how and why, the historian David Young sets out reasons for believing that between 19 and 22 June Coubertin received encouragement from the King of Greece to propose Athens. He certainly sent a telegram to Athens, through the Greek chargé in Paris, on 19 June, and received a reply from the King on 21 June, which Young interprets as giving the go-ahead. The text of the King's telegram reads, 'Très sensible à la demande si courtoise du baron de Coubertin, je le prie ainsi que les membres du Congrès, de recevoir, avec mes remerciements sincères, mes meilleurs voeux pour le rétablissement des Jeux Olympiques. George.'*[8] Young argues that this was a strange message to send before the congress had even taken a decision on the revival of the games, unless it was some form of comment or answer to a message that Athens was in the running for the position of host city. He admits that the evidence is inconclusive, and that we would expect a firmer trail leading to the King.

The congress endorsed the proposal to revive the Olympic Games, provided – always Coubertin's proviso – that they conformed to

---

*'Very touched by Baron Coubertin's courteous request, I send him and the members of the Congress, with my sincere thanks, my best wishes for the revival of the Olympic Games. George.'

modern conditions. Except in fencing, they should be open only to amateurs. They should take place every four years, starting with Athens and then Paris in 1900. The sports represented, if possible, should be athletics (track and field), aquatic sports (rowing, sailing and swimming), athletic games (football, tennis, paume, etc.), skating, fencing, boxing, wrestling, equestrian sports, polo, shooting, gymnastics and cycling. There should also be a pentathlon. A prize for mountaineering should be awarded for the most interesting climb accomplished since the last games. Not all these were to happen, but the syncretic aim was clear. This was not to be an exclusive event.

Before breaking up, the congress nominated a permanent committee to execute its decisions. Vikelas was elected President, in accordance with Coubertin's newly introduced rule that the President of the committee should be from the country where the next games were to take place. He thus found himself the first President of the International Olympic Committee (IOC). Coubertin himself was content to steer the committee as its Secretary General. He knew also that, as senior French member of the IOC, he himself would succeed Vikelas for the four years between the Athens and the Paris games. In the event Coubertin held on to the Presidency from 1896 until 1925.

Coubertin's slate of members of the IOC, most of them absentees, went through unopposed. He described the committee as it evolved as a 'self-recruiting body', like the organising body of the Henley Regatta, with three concentric circles of membership: a nucleus of dedicated active members; a nursery of willing members capable of being educated along the right lines; and finally a façade of people of varying degrees of usefulness whose presence would add prestige and satisfy national pride.

The Paris congress broke up in the confusion caused by the assassination of President Sadi Carnot. It had been a triumph for Coubertin, whose vision, networking and stage management had yielded decisions which were ambitious but realisable. These decisions now had to be implemented.

10 *The first members of the International Olympic Committee, photographed
in Athens. Dimitrios Vikelas, the first President of the IOC, is seated in the
centre, with Coubertin, pen in hand (as General Secretary) next to him. The
other members, standing from left to right, are Gebhardt (Germany), Guth-
Jarkowsky (Bohemia), Kemeny (Hungary), and Balck (Sweden), and seated
Boutovsky (Russia). (From the album of photographs by Albert Meyer, Berlin)*

One man who did not attend the Paris congress was Brookes. He was
too old and ill to do so. He died on 10 December 1895. When he heard
in 1894 of Coubertin's plan to launch international Olympic Games on
a rotating basis, he wrote to Coubertin giving it his full-hearted
approval. But his fate was to be written out of the history books by
Coubertin and Gennadius. Coubertin presumably did not wish to
share the credit with anyone else. Gennadius, when he wrote about the
1896 Olympic Games, attributed them entirely to France and Coubertin. Despite his intermittent twelve-year correspondence with
Brookes, he made no reference to him at all.

When Vikelas reported the decision of the Paris congress to
Phokianos, he wrote that it was the 'consecration of the noble aim of

the Association of raising morale through bodily exercise, but also a manifestation of philhellenic feelings, doubly valuable in the difficult circumstances we are living through, and a new link between Greece and Europe'. Following up in early July, he noted that the first responses of the press had been positive, and advised caution in the public campaign until Coubertin visited Athens in October: 'nothing definite as regards things or persons until then: that is owed to Mr Coubertin'.[9]

Athens was a high-risk choice. The Greek government might block the project. Or it might fail for lack of funding, lack of popular support, government indifference, or defective organisation. Greek athletes might be humiliated by the foreign competition. Vikelas's proposal that Athens host the games had a quixotic element in it.

The first question was whether bankrupt Greece would accept the honour thrust on her by the congress. The matter had to be decided, if only because the Hungarians were rivals for the honour of hosting the games, as a complement to the world exhibition scheduled to take place at Budapest in 1896. Vikelas told his student audience in April 1895 that there were two important reasons for hope: the Crown Prince had allowed his name to be used as an honorary member of the congress, and King George had sent a warm telegram to the congress. These indications were followed soon after the congress by a message from Constantine's aide-de-camp that the Crown Prince had learned with pleasure that the games would be inaugurated in Athens, and that he and his father would offer their patronage.

The plan was for Coubertin to go to Athens in October. In the event Vikelas went first, arriving in late September. As soon as he arrived he realised that matters would not be straightforward. For economic reasons the government refused to take on any commitment to new expenditure. Tricoupis told him that he would have much preferred the question of the Olympic Games not to have arisen. His hesitations were shared by the Committee for Olympic Questions (the committee responsible for the Zappas Olympics, now chaired by the future Prime Minister, Stephanos Dragoumis). Given its name, this body might have been expected to take on responsibility for the whole Olympic affair. Vikelas, who carried on a long and friendly correspondence with Dragoumis, said as much.[10] But the committee had never been enthusiastic about athletics, and was still less so now at a time of national stringency. Dragoumis wanted Vikelas to stop the troublesome Coubertin from coming.

At this point, on 14 October, Vikelas received a telegram from Dr Luys in Paris telling him that his wife's health had suddenly deteriorated; she had oedemas in the thigh, shin and stomach and she was not taking food. He should come quickly. Before leaving for Paris he wrote a letter to Dragoumis expressing his concerns. He accepted that the economic situation was a real obstacle, but argued that the consequences of refusing the honour offered by the Paris congress would be worse than the difficulties Greece would face in hosting the games. Refusal would make the worst possible impression abroad and throughout the whole world of Hellenism. Was it not better to hold the games in Athens and use them to raise national morale, rather than frustrate the goodwill of the international community for Greece?[11]

Coubertin had been working in Paris on the detailed programming of the sports events, corresponding with the heads of sporting federations in France and the UK. On his arrival in Paris, Vikelas tried to persuade him to postpone his visit to Athens for a month or two, in view of the 'hesitations' expressed in Athens. Coubertin would have none of this. He set off for Athens to take up the reins, 'anxious and joyful' at the prospect of the struggle ahead.[12] He received a long, ominous letter from Dragoumis advising him that the Olympic project was a non-starter in Greece's reduced economic circumstances. Besides the economic crisis, the notion of athletic sports did not exist in Greece. He suggested that the games should be put back to 1900 and held in Paris, which had the necessary resources and experience in sporting matters.[13] Characteristically Coubertin ignored this. He claimed to have read the letter only on the boat from Marseilles to Piraeus, when it was too late to turn back.

Prime Minister Tricoupis, who may have been intrigued by this strange French visionary, set aside protocol and visited Coubertin at his hotel. He explained that Greece had insufficient funds to accept the mission which Coubertin wished to entrust to her. Coubertin energetically set about proving the contrary. He blithely told Tricoupis that the expenditure would be comparatively small. He lobbied politicians and journalists. He visited the unrestored stadium, 'a huge mound stripped of its marble', and, later, the Acropolis. He investigated the resources available in Athens and drafted a budget for the games. He spoke eloquently in favour of the games at a meeting at the Parnassus Literary Society. He was instructed by a Greek coachman in how to deal with the Prime Minister. When he returned to Tricoupis, he succeeded in extracting a promise of benevolent neutrality, in the circumstances no small achievement. But there was no promise of official financial support. Coubertin found that he was 'a sort of ball thrown back and forth' between two political parties. Deliyiannis's opposition naturally took the opposite view to Tricoupis. A cartoon in the satirical magazine *Romios* showed the two politicians squaring up to each other as in a boxing match.

Coubertin's allies came from the upper classes close to the royal family. In the absence of the King in Russia, his main interlocutor was the Crown Prince himself, whom he met twice and who confirmed his willingness to support the games. Before leaving Athens, he convoked a meeting on 24 November of about thirty-two prominent Greeks at the Zappeion building. His aim was to form a committee capable of organising the games, under the presidency of the Crown Prince. He consulted Dragoumis about this, and about membership of the committee.[14] Dragoumis attended briefly, to make some introductions, and then left.

The thirty-two men gathered in the Zappeion that day were drawn from the Greek 'establishment' and included, along with a number of Tricoupis's political allies, two close associates of the Crown Prince, Alexander Mercati and George Melas. The former minister and Tricoupis supporter Stephanos Skouloudis left the meeting early and was elected one of the four Vice-Presidents in his absence, to his embarrassment. The date of the games was fixed as 5–15 April 1896. The programme of sports endorsed by the Paris congress was adopted, though not all of them featured in the final programme in 1896. Having established a Greek committee, Coubertin assumed, or pretended, that his work was done. He left Athens to visit Olympia. From there he returned via Italy to France.

No sooner had he departed than the arrangements he had made collapsed in ruins.

6

OLYMPIA REDISCOVERED

The spirit of Greek antiquity has pervaded German scholarship.

Professor Ernst Curtius, excavator of ancient Olympia

Nothing in ancient history had given me more food for thought than Olympia.

Coubertin, *Une Campagne de 21 Ans*

Coubertin's sentimental journey to Olympia can be seen as a necessary and final stage in his journey towards the Olympic revival. But it came, paradoxically, after the crucial decision had been made to revive the Olympic Games at Athens. Athens represented the modern, Olympia the ancient. Coubertin's priorities were clearly shown in the choice to put Athens first.

Olympia lies in an attractive valley in the prefecture of Elis in the north-east corner of the Peloponnese. The little town has grown up around the site of the ancient games. In the early nineteenth century there was nothing there beyond a few huts and cottages.

Olympia is a place of enchantment in the spring, when the Judas trees are in flower among the ruins on the ancient site. It stands in the fertile valley of the Alpheios, a broad river which winds down from the mountains of the central Peloponnese, discharging into the Ionian sea ten miles to the west of Olympia. It is a countryside of olive groves, fruit trees, vineyards and wheatfields, with pine forests covering the flanks of the hills. In ancient times the Alpheios was navigable as far as Olympia, a point of importance for the development of the great Olympic festival.

The Alpheios valley is impregnated with history and legend. Even the river had its mysterious stories. The Greeks personified rivers as gods. Alpheios the river god had a lustful reputation and pursued the nymph Arethusa. Both he and his tributary Kladeos, a narrower stream which joins the Alpheios on the west of the ancient site, can be seen in the museum today in the form of sculptures, solid reclining figures in relief on the east pediment of the great temple of Zeus.

Here at Olympia, some time in the early part of the first millennium BC, the people of Pisa near Elis started to hold competitive games, under the patronage of Zeus. The early history of the games is shrouded in legend. Different versions ascribe the origins respectively to Herakles, the demigod of the twelve labours, and to Pelops, who gave his name to the Peloponnese. The first has it that Herakles cleaned out the stables of King Augeas of Elis by diverting the river Alpheios through them, sweeping out the horse manure and straw in the rushing water. Having completed this labour Herakles laid out the Altis, or sanctuary, on the banks of the river and instituted the first games in honour of Zeus.

The second version is that the games were originally funeral games held in honour of a local hero. Pelops is the most likely candidate. He came to Elis looking for his fortune, and took up the challenge of Oinomaos, King of Elis. Oinomaos had a beautiful daughter, Hippodameia, for whom he had conceived an improper passion. He had been warned, too, to expect death at the hand of a son-in-law. To win his daughter a suitor therefore had to beat the King in a chariot race. The King's practice was to allow the suitor a start while he sacrificed a ram. He would then follow in his own swifter vehicle, and when he caught up, spear the unfortunate suitor in the back. Many had perished in this way by the time Pelops arrived. Their heads were nailed up as a warning to others.

But Pelops was undeterred. He bribed the King's charioteer, Myrtilos, to take the linchpins out of the royal chariot wheels and substitute wax pins. As the wax melted in the heat of the sun during the race, the wheels fell off and the King was thrown to his death. Thus Pelops won the beautiful Hippodameia, who bore him six fine sons, and gave his name to the Peloponnese. 'Now buried by the ford of the Alpheios river,' wrote Pindar, the poet of Greek athletics, in his first Olympian ode, 'he shares in the splendid blood-offerings at an altar visited by countless strangers.'

The start of this unusual chariot race is shown on the east pediment of the temple of Zeus, and can be seen in the museum. It is an appropriate story for a Greek hero, since cunning, exemplified by Odysseus, is a highly prized virtue among the Greeks. Bribery was also to be a recurrent theme of the ancient Olympic Games. The Greek travel writer Pausanias piously commented that it was surely a staggering thing that people should so despise the god at Olympia as to give or take a bribe; but his own writings are full of incidents of bribery or attempted bribery, and the severe fines which it incurred.

The Greeks officially reckoned that the Olympic Games started in (what we call) 776 BC. They grew from a simple foot-race into the greatest festival of the Greek world, a symbol of the unity of Hellenism, attracting thousands of visitors from all corners of the Hellenic world, from Sicily to the east shores of the Black Sea. The five-day programme in the classical period included three foot races of different lengths, a race in full infantry armour, wrestling, boxing and the violent, mixed *pankration*, chariot and horse races, and the pentathlon, consisting of the discus, javelin, long jump, running and wrestling. Many of the details of these events, for example how the athletes jumped with heavy weights in their hands, are obscure. The Olympic truce which held throughout the festival ensured the safety of participants and visitors in transit, though it did not stop Greek states from fighting each other. As the years passed and the festival grew in renown, the sacred site of

Olympia, with its temples to Zeus and Hera, filled with sporting buildings and commemorative statues, many no doubt of indifferent quality.
Pausanias, writing in the second century AD, mentions by name 213 statues of victors, and that must be only a selection.

The games took place at the second or third full moon after the
summer solstice, in the hot season from mid-August to September. This
was the time after the harvest was gathered in, when men could relax
for a time and celebrate. It was hot for the contestants, as Athens will be
hot in August 2004, but a good season for spectators to sleep out under
the stars.

The games continued at intervals of four years without a break until
393 AD, their regularity allowing them to serve as the basis of the Greeks'
system of universal dating. Then the Emperor Theodosius issued an
edict forbidding pagan festivals, and they were closed, done for by the
new and aggressive Christian religion.[1]

The games differed in a number of important ways from the sort of
athletic sports contests which were developing in the second half of the
nineteenth century. They were primarily a religious festival to Zeus.
The contestants in track and field performed naked. The programme,
rules and conditions were different. But there was also a likeness which
appealed both to Greek revivalists and to internationalists such as Coubertin, in the connection with the supposed ancient Greek value of balance of mind and body. Coubertin also took it for granted that the
revived Olympics, like the ancient games, should be for men only –
though women had their own separate games at Olympia, dedicated to
the goddess Hera. In their exclusion of women, at least married women,
even as spectators, let alone competitors, Olympia stood at the conservative end of the spectrum of Greek city states. Coubertin was happy to
allow women as spectators but reluctant to go further. A number of bad
arguments had been concocted by nineteenth-century medical special-
ists to show why sport was bad for women.

All this and much more was known to those who had studied the classical authors. Pindar and Bacchylides had written odes in celebration of

Olympic champions. Thucydides had referred to the early games and the introduction of the practice of competing naked. Even the details of the buildings of ancient Olympia were well known through the writings of Pausanias. But for western Europeans, by the eighteenth century Olympia the place had to all intents and purposes vanished off the face of the earth. After the closure of the games, earthquakes, landslides and floods had completed the work of the Christians, destroying the buildings, toppling the columns of the temples to the ground, flooding the stadium, and finally burying the entire site in mud. The hand of man had also played a part. The Altis was burnt on the orders of Theodosius 11 in 436 AD. The buildings were quarried for masonry for a Christian church on the site of the workshop of the great sculptor Pheidias, who designed the gold and ivory statues of Athena in the Parthenon and Zeus at Olympia. Marbles were consigned to the lime kilns. Gradually the site was forgotten, except by the local Greeks.

With the rediscovery of Greece by western travellers in the late eighteenth century, more British and French visitors began to visit the Peloponnese, making their tour with mules and muleteers and interpreter or dragoman. Many of these visitors were knowledgeable, some were rich and some were acquisitive. They took pleasure in identifying ancient sites.

Richard Chandler, a Fellow of Magdalen College, Oxford, and of the Royal Society of Antiquaries, was sent on a mission to Asia Minor and Greece in the 1760s by the Society of Dilettanti. His instructions were to 'collect informations, and to make observations, relative to the ancient state of these countries, and to such monuments of antiquity as are still remaining', for which purpose he was to keep a detailed journal 'in the plainest manner, and without any regard to style or language, except that of being intelligible'. He was provided with a budget of up to £2,000.[2]

The book which Chandler wrote on his return was in fact stylish as well as erudite. Having travelled round the classical sites of Asia Minor and the Troad, and then Athens, Attica, Delphi and the Peloponnese, he and his companions reached Olympia in July 1766, two and a half years after embarking at Gravesend. By this time they were tired and sick. Like so many visitors in ancient times, they approached Olympia by sea, landing in the bay of Chiarenza. Staying at a monastery for the night, they were preyed on by vicious gnats, and at the next stage discovered that myriads of large fleas had settled in the folds of their garments. It was harvest time and the peasants were working in the fields. Approaching what Chandler assumed to be Olympia by a road through the hills, with views of the river Alpheios, the travellers pitched tent in a cornfield near a ruin. 'Here gnats swarmed round us innumerable, infesting us, if possible, more terribly than before. We endeavoured to sleep, in vain. Our Greeks too called on their Panagia [the Holy Virgin] but were not relieved.'

Chandler knew what was there to be found. No doubt he had a copy of Pausanias's description of Greece in his baggage. Pausanias was an erudite Greek from Asia Minor who travelled from city to city in the mid-second century AD, recording in great detail the monuments of Greece, with their local cults and legends. This was a good time for tourism and observation, for most of the buildings from the classical and Hellenistic periods were still standing. His description of Olympia provides much of the surviving evidence about how the various sports were organised. He told the stories of famous athletes such as the wrestler Milon of Croton, who won the wrestling six times at Olympia and whose exploits still resounded centuries after his death.

Following Pausanias, Chandler described the ancient sanctuary which he knew to be concealed under the earth: the Altis with its temples, the stadium 'in the grove of wild olive trees', the hippodrome, the whole site washed by the copious and pleasant stream of the Alpheios flowing by on its way from the mountains of Arcadia to the sea.

The following morning, Chandler and his travelling companions crossed a shallow brook, probably the Kladeos or one of its tributaries, and started to survey the ground. Their high expectations were disappointed. They found that the land was almost naked.

The ruin, which we had seen in the evening, we found to be the walls of the cell of a very large temple, standing many feet high and well-built, the stones all injured, and manifesting the labour of persons, who have endeavoured by boring to get at the metal, with which they were cemented. From a massive capital remaining it was collected that the edifice had been of the Doric order. At a distance before it was a deep hollow, with stagnant water and brick-work, where it is imagined was the stadium. Round about are scattered remnants of brick buildings, and vestiges of stone walls. The site is by the road-side, in a green valley, between two ranges of even summits pleasantly wooded. The mountain once called Cronium [the modern hill of Kronos, the pine-covered conical hill which dominates the site] *is on the north, and on the south the river Alpheus.*

It was not surprising that Chandler found only fragments, given that most of the low-lying site was buried in silt. But though in no condition to enjoy the experience, Chandler had 'rediscovered' Olympia for the west. It was now only a matter of time before someone dug it up. The age of scientific archaeology was beginning.

Chandler and his companions had had enough:

We had experienced, since our leaving Athens, frequent and alarming indisposition. We had suffered from fruits, not easily eaten with moderation; from fatigue; from the violent heat of the sun by day, and from damps and the torments inflicted by a variety of vermin at night; besides the badness of the air, which was now almost pestilential on this side of the Morea. My companions complained. Our servants were ill; and the captain, whose brown complexion was changed to sallow, had grown mutinous, and declared he would go away with his vessel, as he must perform a long quarantine at Zante, if his return were delayed.

As the exhausted travellers made their way down to the sea, the gnats attacked them again. They sailed for home from Chiarenza on Sunday, 20 July 1766.

Chandler was followed by others who added to his identifications, including the French consul Fauvel in 1787 and the great topographer Colonel Leake, another devotee of Pausanias, in 1805.

Those who took an interest in ancient Greek ruins at this period could be divided roughly into three categories. There were the scientific travellers: archaeologists, architects, natural historians, topographers. There were the collectors of antiquities such as Lord Elgin, who was prepared to violate a building in order to export its marbles for private collections in Britain. And there were the local people who saw the ruins as a useful source of stone for building or for making lime.

As early as 1723 the Frenchman Bernard de Montfaucon had written to Cardinal Quirini, recently appointed Bishop of Corfu, urging him to excavate Olympia, with Pausanias in his hand. Nothing came of this. Others were tempted. The British topographer Sir William Gell, who visited Olympia in 1806 with the painter Edward Dodwell, tried to raise funds in Britain for an excavation, but his scheme was too visionary for the practical British. The eccentric German art historian Johann Joachim Winckelmann had similar ambitions. Winckelmann believed that there was something holy in the noble simplicity of Greek sculpture, reflecting man's true, free and uncorrupted nature, and looked to Olympia for confirmation of his intuitions. But Winckelmann never got as far as Greece. He based his influential reflections on copies of Greek sculpture which he saw in Rome, and was stabbed to death by his male lover in Trieste while planning an expedition to Olympia to excavate.

The first foreigners systematically to investigate the Morea, as the Peloponnese was then generally known, were the French. A French scientific expedition came to Olympia in 1829 and dug for six weeks, carrying away from the temple of Zeus some panels carved in relief (metopes) showing the labours of Hercules. These can still be seen in the Louvre. But the final task of excavating the site fell to Professor Ernst Curtius of Germany.[3]

Curtius, one of two brother historians, was a pious, serious German scholar with a religious sense of mission. The domed forehead and firm jutting jaw of his portrait seem to indicate a man of determination as well as high culture. He believed in the disinterested role which Prussian scholarship, backed by the Prussian state, should play in revealing to the world the noble achievements of Greek culture, of which Olympia was the summit. In 1837 Curtius went to Athens, where he served as tutor in the family of one of young King Otho's Bavarian advisers. He travelled round Greece with the eminent geographer Karl Ritter, picking up a lasting interest in the topography of ancient Greece. He visited the valley of the Alpheios in 1838 and 1840, complaining like Chandler about the sultry and unhealthy atmosphere and the swarms of vicious mosquitoes.

Curtius returned to Germany in 1841, completed his doctorate and embarked on a successful career as a scholar and lecturer. His brand of sentimental enthusiasm, in the tradition of Winckelmann, proved extremely popular. A lecture about the Acropolis of Athens attracted an audience of nearly 1,000, including the Crown Prince of Prussia, later Wilhelm I, and his wife. They were sufficiently impressed to hire Curtius to tutor their eldest son, later the Emperor Frederick III. Under his tutelage the liberal-minded prince became a philhellene.

Curtius firmly believed that Germany, with its serious, disciplined, art-loving spirit, had inwardly appropriated Greek culture, and should have the privilege of recovering the remains of this great site and symbol of ancient Greek art, sport and religion. He believed that Olympia was still a holy place. He launched his revival of Winckelmann's project in 1852 with a public lecture in Berlin, following this with a memorandum to the Prussian government calling for support and funds. 'The spirit of Greek antiquity,' he claimed, 'has pervaded German scholarship.' The enormous job to be done at Olympia might perhaps have been done by the French, but they were soon to be heavily involved digging elsewhere, at Delos and Delphi. The Greeks had neither the means nor yet the interest. The British had avid and knowledgeable collectors, but Curtius disapproved of dilettante collectors. In any case the British were not yet a serious presence on the Greek archaeological scene.

The King of Prussia was impressed. Curtius won permission to negotiate with the Greeks, and the German Embassy at Athens entered into discussions. But it took more than twenty years for the dream to become reality. Instability in Greece, the blockade of Greek ports by Britain and France during the Crimean War, and the obstruction of the Prussian Chancellor Bismarck all delayed the project. Bismarck thought that digging up ruins at Olympia was expensive frippery, especially if Germany was not to be allowed to appropriate the results. But Curtius, with the help of his royal patrons, carried the day. In 1869 the Crown Prince travelled to Athens and lobbied on behalf of Curtius's scheme. He pronounced himself content with the restrictive Greek rules on the export of antiquities. In 1873 there was a scare when the great Heinrich Schliemann, temporarily denied permission to dig at Troy and looking for an alternative site for his genius, bid for the Olympia concession. But finally, in 1874, King George I signed a treaty giving permission for the German excavation. It provided that Curtius should excavate the site and publish his findings. He was permitted to take photographs, but to export only casts and duplicates. This was to be a model for future archaeological practice between host country and foreign scholars.

Curtius and his assistants started to dig in October 1875. Teams of Greek workmen were engaged and moved in on the site. One of those who visited Olympia to see the results was Mahaffy, who used to say of King George of Greece 'Quite the nicest King I know'. Mahaffy visited Greece in the spring vacation of 1877 with his former Trinity College Dublin student Oscar Wilde, now at Oxford. Oscar seems not to have bothered to get leave of absence, and was rusticated on his return, remarking later in life, 'I was sent down from Oxford for being the first undergraduate to visit Olympia.'

11 *Ancient Olympia was excavated by Ernst Curtius in the 1870s. The photo*
   shows the German archaeologists and Greek workmen in 1875. Coubertin
   instructed that his heart should be buried there.

Mahaffy and Wilde approached Olympia on horseback from Pyrgos,
riding up the mule path which follows the sinuous course of the
Alpheios; but instead of the dry gravel beds and parched meadows
which the pilgrims of ancient times would have found in August, they
found:

> ... *a broad and rapid river ... the meadows green with sprouting*
> *corn and bright with flowers, and all along the slopes the trees were*
> *bursting into bud and blossom, and filling the air with the rich*
> *scent of spring. Huge shrubs of arbutus and mastich closed around*
> *the paths, while over them the Judas-tree and the wild pear covered*

*themselves with purple and with white, and on every bank great
scarlet anemones opened their wistful eyes in the morning sun.*[4]

After this the reality was a shock. 'However interesting excavations may
be, they are always exceedingly ugly,' Mahaffy wrote. Instead of grass
and flowers they found great mounds of earth, the Kladeos flowing like
a turbid drain into the Alpheios, wheelbarrows, planks, trenches, and
hundreds of workmen. The passage of years was required before the
excavated ruins became part of the natural landscape again.

But Curtius had struck lucky. An impressive piece of sculpture
turned up early in the dig, the winged *Victory* of Paeonios, which can be
seen today in the museum. This helped persuade the Prussian parliament to vote further funds. Later, when Bismarck finally cut off the
funds, the King, who remained devoted to the project, subsidized the
dig out of his privy purse. In the course of six years of careful excavation, with upwards of 300 workers on the site, Curtius uncovered the
entire sanctuary of ancient Olympia. With the exception of Paeonios's
Victory and the famous *Hermes* of Praxiteles, the free-standing sculptures were disappointing. But as Curtius wrote, the main achievement
was not the individual pieces, but the resurrected vista of the whole area
of Olympia, and the sense of the ancient festival that the site evoked. It
was this that was to turn Olympia into a tourist icon for the twentieth
century.

By the end of the first phase of the excavation, in 1881, visitors could
see from the top of the hill of Kronos the ancient site laid out below on
the sandy level. Scholars and amateur fans of archaeology in western
Europe and America became aware, through press reports and the systematic German publications, of the reality behind the Olympia of history and legend. Real runners, jumpers, javelin and discus throwers,
riders, charioteers and boxers had played out their struggles in this very
landscape. The painted boxers, charioteers and runners of the ancient
pottery were coming to life in Curtius's excavated site. The sculptures of
the temples of Zeus and Hera, as described by Pausanias, could be seen

in the new museum erected near the site with funds donated by the banker Syngros. They were real and some of them were beautiful.

Later excavations completed the picture, in some cases startlingly confirming the ancient sources. Pausanias had written that there was a building outside the Altis called Phidias's workshop, where the sculptor of the Parthenon had worked detail by detail at the colossal ivory and gold statue of Zeus which stood, or rather sat, in the temple of Zeus at Olympia. Pausanias also described the statue itself, which he saw in the temple: a godlike figure of gold and ivory, seated on an ebony throne, wearing a mantle and olive wreath, holding in his right hand a figure of Victory and in his left hand a sceptre with an eagle. The great statue, which became one of the seven wonders of the ancient world, did not survive. The emperor Caligula wanted to carry it off to Rome and replace Zeus's head with a model of his own, but was deterred by supernatural intervention. The statue was finally transported to Constantinople, where it was destroyed in a fire in 475 AD.

Though the statue was burned, the workshop survived under the mud of the Alpheios. In 1958 the German archaeologists excavated the building beneath a Byzantine church which had been erected on the site. They found a black-glazed drinking cup, dating from the 430s, with the two Greek words which mean I AM PHIDIAS'S scratched on the base. Around it among other of the sculptor's working tools were traces of ivory and instruments for working gold. So history again comes to life in Phidias's workshop.

New finds in archaeology had a wide currency, and the German government published annual reports on the nineteenth-century excavations. The knowledge of what was going on was diffused rapidly through the scholarly community. One of those who were aware of Curtius's discoveries was Pierre de Coubertin. He probably absorbed the details through the publications of French scholars.[5] He wrote in his memoirs ten years after the first revived games took place in Athens,

Nothing in ancient history had given me more food for thought

*than Olympia. Germany had brought to light what remained of
Olympia; why should not France succeed in rebuilding its
splendors? It was not far from there to the less dazzling but more
practical and fruitful project of reviving the Games, particularly
since the hour had struck when international sport seemed
destined once again to play its part in the world.[6]*

This retrospective account of how and when he conceived the revival
of the games is certainly not the whole story. But given the part that
Olympia occupied in the construction of the Olympic revival, it was
clearly essential that it should be incorporated in Coubertin's narrative,
and that he should go there. He made his first visit to Olympia in
November 1894, travelling down from Athens to Patras by train. He
described it as a moment of revelation.

*I remember the footpath that climbed snakelike up the little hill
where the museum and hotel were located. A pure air, perfumed
with scents, blew up from the banks of the Alpheus. For a moment
the moonlight animated a vaporous landscape, then a starry night
fell over the two thousand years with which I had come to seek
stirring contact.*

Coubertin had to wait until dawn to discern the outlines of the
sacred landscape of which he had dreamed. The next day as soon as the
first rays of the sun lit up the valley he rushed towards the ruins. His
first impression was of their smallness – not the impression of most visitors to Olympia, it must be said. But he claimed not to be surprised or
disappointed, for

*… it was a moral architecture I was going to gather lessons from,
and it magnified every dimension. My meditation lasted all
morning, while only the noise of the bells of the flocks on the way to
Arcadia disturbed the silence.*

All morning long I wandered in the ruins.[7]

This was Coubertin's semi-mystical introduction to Olympia. He claimed later to have found it sobering. 'On that morning in November, 1894, I became aware in this sacred place of the enormity of the task which I had undertaken in proclaiming five months earlier the restoration of the Olympic Games after an interruption of 1,500 years; and I glimpsed all the hazards which would dog me on the way.'[8] Pressing tasks awaited him in Paris and he did not stay long. He was to return only once, in 1927. But as we shall see, a part of him, his heart, returned again after his death.

7

PREPARATIONS

The celebration of the Olympic Games in Athens will have an
undoubted moral utility for us.

Crown Prince Constantine, speech at the Zappeion, 24 January 1895

The 1896 Games were to be the largest athletic encounter yet held anywhere in the modern world, and the largest public event ever staged in independent Greece. They could not be improvised. After Coubertin's visit of November 1894 there were only sixteen months for preparations. Yet he had left behind him in Athens a situation of controversy and near chaos, in which the arrangements he had set up quickly collapsed. Skouloudis and his colleagues on the committee set up by Coubertin quickly concluded that the cost of the Games would be at least 600,000 francs, not the 200,000 estimated by Coubertin, and that it was unrealistic to expect to raise the necessary sum quickly through an appeal for funds or through a lottery. They therefore offered their collective resignation. For a time it looked as if the games would not take place in Athens.

In the hothouse atmosphere of political Athens, the Olympic Games had now become a nationalist issue. At a parliamentary debate on 6 December, Tricoupis came under pressure from opposition deputies to clarify the government's position. The Prime Minister replied firmly that the government would give the games no support. Dragoumis inevitably took the same line. He claimed that he had no money to offer, since Zappas's properties in Romania had been confiscated by the Romanian government and therefore were producing no revenue; all his committee could do was to put the Zappeion buildings and the stadium at the disposal of the organisers. Against the government's stonewalling, opposition deputies argued, very much on the lines of Vikelas, that the games would bring benefits to Greece's prestige, to national morale, and to the economy through tourism. Failure to take up the challenge, said one, would mean that the Greeks were exposed in the eyes of the entire civilised world as rustic provincials, and – clinching argument – would strengthen the case of the enemies of Hellenism that 'we are not the descendants of the ancient Greeks'.[1]

Vikelas's poor wife Kalliope died in Paris. After settling her affairs, he returned to Athens in late December. Soon after his return things took a turn for the better, which he attributed entirely to the energy and firmness of the Crown Prince. Effectively Constantine took matters into his own hands. He accepted the resignation of the faint-hearted members of the committee, replaced them with members of stronger stomach, and, working with Vikelas, formed a twelve-member Council to supervise the work of the committee and its working groups. From this point on, the involvement of the royal family more or less guaranteed that the games would take place.

In one respect the task now looked easier. Tricoupis resigned on 22 January 1895 over a dispute with the Crown. (The Crown Prince had appeared at a demonstration against the government's taxation policy. Relations between the Crown and the Prime Minister had been deteriorating for some time, and the King was no doubt glad to get rid of Tricoupis, but the Olympics do not seem to have played a part in the affair.) At the general elections which followed in April, Tricoupis's party was decisively defeated and he lost his own seat at Missolonghi, where Byron had died. He withdrew from the political stage, and retired to the south of France. He was succeeded by his old opponent

12 *Theodoros Deliyiannis (1826–1905), an elegant, populist, long lasting politician, Prime Minister of Greece at the time of the Games. He was assassinated by a disgruntled card player who objected to his closing of the Athens gambling saloons. Photo by Romaides.*

Theodore Deliyiannis, who was much more sympathetic to the Olympic project. The new government could not be seen to divert funds from Greece's creditors, but was happy to give indirect support.

However, the Olympic Games were relatively low in the scale of Deliyiannis's priorities. The new government inherited the economic and financial crisis which followed Greece's bankruptcy, and difficult negotiations with the foreign bondholders. As usual, Crete was in a state of crisis which might explode at any moment in armed revolt against Ottoman power. The Bulgarian threat to Greek interests in Macedonia was a relatively new and growing concern to nationalist Greeks.

Constantine was determined that the games should happen. Having dealt with the crisis caused by the organising committee's resignation, he quickly set in place an organisational structure capable of the complex logistical task of preparation. At the pinnacle of this structure was the Council of Twelve, chaired by Constantine himself, exercising a general supervision and coordinating the effort to raise funds. It contained some of the most distinguished figures in Greek political life, drawn mainly from the opposition to Tricoupis, including ministers, future Prime Ministers and Presidents. He appointed as Secretary General Timoleon Philemon, a former Mayor of Athens, member of parliament, journalist and prominent member of Athenian literary and political society, who had revived and developed the Library of Parliament and was the first President of the Greek Historical and Ethnological Society ('not up to the job' was Coubertin's patronising comment later). Reporting to the council was a Committee for the Olympic Games, serving more or less the functions of today's National Olympic Committees. Below this were committees responsible for the particular sports (two of them, the nautical and the shooting committees, chaired by Prince George and Prince Nicholas), and committees for training Greek athletes, for the reception, accommodation and entertainment of foreign guests and athletes, and for the construction of the stadium. Among the archaeologists who joined the latter were the eminent German Professor Dörpfeld, Curtius's assistant and successor in the

Olympia excavations, and the directors of the other foreign archaeological schools.[2]

The Crown Prince set these committees to work on 25 January with a patriotic pep talk at the Zappeion, only three days after Tricoupis's resignation and the appointment of a caretaker government headed by a nephew of Deliyiannis. He told them that, despite Greece's material poverty and the economic problems the country faced, there could only be one answer to the question whether Greece should mount the Olympic Games:

> *It was our duty to accept the charge and show by the facts that we understand the import of international athletic contests.*
>
> *I am also firmly convinced that, despite the insufficient resources at our disposal to give a brilliant reception to the foreign athletes, they will carry home with them on their return excellent memories of our country. We are in a position to show them real progress in all the branches of human activity … Those who visit Greece on this occasion will receive cordial and irreproachable hospitality, which together with the beauty of our sky, will easily make up for any defects. That is why the celebration of the Olympic Games at Athens will have an undoubted moral utility for us.*

The welcome given to this speech in the press two days later by Professor Lambros suggested that the Crown Prince was yoking the Olympics project to a broader nationalist agenda which would play well for the popularity of the royal family. Lambros and others claimed to be moved to tears by Constantine's reference to the city of Athens as 'capital of the free part of Greek lands', with its implied claim on those other parts which were still 'enslaved'.[3]

In the practical tasks of preparation, the council and committees could expect only limited help from Coubertin, who after his visit to Olympia had returned via Italy to Paris, and remained there. On 12 March 1895 he married Marie Rothan, the daughter of a diplomat and author. He could take part only in the international aspects of the preparations, soliciting teams from the United States, Britain and France through his contacts and through the responsible national organisations. He received encouraging news from his contacts in Hungary and Sweden, news of indifference from Russia. He corresponded with Vikelas in Athens, giving advice about the running and the cycle track, the form of invitation card, a variety of problems as they arose. But the main burden of preparation rested on Constantine and the members of the Organising Committee in Athens.[4]

Fund-raising was the most urgent task. Without an adequate stadium there would be no games. The provisional committee had baulked, and resigned, at the prospect of having to raise 600,000 drachmas for the total costs of the games. It soon became clear that this was a gross underestimate.

How was it to be managed? The council launched an appeal for funds to Greeks at home and abroad, using the network of municipalities and of Greek consulates abroad to spread the news.[5] One of the first to contribute, with 10,000 drachmas, was the banker Andreas Syngros. The Greek communities of the diaspora, such as Marseilles, Alexandria and London, were the most productive. Philemon reported later that some Greeks turned a deaf ear on the grounds that the games were a silly innovation which would fall flat. Nevertheless the appeal raised the respectable sum of 332,756 drachmas. But this was not nearly enough for the stadium, let alone the total cost of the games.

The Panathenaic stadium, where the Zappas games of 1875 had been held, provided an attractive setting for sports even with spectators sitting on the grass. But the pretensions of an international Olympic festival required more. The stadium, in Philemon's words, would be the Altis, or sacred enclosure, of the new Olympics. It must be impressive. The architect Anastasios Metaxas, at the outset of a brilliant career, drew up plans for its restoration, closely following the model of the ancient stadium as it had been beautified by Herod Atticus.[6]

The obvious source of funds for the stadium was the wealthy Greeks

13 *The Panathenaic Stadium in the final stage of preparation for the Games.*
The restoration was the work of the architect Anastasios Metaxas. A
workman is doing something to the column forming the base of one of the
herms found during the excavation of the stadium. The different bands of
colour of the benches show the state of the restoration, with white Pentelic
marble at the front, wood for the higher tiers. The photo shows the Rotunda
on the right, beyond the entrance to the stadium, the Zappeion on the left,
and the Royal Palace (now the Parliament building) on the horizon. The
Protestant Cemetery, with cypress trees, was just across the road between the
stadium and the Zappeion.

of the diaspora. The nineteenth century is the great period of Greek
benefactors. Massive fortunes were accumulated by traders, shippers
and bankers in Turkey, Egypt, Russia, Romania and western Europe.
They were responsible for funding the Athens Academy (Sinas), the
Polytechnic (Averoff and others from Metsovo), the Olympia museum

14 *Statue of Georgios Averoff (1818–99), the Epirot benefactor who paid for the restoration of the Stadium, and much else. The statue was made by Georgios Vroutos, and unveiled by Crown Prince Constantine on the eve of the Games. It is still there, with Ardettos hill behind it.*

(Syngros), and a variety of hospitals, orphanages, prisons, libraries and other institutions. Constantine and Philemon now turned to one of the richest, George Averoff.

Averoff (1818–99) came from the small town of Metsovo in the mountains of Epirus, a town which spawned benefactors. He had amassed a mighty fortune in trade and property in Egypt, where he was still living. As well as his contributions to the life of the Greek communities in Cairo and Alexandria, he poured funds into Greece, for the Metsovio Polytechnic School and the Cadets' School (today's law-courts). The historic battleship which Greece procured from Italy and which did good service in the Balkan Wars was bought with his bequest to the nation and named after him. It can still be seen berthed off Phaleron, near the ancient trireme which was reconstructed with advice from British academics and oarsmen.

Constantine sent Philemon to Averoff in Alexandria with a letter appealing for his support. Averoff's response was immediate and generous. He approved Metaxas's plans and his budget of 585,000 drachmas, making a donation of this amount which he later increased to 920,000 drachmas when the initial budget was exceeded. It was the first of successive cost overruns. Work could now start on preparing the stadium, as well as less urgent commissions such as 125 luxury padded cushions for the VIPs.[7]

The committee was helped by two government measures, worth 200,000 and 400,000 drachmas respectively: the exemption of tickets issued by the games from tax, and the guarantee of income from an issue of commemorative postage stamps.

Vikelas came from Paris to Athens in May 1895 to take the temperature following the defeat of Tricoupis in the elections. The day after his arrival he visited the stadium and climbed up to the slope above the corridor, standing among the bushes and thistles and surveying the scene. The stadium was like an ants' nest, with workers down below moving, chipping and tapping as they carved the seats of the front row. Already the lower section was transformed. He felt that New Greece was stretching out her hands to the ancient world through these works.[8] Vikelas returned to Paris in June, where he became involved in a French academic debate on whether modern Greek pronunciation should be substituted for the pronunciation of ancient Greek then used in French schools. When he returned to

Athens in February 1896 he was amazed by the progress of the stadium.

Not everyone approved. The poet Kostis Palamas, author of the Olympic hymn which was played at the opening of the games, accused of barbarism those who renewed ancient monuments by adding new stones: they should be kept in the state to which time had consigned them, including the additions and changes of the passing years.[9]

The council and the special committees commissioned a new shooting range at Kallithea (this also designed by Metaxas, who happened to be an expert clay pigeon shot) and a new velodrome at Phaleron for the cycle races. The latter project gave rise to a dispute over the best site which split the cycling committee between Kallithea and New Phaleron, the latter being more swampy but in other respects more suitable. The twelve-member council finally resolved the issue, as late as October 1895, in favour of New Phaleron.[10] Other public works were put in hand, on the roads, the lighting, the greenery, the bridge over the Ilissos connecting the stadium with the modern city. One source noted fifteen new urinals. As the event approached, the brewer Fix (originally the Bavarian Fuchs) upgraded his production line. Two thousand sheep were imported from the north, but mysteriously the price of meat still rose. The satirical poet Souris wrote of this as a time when one egg cost one pound.

In the prevailing climate of stringency, cuts were made. To Coubertin's chagrin, the equestrian events envisaged by the Paris congress were dropped, because of the lack of facilities. (They will of course take place in 2004, in a new equestrian centre at Markopoulos.) The games were cut from six to five days. Cricket, royal tennis (the *jeu de paume*), the pentathlon and ice skating, all sports which had either been approved at the Paris congress or been mentioned in the IOC bulletin or the preliminary Greek programme, failed to take place. Not surprisingly, cricket, with its longueurs and its British Empire constituency, has never succeeded in staking a claim. The possibility of including association football, though in the end that did not happen, led to the first Greek experiments with football.[11]

Somehow it was all done. Mistakes were made, and coordination was poor, not surprisingly given that the organisers had no experience to guide them; but by the end of March, stadium, cycling track and shooting range were ready. So were the Greek athletes, with the help of the training committee and a programme of trials. So were simple medical facilities, to be provided by a small team of military doctors whose services proved useful in the wrestling, cycling, marathon and pole vault. To some it seemed like a miracle that, when the teams began to arrive, Athens was ready for them. The worries now centred not so much on infrastructure as on participation. Vikelas in particular was concerned that the constant carping in the Greek media would deter foreigners, and wrote to the press on the eve of the games to remind the Greeks of the national importance of the Olympic enterprise. He urged the Greek organising committee to beef up their propaganda and public relations, including with the foreign press.[12]

And the cost? A rough estimate would be rather more than 1½ million drachmas, of which the stadium swallowed 1 million, as compared with Coubertin's first estimate of 250,000 drachmas and the committee's estimate of 600,000. The breakdown was: the stadium (first phase) 1 million; shooting hall 300,000; velodrome 200,000; miscellaneous 100,000. Averoff had paid for the stadium, the fund-raising campaign had raised more than 300,000, and the receipts from the postage stamp issue were 400,000. Further expenditure, on cleaning up and illuminating the city, was to fall to the municipality of Athens, and some expenditure on entertainment to the civil list.

Reflecting in 1895 on the turn of events, Vikelas saw three benefits for Greece in acting as host. First was the stimulus which the games would give to the development of athletic sports in Greece. Second, the games could be an incentive for the development of tourism. 'Through more frequent contact with foreigners, there will come about a more rapid and complete integration in the general community of Europe. I am not looking merely to the wallets of the travellers. I expect a moral benefit from the increasing association with civilisation from outside.' Thirdly, before the games had even taken place they had brought about a more immediate and frequent contact between the heir to the throne and his people, who could now appreciate what Vikelas saw as his enthusiasm and hard work, his honest strength and decisiveness. A conservative and a royalist, Vikelas saw this as a happy omen.[13]

Meanwhile, from the United States and all over Europe the athletes were making their way to Greece. Here was a test of Coubertin's effectiveness in gathering support for the new Olympic Games. The showing was frankly disappointing. Britain, the country regarded as the inventor of modern athletics, and of virtually every internationally recognised sport including football, rugby football, and cricket, was almost absent. As so often in affairs of international significance involving Europe, she had missed the bus.

The reasons were set out after the games by one G.S. Robertson, an Oxford man who described himself as a 'Competitor and Prizewinner': the competition he entered was the discus, and the only prize he won was for delivering at the closing ceremony of the games a Pindaric ode which he had composed in ancient Greek.

Robertson argued that the 'international perspective' of the committee (the IOC) was at fault:

> *They seemed to suppose that the participation of all nations was of equal importance to the success of the games. They did not consider, or, if they did, they gave no indication of having done so, that every nation except England and America is still in an absolutely prehistoric condition with regard to athletic sports. Unless England and America took a large share in the Olympic*

meeting, it was bound to be an athletic failure. In this matter the committee pursued the suicidal policy of devoting the greater share of their attention to Continental athletes. The original programme and book of rules was printed in French ... no edition of the rules was ever issued in English till very shortly before the games, when a private firm produced one.[14]

The purpose of the Olympic Games was to draw in a wide spread of athletes from many countries. However, Robertson had a point. Coubertin himself fully recognised the importance of Britain and the US in theory, but seems to have neglected them in the period between the Paris congress and the games, leaving the initiative to Sloane in America, and Herbert in Britain. He seems not to have acted on Vikelas's advice to recruit the prominent British classicist Professor Richard Jebb of Cambridge University as a helper, analogous to Sloane, in the British universities.[15] He wrote letters to British newspapers, which published them with sympathetic comment tinged with irony. 'They did not believe in the Olympic Games,' he justly observed.

Robertson pointed out that the two British IOC members, Charles Herbert and Lord Ampthill, had no connection with the old universities, which were the natural recruiting grounds, given that the games would take place in the Easter vacation. This was not strictly true: Arthur Russell, 2nd Baron Ampthill, educated at Eton and New College Oxford, had rowed in the winning Oxford eights in 1890 and 1891, in which year he was President of the University Boat Club. He could surely have recruited in the university if he had wished. But in 1896 he was embarking on a new political career as Assistant Secretary at the Colonial Office. In the end an 'obscure notice' was posted up at Oxford and a paragraph inserted in an unimportant Oxford journal; but it was not until March that any direct appeal was made to the Presidents of the university athletic clubs.

Robertson concluded that 'English athletes, seemingly, waited to be invited to go to Athens and consequently never went. Those who did

15 *The Princeton University team in the stadium: from left to right, Lane,*
   Jamison, the captain Garrett holding a shot, and Tyler with pole. Garrett
   won two silver (i.e. first place) medals for the discus and the shot put, and
   came second in the long jump and high jump, Tyler came second in the pole
   vault, Jamison second in the 400 metres, Lane fourth in the 100 metres.
   (Meyer album.)

go, did not go as representatives of any club, but for the most part, as
private pleasure-seekers.' No doubt the British thought they did not
need the Olympics. The blame for complacency falls on the IOC representatives and the university athletic clubs, with more on the former
than the latter. Neither Herbert nor Ampthill bothered to attend the
games in Athens. They therefore missed also the session of the IOC
which took place during the games. The British absence was a blow to
the credibility of the Athens Olympics, but it was not to be fatal.

The other major player in track and field was the United States. Here
Coubertin was luckier and more effective. His friendship with Professor Sloane of Princeton University paid off. The decision for the uni-

versities was not easy, for financial reasons and because the timing of the event in April virtually ruled out seniors approaching graduation. But Princeton and the Boston Athletic Association, with a high proportion of Harvard athletes, decided after considerable soul-searching to go to Greece.

It was only on 16 March that the manager of the Princeton team finally made a surprise announcement that the University Track Athletic Association would send a team to Athens, thanks to a generous anonymous donor who had solved the team's financial problems. The university faculty had given leave of absence. The team of four consisted of Robert Garrett Jnr, scion of a wealthy family, Albert C. Tyler, Francis A. Lane and J.H. Colfelt, a 'plucky little freshman quarter-miler' who had recently run a quarter mile in 50 seconds. The generous donor was the Garrett family. Unfortunately the parents of the plucky young freshman Colfelt would not allow him to go. This left Garrett with an awkward hole in his team, which he filled with Herbert Jamison, not in the same class as a quarter-miler as Colfelt, but the best who could be found.

Meanwhile at Boston, according to the sprinter and hurdler Thomas Curtis, when Coubertin's invitation arrived, the powers of the Boston Athletic Association went into a huddle and decided that the BAA had a pretty good track team which had met with reasonable success at home and that the Association could afford to send a group of five athletes and a coach to the games.[16] According to the jumper Ellery Clark, 'the whole idea sprang from a chance remark uttered in jest' by the long-distance runner Arthur Blake, at the club's annual games in January 1896. Blake joked that he was too good for Boston and ought to go over to Athens to run the marathon there. A senior member of the club took things forward from there.

The BAA sent Curtis, Blake, T.E. Burke, a short- to middle-distance runner and the best athlete in the team, Clark, who as a senior-year student had to persuade the Dean to give him leave of absence, W.W. Hoyt, a pole vaulter, and John Graham as trainer. They were accompanied by

J.B. Connolly of the Suffolk Athletic Club, a Harvard dropout who decided to finance his own way to the Olympics. Blake, Clark and Hoyt were present or former Harvard students, Burke was from Boston University, and Curtis from MIT.

Some of these, especially Burke, were impressive athletes. 'Tall and slim, yet wiry and rugged at the same time', in the description of one of his teammates, with an enormous stride in the quarter-mile, Burke won a raft of intercollegiate events and was a formidable competitor.[17] But taken as a whole, the American team was not of the highest international standard. Of the Princetonians, only Colfelt, now reluctantly withdrawn, and Garrett in the shot put were of the top class. The IAAA records of United States university athletics during the two years before the 1896 games show Princeton lagging behind Yale, the University of Pennsylvania and Harvard in the points table. To be capable of beating the very best international competition, the Americans would have had to send a combined team including the best of the universities and clubs. It became clear that this was impossible when the New York Athletic Club decided not to send a team because they could not reach peak fitness in time for an event so early in the year. The Americans were made nervous by reports such as that in the *Alumni Princetonian* of 25 March, that England, France and Germany would each have five times as many men in the games as the United States. They need not have worried.

On 25 March the American team embarked on the German liner *Fulda*. They were accompanied by Robert Garrett's mother with a party of young ladies, but not by Sloane. The Princetonians took supplies of drinking water and rigged up an improvised gymnasium and track on board the steamer. The second cabin deck was cleared of all movable objects and the Princeton team practised twice a day in sweaters and rubber shoes. They walked and skipped with skipping ropes, practised starts, and exercised with dumb-bells. When it was possible they practised vaulting, hurdling and high jump too. The Bostonians also turned out for daily practice.

The *Fulda* made landfall at Gibraltar, where the team was able to get some more serious practice, and steamed on to Naples. From there the Americans continued by train to Brindisi, took the boat to Piraeus and reached Athens only two days before the games were to begin, on Saturday, 4 April. They were in fair shape, though the welcome threatened to undermine that:

> There were speeches – cordial, we had no doubt; lengthy, we were certain. There was champagne – much of it – and until we were able to explain the reason for our abstinence, international complications threatened. Even then, I think our hosts scarcely understood. Training? What did that signify? A strange word. Come, a glass of wine, to pledge friendship. No? Very well, then, so be it. Strange people, these Americans![18]

A part of the legend of the American participation in the first Olympics is that they intended to arrive earlier, so as to have time to train, but mistook the dates, failing to note that the prevailing calendar in Greece, the Gregorian, was twelve days ahead of the western Julian calendar. This story, which was used to add drama to the NBC TV film about the 1896 Olympics, has everything in its favour except convincing evidence. The *New York Times* had reported on 17 March that the team would arrive at Athens the day before the great athletic carnival opened on 6 April, and so they did, albeit by a complicated route.[19]

Some of the team strolled down to the stadium on the Sunday afternoon to get the feel of it. Garrett saw a discus lying on the ground, picked it up and tried it out a few times. He found that it was easy to handle, and decided then and there to take part in the discus competition.

Athletes from continental Europe were also making their way to Greece. The Hungarians were the first to arrive, some three weeks before the games, and seemed to some observers to have taken over Athens as they strode around town with blue and white national ribbons in their buttonholes.

The Germans almost failed to come at all. There had been tension between Coubertin and the German sporting establishment since before the Paris congress. Soon after the congress Coubertin was reported as making rude remarks about the Germans in an interview published in the Paris press. So far as he was concerned, the Germans could stay at home. This time-bomb exploded when a big gymnastic club, the Central-Ausschuss zue Foerderung der Jugend und Volksspiele, wrote to the Greek organisers of the games refusing the invitation to take part because of Coubertin's offensive remarks. The refusal was published in the *National Zeitung*. A first-class row brewed up in the German and Greek media. Bourchier reported in *The Times* on 4 January that the words attributed to Coubertin had caused a 'veritable storm in Greece and Germany'. Coubertin shot off a denial that he had used the words complained of, copying it to the Crown Prince, the Greek Minister in Berlin, the *National Zeitung*, his German contact Gebhardt, and uncle Tom Cobley and all. On the German side, some of the turners objected to Coubertin's universal conception of sport, regarding turning as spiritually superior. Others, who saw Germany as the spiritual heir of ancient Greece, were attracted to the antiquarian and Hellenic aspects of the proposed games.

It was important for Greece, not least for the royal family, that Germany should take part. After all, the Crown Prince was married to the Emperor's sister. 'It is unfortunate that there can be no system for the spontaneous generation of Crown Princes, so that Balkan monarchs need not seek consorts in countries whose interests are widely different,' was William Miller's comment years later on the effects of Constantine's marriage.[20] For the Germans it was important that the games should be seen to be Greek and not French. Some discreet lobbying by the royals and the Greek Minister in Berlin, and an approach by Philemon, the Secretary General of the games, calmed the waters. On 21 March Dr Willibald Gebhardt, Coubertin's Berlin contact, and his unimpressive team of three track and field athletes and ten turner gymnasts set out for Athens.

The German row marked the end of Coubertin's honeymoon with Greece. It was not surprising that there should be tensions. He did not visit Greece between November 1894 and his return for the games in April 1896. The main burden fell on the Greeks, who must have felt that while they were doing the work the glory would redound to the Olympic movement and Coubertin. On his part Coubertin began to feel that he was being cut out by the Greeks, who were getting above themselves. His writings are sprinkled with disobliging remarks, not about Vikelas, with whom relations remained good, but about Philemon, the Secretary General ('an active man, shrewd, a good administrator I believe, but with a jealous and proud character. He felt inadequate and that annoyed him'). He suspected Philemon of enjoying the row over the Germans, and not believing Coubertin's protestations of denial. The tension with the Greeks was to break out later in a major disagreement over the future of the games.

Given Coubertin's position, one might have expected at least the French team to be impressive. But he had to struggle even to get together the team of thirteen which actually attended the games, and their participation was in doubt up to the last moment. French preparations were complicated by French infighting. The marksmen of the Union of Shooting Clubs (Union des Sociétés de Tir) objected to shooting being simply one element in a wide-ranging sporting programme. Their President wrote to Coubertin, 'It is almost incredible that the organisers of the Olympic Games should have imagined that the Union

Nationale de France would agree to become an appendage of their committee and that shooting would be a mere branch incorporated and fitted into a whole series of sports.'[21] Coubertin took this sort of thing in his stride.

A few others made their way from Sweden, Denmark, Austria and Switzerland, and Greeks from the diaspora arrived to compete under the flags of Egypt, Cyprus and even Smyrna in Turkey. One unfortunate Italian, Carlo Airaldi, walked all the way from Milan to Dubrovnik, thence proceeded by boat to Patras, and then walked from Patras to Athens, as part of his training for the games. On arrival he was declared ineligible, under the rules on amateurism. It is not recorded whether he walked back home again.

One of the commissions set up by Constantine had charge of training and selecting the Greek athletes. A number of preliminary events were held, including a sports meeting on Tinos in summer 1895, organised by the National Gymnastic Association. A fortnight before the games began, *The Times* reported on 23 March 1896 that the King and Crown Prince and more than 35,000 people attended the official trials in the stadium. The winner of the marathon race – 'an interesting event' – completed the course in 3 hours 18 seconds. In the printed programme for these 'Panhellenic Trial Games', Spyridon Louis is listed, with the wrong initial D, as no. 31 of thirty-three entrants. He is described as 'Amarousiot', i.e. a man from Maroussi, as opposed to most of the entrants who were identified as representing one or other athletic club.[22] Louis did not distinguish himself in the trial race. As the games approached, Olympic fever spread through Athens and on every pavement and square men and boys could be seen practising sports, in imitation of the athletes selected for the games.

The centres of Greek athletic preparation were the established clubs, the PGA and the NGA. But 'established' does not mean stable. There were tensions in the Greek world of athletics, which came to the surface in 1895 with the establishment by Constantine Manos of a new club, the Athens Athletic Club (AAC). Manos, an intellectual who had studied at Leipzig, Heidelberg and Oxford, and was making a name as a demoticist poet, was one of the élite young men enlisted by the Crown Prince to prepare for the games. His father, Colonel Thrasyvoulos Manos, who had played a part in the ousting of King Otho, was a member of the Crown Prince's twelve-man Olympic Council. Constantine Manos was one of the secretaries to this council, and enjoyed the favour of the Crown Prince.

Manos's AAC was dedicated to the principles of amateurism, which until recently had not greatly bothered the Greeks, but which Manos carried to absurd lengths. He published an article claiming that NGA and PGA members should be excluded from the Olympic Games because they employed professional trainers. Chrysaphis and Phokianos, the professionals in question from the NGA and PGA respectively, responded strongly. The IOC had to rule that amateurism was an attribute of individuals, not clubs.[23]

Manos seems to have been trying to poach athletes from the older PGA and NGA, and if possible to monopolise the training of athletes for the Olympics. He succeeded in virtually taking over the public gymnasium for his club, and squeezing out Phokianos. He tried to introduce English dietary principles. The athletes were given drinks made of cola extract, with alleged medicinal benefits.[24] Manos concentrated on track and field events and the pentathlon, disapproving of the introduction of gymnastics and the 'ugly' sport of cycling as unsuited to the Olympics, though he conceded their physical benefits.[25] One historian describes the Manos trials as occasions when well-dressed people talked French to each other; but the results of the Athens trials in March show that Manos's athletes had considerable success in track and field.[26]

Vikelas had hoped that the Olympics would encourage tourism.

Greece had already been on the map for Thomas Cook for some years. In spring and autumn his boatloads of tourists – Cookies and Cookesses – were disembarked at Piraeus and headed for the Acropolis, carrying their cameras and wearing their sun helmets. Now Cook was appointed official agent for the Olympic Games. But for travellers from Britain it was a long way to travel for a new event with uncertain hopes of success and not much British involvement. The idea of the Olympics appealed more in France, where the Paris congress had made some impact on the media. A boatload of visitors set off from Marseilles for Greece on the *Senegal*, among them the art historian Gustave Larroumet representing *Le Temps*, and the writer Jacques des Gachons for *Le Journal*. The right-wing nationalist author Charles Maurras, who was commissioned to report on the Olympic Games by *La Gazette de France*, travelled separately.

None of these men was a sports journalist. They and their journals saw the games in the exotic context of Greek history and travel to the Levant. Their reporting reflected this, though Maurras at least, unlike Larroumet, watched the games and found them interesting. The visit of the *Senegal* was the first of a series of cultural and educational cruises to Greece and the Levant organised by Louis Olivier, the pacifist founder of the *Revue Générale des Sciences*. These forerunners of the British Hellenic Travel Club and Swan Hellenic cruises allowed adventurous French visitors to explore classical, and increasingly Byzantine, sites in reasonable comfort. They enjoyed the expert guidance of the director of the French School at Athens and the great Hellenist Charles Diehl.[27]

8

ATHENS REVIVED

A stay in Athens is, so far as external conditions are concerned,
similar to a stay at Naples or Palermo. Like these towns, the Greek
capital affords all the conveniences which most travellers find
necessary for comfort.

Karl Baedeker, *Greece: Handbook for Travellers*, 2nd revised edition, 1894

A journey in Greece is full of interest for a traveller of every
character, except indeed for a mere idler or man of pleasure.

Murray's *Handbook for Travellers in Greece*, 6th edition, 1896

The Athens which awaited the intrepid Olympians was very different from the huddled little township of Byron's time, or even the
immature capital of King Otho, so abused by visitors such as Thack-
eray. It was a handsome, well-laid-out city of about 130,000 inhabitants,[1] with the public buildings, theatres and shops appropriate to a
capital city, and the conveniences which the great Baedeker regarded as
important to his readers. However, and agreeably for the Athenians and
for visitors, it was still compact. The broad olive grove which covered
the Attic plain between Athens and Piraeus came close to the city at
Kolonos on the north-west side.

The city had recently become more accessible to visitors from the west. The Corinth canal, the greatest achievement of Tricoupis's modernisation programme, opened on 6 August 1893. At a stroke this cut 202 miles off the distance for steamers travelling from Brindisi to Piraeus. The traveller could either proceed by steamer through the canal to Piraeus, or could disembark at Patras on the gulf of Corinth and proceed from there to Athens by train in seven and a half hours. Athens had now been brought by the railways and the canal within four days of London. French visitors travelling by steamer from Marseilles took slightly longer, completing the journey in five days.

Athens in the 1890s had a royal palace, which dominates many of the early photos of the city. It had the handsome threesome of public buildings by the Danish brothers Christian and Theophile Hansen, the University of Athens, the Academy and the National Library. It had ministries, an observatory, a polytechnic, a railway, a foundling hospital and orphanage, a shaded national garden laid out by Queen Amalia at the suggestion of King Ludwig I of Bavaria. Some of the more impressive buildings were paid for by wealthy Greek benefactors from the diaspora. As well as the many domed Byzantine churches – tempting prey for demolition and development – and the new Metropolitan Cathedral, there were churches for the Catholics, the Russian Orthodox and the English Protestants, and a spacious, shaded cemetery for the Greeks, with a separate cemetery reserved for British and German Protestants. The Great Powers were represented not only by their legations, but by the French (1846), German (1874), American (1882) and British (1886) schools of archaeology and Hellenic studies, the latter two built on the undeveloped slopes of Mount Lycabettus, where until recently sheep had grazed.

Above all, for the foreign visitor, Athens was its ancient monuments, which the conveniences of the modern capital were there to serve. It was the monuments and the ancient history they represented that brought educated people to Greece, because they had heard and read so much about them and they saw them as their own heritage. For this reason Murray and Baedeker included not only minutely detailed accounts of the ruins of antiquity but also learned introductory essays on Greek art, sculpture, archaeology and history by the foremost authorities of the day. Now Athens could also boast of a modern National Archaeological Museum, completed in 1889, to house not only the treasures of Athenian sculpture and art but also the exciting new discoveries of Heinrich Schliemann from Mycenae, including the death mask in beaten gold which he claimed to be of Agamemnon.

The interested traveller in the 1890s could find plenty of 'new' antiquities, and new theories about the ancient city. Murray referred to the 'energy with which archaeological research has been conducted during the last few years, both in the Greek provinces and in the capital, and the extensive provision made for the reception of newly found works of art'. The accumulated earth upon the Acropolis had been searched down to the naked rock, revealing a mass of evidence about the ancient structures, and a collection of fine archaic statues. The medieval and Ottoman relics had been cleared away, including the so called Frankish (actually Florentine) tower which is a prominent feature of early drawings of the Acropolis. Through this purgation, an expression of the nationalism of the new state, the Greek nation reclaimed part of its own ancient heritage, and presented it to the outside world. Only Vikelas and a few foreigners complained that the archaeologists had gone too far.

The foreign schools of archaeology played an important part in this process of revelation, in particular the French, on the Acropolis, at Delphi and on Delos, and the Germans in the Agora, at Olympia and later in the Kerameikos. Murray felt obliged to defend the relatively low-key role of the British School by pointing out that it was grossly underfunded compared with the French, German and American Schools. Some things never change.

A number of Greek and foreign observers, including Vikelas, the American consul George Horton and the historian William Miller left descriptions of Athens in and around the 1890s. Each observer had his own conception of Athens. One of the more fanciful accounts was the

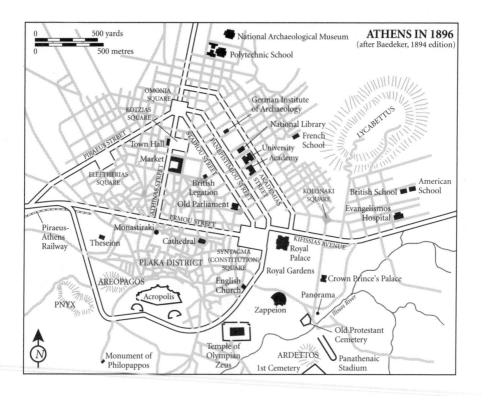

invition of Freddy Benson, who spent three winters in the 1890s at the British School as a budding archaeologist, and went on to become a fashionable society novelist. Freddy's brother, the schoolmaster author Arthur Benson, said that inaccuracy was a Benson family failing. It was certainly a characteristic of Freddy, whose Athens is a fantasy city:

> *Athens, with its high-born princes, and its national pride, and its army dressed in Albanian costume … its fleet of three small cruisers, its national assembly of bawling Levantines, and its bootblacks called Agamemnon and Thucydides, was precisely like the fabulous kingdom of Paflagonia in the 'Rose and the Ring', or some Gilbertian realm of light opera.[2]*

The most reliable picture available to the reader of English was the factual but still sometimes exotic language of Baedeker's and Murray's *Handbooks*, the two guidebooks which, in successive editions, helped the middle-class western traveller to cope with the complexities of Greek drachmas, gold francs, dragomans, hotels and cafés, humble khans and flea-ridden bedding. They drew a sharp distinction between civilised Athens and the rough provinces, where brigandage and the taking of hostages had not long been suppressed.

Not that Baedeker or Murray wished to put off their clients from travelling outside the capital. On the contrary, they provided a wealth of practical information designed to make journeys into the interior and the islands tolerable. They described how to negotiate with guides and muleteers. They wrote about horses, English servants (useless), security and brigandage, money (if you need 5 drachmas, cut a 10-drachma note in half), appropriate dress ('a suit of grey tweed, such as is used by sportsmen at home, and an overcoat of some moderately thick or water-proof material') and precautions against fleas and bed-bugs ('The pests which render night hideous include not only the flea (*psíllous*), with which the traveller in Italy has probably become more or less familiar, but also bed-bugs (*koreoús*), lice (*psíraes*), and other disgusting insects, winged and wingless. The best remedy against the attacks of these enemies of repose is good Insect Powder (Persian or Keating's), which should be plentifully sprinkled on the traveller's clothes and bedding.' Baedeker). Murray's weapon against vermin was a complicated apparatus consisting of a calico sheet sleeping bag attached to a muslin canopy stretched on a framework of cane, as a mosquito net. This contraption, illustrated by Murray, was invented by Mr Levinge and sold by Messrs Maynard and Harris of Leadenhall Street for one pound five shillings. ('The whole apparatus may be compressed into a hat-case.')

The countryside and the islands provided some of the most interesting, challenging and aesthetically satisfying experiences which Greece had to offer, including Olympia itself. Some of Baedeker's injunctions, such as the need for woollen underclothing as a

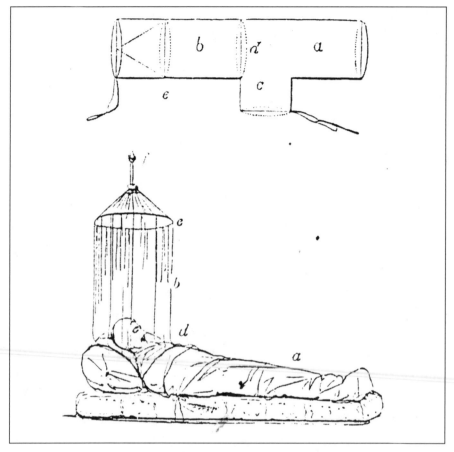

16 *Mosquito net, as recommended for travel in Greek lands (*Murray's
Handbook for Travellers in Greece*)*

preventive of chills, may seem fussy by modern standards. But everything he wrote rested on hard practical experience and most of it was
useful and necessary.

As to Athens, Baedeker was encouraging. There were several excellent
hotels of the first class, notably the Grande Bretagne in Constitution
Square, a distinguished building designed by the Danish architect
Theophile Hansen, where the traveller could stay, with full board, for
12–15 francs, the equivalent of about half a sovereign. (Today's rate at
the same hotel, which has been lavishly modernised for the 2004 games,

is 427 euros – about the same number of dollars – for a room without meals.) The owner of the Grande Bretagne, Stathis Lampsas, had recently launched '*diners-dansant*' for the winter season. The hotel had become a centre of attraction for Athenian society. It was the choice of Coubertin and the members of the IOC.

The capital had the conveniences of a modern European city, say Florence or Naples. It was (and is) both the political centre, and a city of restaurants, cafés, confectioners and entertainment. A military band played in Constitution Square three times a week. The cafe was a place for men (not women) to relax. They could smoke cigarettes or a narghile pipe, or read the English or French newspapers at the much frequented Zacharatos, on the corner of Constitution Square and Stadiou Street. In the evenings people would walk out to the cafés in the Zappeion gardens, the Ilissos garden, or at 'The Columns', near the temple of Olympian Zeus.

The Athens of the 1890s was a city in transition, a mixture of the old and the new, 'new' meaning western European. The traditional *fustanella*, or kilt, was disappearing from the streets (Miller saw only one *fustanella* in the parliament of 1904), as were the baggy trousers known as *vracha*. The American popular lecturer Burton Holmes, who was in Athens for the games, wrote that the men as a rule were dressed like the average civilised man in any land, that is badly; the women aped Paris fashions; and the officers were well-groomed and tightly laced, typical continental *militaires*. But the *evzones* were an exception, 'a delight to the eye with their bright red fezes, long blue tassels, short embroidered jackets, fustanellas of innumerable pleats, and tsarukia [slippers] of red leather with tufts of red upon the tips of the turned-up toes'.[3]

The social life of the elites had changed since the time of Otho. The new rich, many of them immigrants from the diaspora, were treading on the heels of old families with credentials dating from the war of independence. Handsome neo-classical houses were built for them by Greece's native and foreign architects, their gardens adorned with fragments of ancient ruins unearthed in the process of construction.[4] The number of priests, with their stovepipe hats and beards, and the number of army officers to be seen on the streets of Athens was much greater in proportion to the population than in most European countries. In 1894 the first workers' May Day gathering took place, provoking arrests by the police. In the family, men dominated, girls were secluded; but there were stirrings of female emancipation reflected in the *Women's Daily*, which first appeared in 1887, edited by a 'new woman', Kallirrhoe Parren, who campaigned tirelessly to improve the status of women in Greek society. She commented sharply that women had been left out of the Olympic programme, 'as they are always left out'.[5] But the inclusion of gymnastics in girls' education in the late nineteenth century had unlocked a door which Parren and others were able gradually to push open.

As the century progressed there were growing opportunities for leisure pursuits. The Athens to Phaleron road was the favourite carriage promenade, followed almost daily by the King and Queen, from whom the fashionable world took their cue. The King would walk up and down the beach at Phaleron followed by his dachshund. People would drive down to Phaleron in the winter in landaus, drags, barouches, ride down on horses, or, if they were modern and adventurous, on bicycles or tandems. The promenaders would return at sunset, the drive or ride broken perhaps at one of the inns on the road. The roads were rough, and cycling was still a hazardous novelty. The American Consul, George Horton, was a keen cyclist. He decided to enter for the Olympic cycling events but was put out of contention by an accident shortly before the games.

New Phaleron was the summer bathing resort, with bath-houses, a hotel, a bandstand on a platform, and the novelty of electric lighting. Athenians travelling down on the open tram for four cents a ticket might find the King on board. But after 1869 more and more people would travel between Athens and Piraeus by the steam railway, which opened in that year, making eight sorties a day at a price of 1 drachma (first class). It was electrified in the early twentieth century. The warships of the Great Powers, British, French, Russian, American, could be seen riding at anchor in Phaleron bay. Sometimes after dark they would light up the Acropolis with their searchlights.

In the afternoon the city was deserted, the people enjoying their siesta. In summer people would go to one of the garden tavernas on the outskirts, for a convivial evening of food, wine, talk and song. Or they would patronise one of the many open-air theatres, presenting drama, puppets, or the Karaghiozis shadow plays which enjoyed a revival in the 1890s. The villain was always a Turk. In the winter there were covered theatres in the middle of town. French and Italian opera and operetta could be enjoyed. The first showing in Athens of the revolutionary new technology, moving film, took place in 1896.

There was a fizz about the city's intellectual life. Although Athens was open to influences from western Europe, it was still much like a village where everyone knew everyone else. The media were sharp, satirical and often scurrilous. A new 'generation of the '80s' was making itself heard. It was a society of small magazines, literary cafés such as Yiannopoulou's on the corner of Stadiou Street, and literary clubs such as the Parnassus, where Palamas, Vikelas and their friends would read lectures and new poems and debate the issues of the day. A group of intellectuals associated with the journal *Estia* formed around Professor Nikolaos Politis, the father of Greek folklore studies, which were integral to the new interpretations of Greek identity and national continuity. They met on Saturday evenings at a German tavern in Omirou Street to discuss the development of a truly Greek literature and art, reflecting not just the classical past but all the complex currents of Greece's history, foreign occupation and racial mixing. Kostis Palamas, the representative voice of the new generation, was among the habitués. Phokianos, with his loud voice, would entertain the company with songs.[6]

Apart from the 'national questions' in politics – Crete, Macedonia, the fate of 'enslaved Hellenism' – the most impassioned debate was about the language. This was the time of reaction by young literary lions against the archaising Greek known as *katharevousa*, the language of the law, education and most of the press, in favour of a demotic Greek thought to be closer to the language of the people, whatever that was. (The *katharevousa* had been devised as a unifying measure partly because there was no standard popular language.) The extreme exponent of demoticism was the writer Yannis Psycharis, professor of modern Greek and author of the controversial book *My Journey*, who lived in France. Palamas became the leading poet of demotic Greek. Another of the demoticists, Alexander Pallis, was at this time translating Homer's *Iliad*. Five years later his translation of the gospels led to riots at the university and the burning of his books. Constantine Manos, the young athlete and poet who had thrown himself into the preparations for the Olympic Games, was another demoticist. Vikelas himself adopted a moderate, simple form of purist Greek and wrote a short poem sensibly arguing against linguistic extremes.

The city was still compact enough for the visitor to walk easily from one end to the other. Cabs were plentiful at 1 drachma a trip. Between Constitution and Omonoia Squares, four-seated wagons known as *vis-à-vis*, drawn by lean horses, plied their trade with much hissing, cracking of whips and cursing. The centre of Athens was served by a network of trams, which also connected the city with Piraeus.

The evenings in Athens had a seductive charm, with the mild climate, the open air cafés, the scents of orange blossom and jasmine. It was a city on a human scale. The problems, referred to by Greeks and foreigners, were the glare of hot sun off the walls and pavements, the dust and litter, the lack of water, the cracked and uneven surface of the pavements – a problem then as now. But a bootblack or shoeshine boy would polish up your dusty shoes for less than a penny (5 lepta), and go on in the evening to the Night School for Destitute Children.

The sharpest critic of the state of the city was the writer Emmanuel Roides, author of the scandalous novel *Pope Joan*. He mocked the poverty of content of the Zappeion exhibitions, shops and cafés compared with the luxury of the new buildings which held them. In a series of articles on 'Walks in Athens' he painted a grim picture of the filthy drain which ran down Voulis Street, the foul smells, and the way in which shops and workshops invaded the pavements, so that pedestrians had to brush past the carcasses hanging outside the butchers' shops which dripped blood on the pavements. He joked sourly about the newspapers' pleas to the Athenians to clean up the streets before the Olympic Games, for the sake of appearances before the foreign visitors. There was a tribe which only changed its clothes and hunted its fleas before great religious feasts: perhaps it was only on the occasion of the Olympic Games that the Athenians should have the privilege of pure air and clean streets.[7]

Malaria was endemic in the countryside but the climate of Athens was famed as healthy. For those who did fall ill, there were doctors and chemists aplenty. There were booksellers which sold English, French and German books. Newspapers could be bought on the pavements for 5–10 lepta. Baedeker commented optimistically that they would be read 'without difficulty by those who understand ancient Greek, and the discussions about modern affairs in classic diction will be found entertaining'. For the clubbable British, there was even the Athens Club, to which strangers were admitted if introduced by a member. It still exists, a sombre and traditional place which provides a good meal in the middle of town.

Murray and Baedeker were writing for the educated, well-provided tourist from western Europe, whose first interests were in comfortable accommodation, tolerable food and the facilities to visit the classical ruins in comfort. One has to look elsewhere for a picture of the look and feel of vernacular Athens at this time. George Horton described being woken in the early hours in summer by the fruit and vegetable street-vendors crying their wares in Greek, Turkish and Italian. Among the items on offer were bundles of fat pine kindling wood (*dadi*) and a hot herb drink known as *salepi*. 'In no other city of the world are the street cries so varied, so harrowing, so vocally picturesque,' Horton wrote.[8] This was still the case in the 1960s in the narrow streets on the higher slopes of Mount Lycabettus.

Away from the central hotels and government buildings, the city had much of the squalor and the exotic charm of provincial life, and some of the violence associated with rapid urbanisation. Most of the inhabitants were first- or second-generation immigrants from the country, attracted by the prospect of jobs, or non-jobs, in the public service, provided through the intervention of their patrons in parliament. In the native quarters around the north slopes of the Acropolis, the Theseion, the lower slopes of Lycabettus and the Phaleron road, families lived in two-storey houses of stone and stucco with adobe walls, a tree or two, and pots of flowers in the courtyard of beaten earth. This was the Athens described by Alexandros Papadiamantis from Skiathos, the greatest of Greek story-writers.[9] The women would fetch water from a common neighbourhood hydrant. Water from the Athens aqueduct was regarded as pure, but demanding customers could order water through the hotel porter from the springs at Kaisariani monastery. This was brought down to Athens every day in casks.

In the Anaphiotika area of the Plaka on the northern slopes of the Acropolis, Burton Holmes found 'the abode of poverty, the headquarters of the laundresses of Athens', where the newly washed linen of the Athenians was hung out to dry upon the sacred slope of classic Athens – the sort of rhetorical contrast between ancient and modern which always appealed to western visitors.[10] The Plaka was the area where the visitor could most easily find the picturesque, which he or she had been taught to expect from engravings and drawings which included Greeks in *fustanellas*, ladies in traditional costume, the life of the former Turkish bazaar. Visiting Athens ten years earlier, the Cambridge classicist J.E. Sandys strolled with his wife through a curious narrow street, the shoemakers' market, which was gay with long rows of bright Albanian slippers of scarlet leather, 'with the toe turned up in front like the prow of a gondola', before leaving this quiet area for the 'gloomy and grimy and noisy street of the blacksmiths'.[11]

As the games approached, they began to influence the look of the city. The reconstruction and marbling of the ancient stadium was only part of this. The new Mayor of Athens conducted a hurried campaign to clear rubbish, water the streets, improve the lighting and erect street signs. Theatre troupes and street performers began to move in from the provinces. Visitors from the country brought with them food products to sell to the presumably affluent foreigners.

The most spectacular innovation was a panorama of the siege of Paris in the Franco-Prussian war of 1870. Panoramas were popular attractions and this one had already been shown in the Champs Elysées in Paris and then in Boston. It was packed in sections in enormous boxes and transported on carts through the streets of Athens, to the accompaniment of trumpets and drums, and set up at the bottom of Herod Atticus Street near the Ilissos river, just opposite the ancient stadium. The drama of the 1870 siege of Paris was a 'natural' subject. Visitors and Athenians, who included members of the royal family, could read in a sixteen-page booklet about the dramatic events of the siege, the efforts of the Parisians to build defences and procure food, together with a detailed key to the six sections which made up the panorama, and a history of the invention of panoramas. The Athens panorama lasted well into the twentieth century and can be seen, a massive rotunda of lath and plaster standing across the street from the stadium, in postcards of the period.[12]

This was Athens in the early 1890s. Baedeker printed in his 1894 edition a panoramic view as seen from Mount Lycabettus, showing an elegant, uncrowded city of neo-classical buildings, many of them standing in their own space, the city reposing in the Attic plain with the distant view of the island of Aigina and the mountains of the Peloponnese. The contrasts of the late nineteenth and early twentieth century and some of the life and society of the Athenians are caught in the pictures of early photographers, such as Petros Moraitis, Felix Bonfils, James Robertson and Fred Boissonas.[13] Moraitis shows the purified state of the Acropolis, the variety of costume, the view from the Acropolis across bare ground to the wooded First Cemetery, the severe groups of bourgeois ladies and of college graduates. The cemetery itself, with its elaborate neo-classical marble tombs set among cypress trees, captures the spirit of nineteenth-century Athens, and of those severe ladies, better than any other monument. In Moraitis's photograph it is set apart from the city. Today it is a place of peace and reflection in a noisy, concrete labyrinth.

Athens was also a capital city of politics and faction, newspapers and literary coteries; over-supplied with doctors, lawyers and other graduates, as was picked up by the monarchist Charles Maurras during his visit for the Olympic Games:

The kingdom of Greece is the prey of the parties. Intelligent, patriotic, still sustained by an old and traditional organisation (some deputies are elected to the Chamber from father to son), pretty well unsullied by any socialist fever, Greece maintains at Athens two thousand students of philosophy, law or medicine, all of them aspiring public servants and aspiring parliamentary deputies. This people of barristers, priests and doctors will never find in the entire East a sufficiently large number of people to preach to, of clients to cure and to advise. What will sustain so numerous a bourgeoisie? These modern Athenians would need slaves.

I am very much afraid that the State may, finally, have to work and pay for them. This State reduced to the function of provider and nurse will lead fatally to civil ruin. The employees of the State are already numerous. They all play politics. They will do so even more, and their number will increase: however slender the resources from which their salaries come, modest or small today, these will increase at the same rate as they do. Such is the destiny of a country where the mob has too much influence. Internal troubles give rise to political deals to the detriment of the public interest. But these absurd deals cause new quarrels, which themselves tend

*to produce further onerous compromises. And so on, until it all
ends in general degeneration or the entry of the Foreigner on the
scene.*

*Not having their own national dynasty, Greece has chosen a
king from abroad. This king renders her big services. Royalty here
… exists above all in order to hold a balance between the factions.
Personally esteemed for his good humour, finesse and discretion,
surrounded with devotion which I could not help noticing, King
George is blamed for his extraordinarily modest use of his
constitutional prerogatives.*

– Why are you against the king? I said to someone.

*– Because he does nothing, he says nothing, he does not make
enough use of his power.*[14]

Maurras noted an ineffable confidence in the qualities of the people:
what was good was their own work, what was bad was a consequence
of a bad administration and a bad state. He found 'deluded' republicans who thought that the abolition of the monarchy would improve
things.

The confidence that Maurras noted might also have been called fool-
hardiness. It was the feeling tapped by the National Society, which in
September 1895 had started recruiting prominent civilian members, in
small numbers at first. Among the first civilians to be sworn in (eight
out of 130 members in January 1896) were Georgios Drosinis, the editor
of *Estia*, and Anastasios Metaxas, the designer of the restored stadium.
Drosinis was sworn in by the young officer Pavlos Melas, who became a
national hero, and lost his life, in Macedonia. He in turn recruited most
of the *Estia* group of writers. The eminent Athens University scholars
Spyridon Lambros and Nikolaos Politis joined in the spring. Both were
closely connected with the Olympics, contributing chapters to the official book of the games. Lambros was Secretary of the Committee for
the Preparation and Training of Greek athletes. In 1897 he was to
become Acting President of the National Society. Politis, the folklore

scholar at the centre of the *Estia* dining group, became a member of the Committee for Athletic Events and Gymnastics.[15]

Other literary figures who were sworn into the society were the poet Palamas, and Vikelas himself. For the moderate Vikelas this was an uncharacteristic act. He had held out for a year against the arguments of Melas before giving in and joining, largely as a fund-raiser. He immediately realised he had made a mistake – 'the biggest mistake of my life' – in joining a secret organisation within which he had no influence and of which he did not even know the names of the leaders. He resigned.[16] That men of this calibre from the intellectual world of Athens were joining a secret society shows how rapidly and deeply the country was being carried away by a literally irresponsible form of nationalism. Crown Prince Constantine, to his chagrin, was one of the few who because of the policies of the society could not become a member.

For several months the usually peaceful street of Herod Atticus, next to the royal gardens, had sounded all day long with the rattle of heavy wagons bringing blocks of marble from the quarries on Mount Pendeli, north of Athens. Wagon after wagon crossed the Ilissos bridge. Gradually the rows of marble benches were rising in the stadium, up to the level of the corridor dividing the lower seats from the higher.[17]

The world outside was becoming aware of the forthcoming Olympic Games through reports in *The Times* and other journals of record. The archaeologist Charles Waldstein, former director of the American School, wrote to *The Times* on 19 March contradicting rumours that the site and buildings would not be completed before the games began and that the games would be a failure. Having inspected the stadium and the rifle ranges he was happy to congratulate the organisers and the architect on the energy and intelligence with which the work had been pushed forward and the stupendous effect produced by the stadium. Given Waldstein's credentials this was useful testimony.

A dyspeptic correspondent of the *New York Times* of 29 March, named Bigelow, gave a different impression. He had searched for the classic Ilissos and other things which his college learning had taught him to expect:

> *There were plenty of old tin cans and rubbish scattered where once the silvery Ilyssus sparkled to the sea; the Groves of Academe reminded me of picturesque bits in shanty town. Mars Hill I could have matched in the outskirts of any American town … The town of Athens was enveloped in clouds of dust, which blew furiously up and down her streets, stopping up eyes ears and noses with most irritating thoroughness – for, so far as paving and sprinkling are concerned, Athens might be considered on a par with provincial cities of Algeria or New York.*

According to Bigelow the Greek army wore shabby uniform; the democracy was bogus; the games would be crooked; and the Greeks knew as little about amateur sport as the Chinese. But it turned out that his visit to Athens had been on the occasion of the wedding of the Crown Prince to Princess Sophie in 1889, so his strictures could be ignored.

On 6 April, to mark the opening of the games, the London *Times* published a two-column think piece from their Special Correspondent which gave a thoughtful account of the origins of the new festival and its preparation. The article bears the stamp of *The Times*'s eccentric Balkan correspondent James Bourchier, one of whose interests was archaeology.

Bourchier paid tribute to Coubertin. He regretted that the festival could not have been celebrated at Olympia among the monuments of ancient grandeur brought to light by the German archaeologists, but accepted that this was impossible: modern visitors could not be expected to bivouac in the fields or under the portico of a temple like visitors to the ancient games. Athens was the only place capable of supplying modern comforts.

From another point of view there could be no more desirable choice than the city of Pericles and Phidias, where all that was greatest and best in Hellenic civilisation attained the highest degree of perfection, and where to this day, intact in its essential features, the ancient *stadion* exists, looking across the waters of Ilissos to the venerable ruins of the Parthenon and the stupendous columns of Olympian Zeus.

Bourchier castigated the British for not coming:

> *It is greatly to be regretted that England, the home of latter-day athletics, will be very inadequately represented at the festival, and that Oxford and Cambridge, where the physical and mental training of ancient Greece has found its nearest counterpart in modern times, will hardly be represented at all.*

Despite the lamentable absence of the British, Bourchier concluded that the games would be a success.

Coubertin arrived in Athens in March. He wrote a rapturous 'Letter from Athens' for a French journal, welcoming the Athenian spring with its soft breezes and sweet-smelling flowers:

> *Everywhere people are shining up the marble, applying new plaster and fresh paint; they are paving, cleaning, decorating.*
>
> *The road to the stadium is in full dress with its Arc de Triomphe and its Venetian matting. But this is not the favorite promenade. Interest is elsewhere, on the shores of the Ilissos, until now disdained. Every evening about five o'clock the citizens come here to cast an appraising eye upon the work being done at the stadium. As usual, the Ilissos is without water, but this passes unnoticed. A monumental bridge spans the celebrated stream and gives access to the great plain upon which they are restoring the ancient stadium.*

Coubertin noted that the Hungarians had arrived, to an enthusiastic welcome. The Germans, Swedes and Americans were expected that day. The news had just come though that the Paris Municipal Council had voted funds for the French team to come, so French participation was assured. He made no reference to the British.[18] But the *Illustrated London News* of 4 April showed where British priorities lay. It reported that Oxford beat Cambridge in an exciting boat race in bad weather, and printed a whole page of photos of the Oxford and Cambridge athletics match.

There was a last-minute scare caused by reports in March of a few cholera cases in Egypt. Strict quarantine was imposed on visitors from that country. The prospect of the games brought on a fever of imitative sport in the streets and parks of Athens. Coubertin and other visitors were amazed to see young boys and men running, jumping and throwing improvised stones on every street corner. It was the thing to do.

9

THE GAMES BEGIN

THE OLYMPIC HYMN
To Samaras, who gave it wings

Ancient immortal Spirit, pure father
Of the beautiful, the great and the true,
Come down, appear and light up here
The glory of your own land and sky
The track and the wrestling struggle and the shot,
Shine on the onrush of the noble Games,
Crown them with the unwithering branch
And shape the body to be worthy and iron strong.
Fields, mountains and seas shine with you
Like one great temple of white and purple,
And to worship you, ancient immortal Spirit,
Every people runs to the temple here.

Kostis Palamas

Sunday 5 April (24 March old style) was Easter Day for both the Orthodox and the Catholic and Protestant churches. Easter is the shining feast of the Greek Orthodox. It was an auspicious day.

A temporary wooden bridge had been thrown across the Ilissos river.

17 The entrance of the Stadium, decked out for the Games. The statue of Averoff, with wreaths laid at its base, can be seen directly below the line of the Parthenon. The organisers have been lavish in providing modern pieces of ancient statuary, of Muses, gods and goddesses etc. Phokianos's gym is the low-lying building between the two right hand flagpoles.

From the morning on, according to the official report on the games, crowds began to converge on the stadium, which filled up well before the hour set for unveiling the statue of the great benefactor Averoff.[1] Inside and outside the stadium was a throng of spectators, members of the Council of Ministers, the IOC and the Greek committees, sportsmen, officials and police. The special crews of ushers recruited for the games stood out in their cherry-coloured coats, black trousers and white helmets. The clouds looked threatening, and umbrellas were raised.

At about eleven o'clock the Crown Prince and Prince Nicholas arrived. By now it was pouring with rain. Philemon, the Secretary General, pronounced a eulogy of Averoff, who had declined the invitation to attend on grounds of health. In his reply, the Crown Prince praised the generosity of the man who by paying for the restoration of the stadium had enabled the revival of the Olympic Games to take on a Greek national character. Constantine then unveiled the statue, which with its extended right arm seemed to be inviting the crowd to enter the stadium. The President of the Philharmonic Society of Athens and the President of the Hungarian team, Kemeny, laid wreaths at the foot of the statue.

Monday 6 April, which is 25 March in the old style calendar, dawned fair. The 25th of March is the Greek National Day, on which the outbreak of the War of Independence is celebrated. In the morning the royal family and officials went to the cathedral for a solemn *Te Deum*.

The streets of Athens had a look of extraordinary animation. All the public buildings were draped in bunting; multicoloured streamers floated in the wind; green wreaths decked the house fronts. The two letters 'O A', the Greek initials of the Olympic Games, and the dates, 776 BC–1896 AD, indicating their ancient past and their present renascence, were everywhere.[2]

The crowds began to gather in the streets. They besieged the Melas house, where the offices of the committee were distributing tickets, and formed crowds round the ticket touts on the streets. Tickets were available at a variety of cafés, shops and tobacco merchants, at 2 drachmas, or 1½ drachmas for the inferior seats high up in the stands. The crowds were good-humoured. Bands from Zakynthos, Lefkas, Patras and other towns and islands played jolly music.

From noon people began to fill the benches. As they drove through the city to the stadium, the American athletes began to realise the magnitude of the whole affair. The organisers had put up a barrier in Herod Atticus Street to control the traffic. Colonel Metaxas's special police saw to it that order prevailed in the stadium. The scene was magical:

> ... *the various outfits of the ladies, their varied coiffures, the movement of their fans amid the black mass of several thousand*

18 *The crowded Stadium, taken probably on the opening day of the Games, from near the Ilissos bridge at the bottom of Herod Atticus Street. Ladies carried parasols when the sun shone, umbrellas when it rained.*

spectators, the brilliant uniforms and the plumes of the officers, the striking colours of the floating flags, the lively semi-circle of spectators who, without tickets, occupied the top of the hills surrounding the stadium, all this made a most curious and imposing ensemble. Most of all the little hill which dominates the right side of the stadium presented a picturesque spectacle: seen from inside the stadium it seemed to be a pyramid of heads. The decoration of the stadium was truly splendid. At the entrance were placed upright masts, surmounted by banners and ornamented with shields; on each side of the façade were tripods taken from ancient art; all around the stadium were flagpoles adorned with shields; on each side of the sphendoni [the curved end of the stadium] *were placed the two herms discovered during the excavations. The rows of seats were covered with little cushions for*

*the spectators to sit on. In the arena and on the course members of
various committees, the chief officials and other functionaries were
walking around. Then the bands entered playing various pieces of
music.*[3]

At 3.15 p.m. the King and Queen arrived and were greeted by the Crown
Prince. The band played the Greek national hymn, and the royal family
and court officials, ministers and ecclesiastical dignitaries took their
seats in the reserved places in the front row of the *sphendoni*. By now
the stadium and the higher slopes of the Ardettos hill were full, with an
estimated 80,000 spectators and a massive show of police. The athletes
stood on the track in a double line, in their own national groups, awaiting the action.

In preparing for the event the IOC, working with the Crown Prince
and his committee, had drawn on Greek protocol, their own common
sense and precedents from the Zappas Olympics, to work out a simple
and dignified ceremony. Clearly Coubertin played a major role. He
claimed in his *Olympic Memoirs* that most of the protocol for the opening and closing ceremonies, the hoisting of the winner's national flag at
the prizegiving ceremony after each event, and so on, dated from the
period of his first visit in late 1894.[4] This is not wholly accurate,
because there was no prizegiving ceremony after each event in 1896.
However, the opening by the Head of State, the playing of an Olympic
hymn, the raising of the national flags of winners' countries, the conscious striving after a solemn and ceremonial effect, were all present in
1896 and were the foundation of the future ceremony which is an integral part of the Olympics. Though they did not know it, the pioneers of
1896 were helping to establish a new tradition of ritual for the twentieth
century's greatest secular cultural invention. The elements added later
include the flag with its five rings (1920), the Olympic oath (1920), the
Olympic flame burning throughout the games (1928), and the torch
relay (1936).

The Crown Prince made a short speech on his familiar theme. Greece had no choice but to take up the challenge of the Paris congress's decision that the Olympic Games should take place at Athens. He asked indulgence for any defects in the organisation, due to lack of time and experience. Through these games Greece was today 'binding herself more closely to the rest of the civilised world'. He welcomed the athletes from other countries. The revival of the games should confirm the reciprocal bonds of friendship between the Greek people and other peoples. The games should revive physical exercise and raise the moral feelings of Greek youth, helping to create a new generation of Greeks, worthy of their ancestors.

At Constantine's invitation, the King spoke: 'I declare the Games of the First Olympiad of the modern era open.' For Coubertin it was a thrilling moment. The bands and the choir of 150 voices, under the direction of the composer Spyridon Samaras, struck up the Olympic hymn which had been commissioned two years before, at Vikelas's suggestion, from Greece's greatest poet, Palamas. It is now played at every opening ceremony, though it took sixty years to be accepted as the official anthem of the Olympic movement at Melbourne in 1956.[5] The crowd was so pleased with this first performance that the King called for a repeat. When the bands and extras vacated the arena, twenty-one competitors in the 100-metre dash emerged from the dressing-room beneath the tunnel at the end of the arena, and the games began.

Charles Maurras was one of those who watched these proceedings. He commented that of the 80,000 or so spectators, a good quarter were particularly lucky, in that sitting high up on the eastern side they had a superb view not only of the games but also of the columns of the temple of Olympian Zeus, the ruins of the theatre of Dionysos, and the Acropolis crowned by the Parthenon.[6] Maurras had come to mock at the 'cosmopolitanism' of Coubertin's games. Cosmopolitanism was a boo word with connotations of racial degeneracy and anti-semitism. But as the games proceeded he found himself drawn to some surprising conclusions. He was clearly fascinated by the royal pomp and pageantry which he saw below him. He described the King taking his place on one of the thrones set in the middle of the front row at the end of the stadium, and placing the young King Alexander of Serbia on the other throne.

On the left of King George is the Princess Royal, wife of the Crown Prince and sister of the German Emperor. She is a very handsome person with fair hair which shines with a strange éclat in the Greek air. Her two children, dressed in sailor suits like all the little boys in the world, lean languidly against the knees of their governess. On the right of the young King of Serbia is Princess Marie, daughter of the King of Greece, pink and white like Gretchen. Her betrothal to Grand Duke George of Russia was celebrated last week. He is on the right of his fiancée. He is a tall man with a big brown moustache. All the Athenian ladies regret that he hides his face under the vizor of a cap …

After the Grand Duke, continuing to the right, there are the remaining royal princes, who are also dressed as sailors. Their transparent complexion and pale blue eyes, like those of their sister, evoke northern climes.

I think all these people are becoming hellenised quite quickly. The Greek people absorb and assimilate any and all barbarians, and this ruling family seems absolutely disposed to put up with anything. There is no hellenic whim to which the King is not ready to lend himself with a good grace, and his three elder children, as they circulate in the stadium, seem popular.

The heir presumptive is President of the Games. And he really presides. No detail escapes him. Strapped tightly in Prussian style into his uniform of an Infantry General, Crown Prince Constantine wishes to keep an eye on everything himself. He is seconded closely by his brother Prince George, in the uniform of a naval Captain …

Maurras's observant, snobbish eye ranged further over the front row of the spectators, taking in Prince Nicholas, the artistic member of the family, the King's ADC Colonel Papadiamantopoulos, who was apparently related to the French-Greek poet Jean Moréas, the ambassadors with their wives, members of the government and their families, and in the second row members of parliament with their wives and daughters.

We can still see in old photographs the packed stands on this first day and on the day of the marathon race. Following the events was not altogether easy, particularly for those high in the stands, and for foreigners who could not lay their hands on the printed daily programmes (of which there were Greek and French versions) and could not quickly pick up from the Greeks what was happening. A French spectator from the *Senegal* wrote that there were empty spaces at the sides of the stadium, but that the surrounding hills were covered with spectators, keen to watch for free. 'Although a bit boring, the games are arousing much interest. As for me, I am seated too high up; at this distance, the competitors look like agitated insects.'[7]

Contemporary photos and reminiscences suggest that the scene was more like than unlike a modern athletic meeting, though the athletes' clothing was heavyweight by modern standards: they wore flannel shirts, thick, short socks and canvas running shoes. The athletic equipment business was beginning to take off. The substantial advertising section by Spaldings in the back of their booklet about the 1906 Athens games contains advertisements for every variety of equipment: finest calfskin running shoes for $5, kangaroo leather cross-country shoes for $5.50, a sixteen-foot hollow spruce vaulting pole for $10 (the American poles in 1896 were much superior to others), running pants in sateen $1, best worsted quarter-sleeve shirts $3, cotton sleeveless shirts $1, and so on.[8]

As to athletic standards and techniques, there were enormous differences between the competitors. An American athlete remarked later that 'the Greeks had not got it'. While the Americans and British had evolved a method of hurdling which took the whole course in one rhythm, the Greek hurdlers still took each hurdle as a separate event, landing on two feet before setting off again for the next. A well-known photo of the start of the 100-metre dash shows that only the Americans had developed a start from a crouch; others simply bent slightly forward in anticipation of the gun. (The photo, incidentally, is probably of a heat, not the final, because what looks like the winner of the final, Burke, can be seen standing at the left behind the runners, keeping himself warm in an overcoat.) The official timekeeper, Charles Perry, was the same Englishman who had come out to prepare the track and help train the athletes at the Athens Athletic Club. Accurate records were kept, so far as we can judge, though the timekeeping for the marathon posed special problems. But, although all the winning times were by definition Olympic records, they were not particularly impressive, because for the reasons set out by Robertson and others, the athletes who made their way to Athens were self-selected and most of them were not the best of their generation.

The first event in revived Olympic history was the 100 metres heats. Francis Lane of Princeton won the first heat in 12.2 seconds.[9] Tom Curtis of Boston won the second heat from a Greek athlete from the AAC, Halkokondylis. Burke won the third heat. The American team cheered their winners. A pattern was being set. The superior training and experience of the American university athletes were paying off.

Thirty-six years later Curtis, who was primarily a high hurdler, wrote a lively account of the games in which he described his heat:

> *Entered in the heat with me were a German, a Frenchman, an Englishman, and two Greeks. As we stood on our marks, I was next to the Frenchman, a short stocky man. He, at that moment, was busily engaged in pulling on a pair of white kid gloves, and had some difficulty in doing so before the starting pistol. Excited as I was, I had to ask him why he wanted the gloves. 'Ah-ha!' he answered, 'zat is because I run before ze Keeng!'*
>
> *Later, after the heat was run, I asked him in what other events he was entered. He was in only two, 'ze cent metre and ze marathon,' to me a curious combination. He went on to explain his*

19 *The start of one of the 100 metres heats on the first day of the Games,*
showing the different styles of starting technique. This is generally thought to
be the final of the 100 metres, which was won by the American Tom Burke,
identified as the second athlete from the left, with rippling upper arm
muscles, who is making a modern crouching start. But others claim plausibly
that Burke is the standing figure on the extreme left, dressed in a long dark
overcoat, in which case this must be a heat, not the final. The Rotunda,
which contained a panorama of the siege of Paris, is in the background.
(Meyer album)

method of training. 'One day I run a leetle way, vairy queek. Ze
next day, I run a long way, vairy slow.'[10]

The story illustrates the fallibility of human memory, the desire to
embroider a good yarn, and the historian's problem in dealing even
with eye-witness sources. As related, it cannot be true, because there
was no Frenchman in Curtis's heat. There was a Frenchman, called
Grisel, in Lane's heat, who may possibly have been the man with the
white gloves. Or possibly it was the middle-distance and marathon
runner Lermusiaux, who did not take part in the 100 metres at all.

20 *The famous 'discobolus' or discus thrower: a Roman marble copy probably of the fifth century BC bronze original by the Greek sculptor Myron. Greek athletes of the late nineteenth century modelled their style on the symmetry and elegance of Myron's sculpture.*

Next came the triple jump. There is some debate in the sources as to whether this was a hop, skip and jump or a hop, hop and jump. The ebullient American James Connolly from Boston claimed that he was trained for the former but found on arrival that he was expected to jump the latter. Be that as it may, he won, with a distance of 13 metres 71 centimetres, thus becoming the first Olympic champion in the revived Olympic history. The American flag was run up the mast near the stadium entrance by sailors of the marines. The crowd cheered loudly and the American athletes cheered their victory in their own way, with loud 'ra-ra-ras', a feature of the games which forcibly struck every non-American observer. The King even invited the American team to perform their cheers, or 'war cries' as he called them, at one of the official receptions.[11] As yet the playing of the national anthem of the winner had not entered the Olympic repertory.

Following the 800-metre heats, won by Flack of Australia and Lermusiaux of France, came the discus competition. The Greek spectators took an intense interest in this, because they regarded it as their own sport and expected it to be won by a Greek. The event was modelled on what was known or guessed about the ancient Greek discus throw, and Greek athletes modelled themselves on the famous discobolus, or discus thrower, of the sculptor Myron (or rather on Roman copies, since Myron's work was lost). Greek hopes rested on two promising athletes, Versis and Paraskevopoulos. The entry was international, including athletes from the US, England, Sweden, Denmark and Germany as well as Greece. The American was Robert Garrett Jnr, the Captain of the Princeton team.

By now the sun was going down and the early April air was cool. As the competition began it became evident that some of the entrants had no idea how to throw the discus. The Greeks on the other hand were elegant and competent, and won applause for the formal beauty of their style. The Princetonian athlete A.C. Tyler described the scene for the Associated Press:

> *The efforts of the English novices were ludicrous. Garrett had*
> *practised a little during the forenoon; but he had not seen a discus*
> *before to-day. Consequently you may imagine our joy when the*
> *American competitor's first hurl was 27 metres, 53 centimetres. The*
> *Greeks almost tied themselves in knots in preparing for a throw,*
> *and then suddenly stretched out, and the discus sailed through the*
> *air. The best Greek threw 28 metres, 51 centimetres. Garrett's*
> *second and third tries were unfortunate, the discus first flying*
> *crooked, and the third time dropping from his hand as he pitched.*
> *But Garrett's first effort was sufficient to secure him a place in the*
> *finals. His two opponents were native Greeks, and one of them was*
> *the champion for many years of discus throwing; the other Greek*
> *was a famous weight-lifter. Both were men of magnificent*
> *physique. The Greek champion, in the finals, threw first and scored*

21 *Robert Garrett of Princeton University, posing with discus. He won the event on the first day with a throw of 29.15m. The discus was presented to him and is now to be seen at Princeton. The photo is conventionally printed this way round, showing Garrett throwing right handed, but with the miniature US flag on his chest the wrong way round. If he actually wore the flag the right way round, then Garrett was left-handed. (Meyer album)*

28 metres, 88 centimetres. Our champion, Garrett, followed with 28 metres, 72 centimetres. The third man was so provoked at Garrett's success that he was only able to throw 27 metres, 48 centimetres. The champion of Greece then threw the discus 28 metres, 95½ centimetres, and the other Greek hurled it 28 metres. Then came the final effort, and we all held our breath as Garrett carefully prepared for the throw. By this time he had caught the knack of hurling the discus, and had complete confidence in himself. He put all his energy into the last cast, and as the discus flew through the air the vast concourse of people were silent as if the structure were empty. When the discus struck there was a tremendous burst of applause from all sides, and we joined in with right good will. The applause of the Greek champions, however, was decidedly feeble. The throw was measured, and the announcement was made that Garrett had thrown 29 metres, 15 centimetres, and had beaten the Greeks at their own game.

Garrett's winning discus can still be seen at Princeton. Many years later he presented two discuses to his old university, where they are on display today.

The damaged one was lying on the ground in the stadium when we Princeton youngsters visited it the afternoon of the Sunday before the games. I experimented with it a few times and then determined to take part in the event just for the fun of it. The other undamaged discus was the one used in the games, if my information is correct. Immediately after the games were held the Greek authorities had a monogram placed on one of the brass plates and present[ed] the discus to me.[12]

After the 400-metre heats, won by the Americans Jamison of Princeton and Burke of Boston, the first day of the sports ended and the royal family retired. That evening the city was flooded with light, in celebration of the return of the games and in welcome to the visitors from abroad.

10

THE GAMES CONTINUE

A striking contrast in truth – the bicycle at the foot of the Parthenon.

Coubertin, Letter from Athens

Only the Marathon race recaptured the excitement of that first day. The intensity could not be sustained through a week of sports, some of them made tedious by lack of information, long delays, lack of skills, or bad weather.

It had poured with rain during the unveiling of the Averoff statue on Sunday 5 April. Dark clouds hung over the stadium on the afternoon of Monday, the first day of the games. The Wednesday was the coldest day since February, with a sharp north wind cutting across the Phaleron plain where the bicycling and lawn tennis contests were held in the velodrome. On Thursday 9 April the Athenians woke to see Mt Pendeli covered in snow almost down to the base, an unusual phenomenon for April. On Monday 13 April a southern gale blew steadily, forcing the postponement and finally the cancellation of the boating events at Phaleron. The prizegiving ceremony was postponed from Tuesday to Wednesday because of heavy rain again. The King was said to have remarked in advance that there was often bad weather around Independence Day. Even so, this was an unusual run of bad luck for the organisers.

The cold gave rise to one of the legends of the games. The American swimmer Gardner Williams had entered as an individual, unconnected with Princeton or Harvard, for two of the swimming events:

> *He had traveled 5000 miles for this event, and as he posed with the others on the edge of the float, waiting for the gun, his spirit thrilled with patriotism and determination. At the crack of the pistol, the contestants dived headfirst into the icy water. In a split second, his head reappeared, 'Jesu Christo! I'm freezing!'; with that shriek of astonished frenzy he lashed back to the float. For him the Olympics were over.*[1]

There were some empty spaces in the stands as the initial excitement wore off, provoking demands that the price of tickets be reduced.

The track and field events continued in the stadium throughout the week, interspersed with weightlifting, wrestling and gymnastics, ending with the climax of the marathon finish on Friday. There was fencing at the Zappeion on Tuesday and Thursday; shooting at the Kallithea range from Wednesday to Saturday; cycling in the velodrome; tennis at Ilissos and in the velodrome; swimming at Piraeus on Saturday. On Sunday there was a road race for the cyclists from Athens to Marathon and back.

The track and field events were the most popular of the Olympics, watched by keen crowds in the stadium. Not being able to secure agree-ment on international rules, Coubertin adopted the principle of sub-sidiarity, using French rules (of the USFSA) for the races, English (AAA) for the jumping and throwing, and other rules as appropriate for other events. The field of competition was wider than ever before, with eleven nations represented, of which only the US (ten) and Greece (twenty-seven) had ten entrants or more. The contestants found the track prepared by Charles Perry problematic. It was shorter than the standard modern track, about 330 metres in circumference, and the turns were very sharp. The American athletes complained that it was too soft. The races were run clockwise, contrary to the growing trend for anti-clockwise direction.

As the events proceeded, the American predominance was confirmed. An old priest who sat two rows in front of Rufus Richardson, the Director of the American School, kept turning and asking, with smiles, 'Is that one of yours?' – adding, when the answer was yes, 'Yours are doing well.' On the afternoon of Tuesday, the second day, they won three events: the long jump, the shot put and the 400 metres.

Robert Garrett took the field again on the afternoon of Tuesday, for the long jump, followed after a short interval by the shot put. He came second in the long jump to the Harvard athlete Ellery Clark. Having come 5,000 miles to take part, Clark fouled on his first two jumps. He was put off his stride by a ruling of Prince George forbidding the marking of the spot in his run up where he began to run his hardest. 'It was little short of agony' awaiting his final attempt, which was the winning jump.[2] In the shot put, Garrett put in a winning first throw. The Greek athlete Miltiades Gouskos threw strongly with his third throw, so that the crowd thought he had won. When the responsible official hoisted the Greek flag, they cheered. But it quickly proved that this was a mistake and the Stars and Stripes replaced the blue and white Greek flag, to the disappointment of most onlookers. Nevertheless Greece won second and third place, and was beginning to haul in the medals.

In between these two events was the final of the 400 metres. Tom Burke, who was probably the best athlete in the American team, had beaten the British champion Edgar Bredin in the 1895 match between the New York Athletic Club and the London Athletic Club. Bredin, who held the world record, turned professional and was ineligible for Athens. Burke won the 400 metres comfortably in 54.2 seconds, followed in at a distance by Herbert Jamison of Princeton. The slow time, well below Burke's best, confirms the slowness of the track.

The American monopoly of the silver (equivalent of our gold) medals was broken by Edwin (Teddy) Flack of Australia, an accountant who was working in London at the time of the games and trained with the London Athletic Club. He carried off the 1,500-metre race late on Tuesday afternoon, winning from Arthur Blake and the Frenchman Lermusiaux. Two days later Flack repeated his success in the 800 metres.

The crowd was chagrined by the failure of the Greek athletes to win silver medals, but all accounts agree on their sporting reactions. The Prime Minister was said to have turned to the American Minister after the third or fourth American victory and jokingly asked why Columbus had discovered America. But actually the Greek record was none too bad. They had many more entrants than any other nation, and they took ten medals in track and field to the Americans' seventeen – one first in the marathon, three seconds and six thirds.[3]

The Americans again took silver in the finals of the 100 metres sprint and the 110 metres hurdles, the high jump and the pole vault, all of which were carried out on the Friday. Burke easily won the 100 metres from the German Fritz Hofmann. In the hurdles Curtis just beat the confident Englishman Grantley Goulding, whom he conceded was technically a better hurdler than himself, though not so strong a runner.[4] Clark won his second medal in the high jump, with Garrett and Connolly equal second. Welles Hoyt defeated Albert Tyler in the pole vault, with two Greek vaulters equal third. This event was interrupted by the commotion caused by the entry of Spyridon Louis into the stadium at the end of the marathon.

Even outside the track and field programme, most of the events attracted quite large crowds. On Tuesday morning the centre of attention shifted to the Zappeion building, where the fencing was to take place, in the presence of the King and the Crown Prince. This was the only event which admitted a separate category of professionals, the fencing masters. It was dominated by the Greeks and the French. The foil was won by a Frenchman, Gravelotte, who was said to have celebrated his victory by drinking a glass of retsina wine on the Acropolis. In the foil event for professional masters, the Greek Leonidas Pyrgos beat the Frenchman Jean Perronet, and became the first Greek athlete to win an Olympic first place in modern times. Greeks took first and second place in the sabre event, held on 9 April.

On Wednesday morning the cavalcade moved to the suburban village of Kallithea for the inauguration of the new shooting range. In traditional Greek style, the building with its dressing rooms and terrace was first blessed by the Bishop of Cephalonia. Queen Olga arrived with her daughter Princess Marie and her fiancé the Grand Duke George. The Queen fired one shot from a flower-bedecked rifle. The events, which took place under an amazingly complicated scoring system, were dominated by Greek competitors, twenty-eight of them against only three from the US, two from Britain, and a few others. A number of amateurs seem to have entered for the shooting just for the fun of it. The competitors included, for example, Charles Waldstein, previously director of the American School, and Anastasios Metaxas, the architect of the stadium and shooting gallery, who as we have seen was a member of the secret National Society. The Greeks, with a strong team of students which had practised with the help of the future Foreign Minister George Streit, took the first five places in the military rifle event.

The pistol events were dominated by the American brothers John and Sumner Paine. John Paine, a member of the Boston Athletic Association, travelled out to Athens via Paris, where he picked up his brother Sumner, who was performing in a Paris shooting gallery that summer. They brought with them to Athens a wide variety of weapons, including a Colt army revolver, a Smith and Wesson Russian revolver, pocket guns and .22 calibre pistols. In the military pistol event John Paine beat his brother. He then stood down from the free pistol event, allowing Sumner to win from a Dane. In the third pistol event the two brothers stood down when they discovered that their weapons were not of the prescribed calibre.

Tennis took place at the Athens Lawn Tennis Club near the Ilissos river, and in the velodrome. None of the top tennis players (most of whom were British) attended. A young British player called John Pius Boland, later MP for South Kerry in Ireland from 1900 to 1918, was in

Athens on holiday at the invitation of Constantine Manos, whom he had met as a student at Oxford. He appears to have entered the tennis tournament on impulse. Boland beat the Egyptian Greek Dionysios Kasdaglis in the men's singles final, and partnered by a German won the doubles, also from two Greeks.

Of all the events in the 1896 Olympics, the weightlifting, for which there were as yet no internationally agreed rules, came nearest to an ugly dispute, not so much because of the athletes as because of arguments between a disputatious British judge and Prince George, the chairman of the judges. In the first event, the two-hands lift, the Dane Jensen beat the British weightlifter Launceston Elliot on 'style', both having lifted the same weight of 111.5 kilograms. In the second, the one-hand lift, the order was reversed. Elliot, a large, fair, handsome young man, was much admired by the Greek crowd.

Elliot cropped up again in the wrestling, a Greco-Roman event which took place, like the weightlifting, in the stadium. Again there was some nastiness. Elliot was beaten in the first round by the wiry German Carl Schuhmann, and disputed the result. The German went on to beat the Greek Tsitas after a long-drawn-out final, which lasted for forty minutes before darkness fell, and was then postponed to the next day, when Schuhmann took fifteen minutes to clinch victory.

These two events show how much depended on the skill and firmness of the judges. Prince George and his team acquitted themselves well. The aura attaching to royalty may have helped sustain his judgements; it does not seem to have prevented the athletes from disputing the rules. Prince George, who was immensely big, made a great hit with the crowd during the weightlifting by picking up one of the heavy dumb-bells in one hand and shifting it.

Swimming events at 100, 500 and 1,200 metres freestyle took place on the Saturday in the attractive bay of Zea, where today is the marina from which hydrofoils, the 'flying dolphins', set off for the islands of the Saronic Gulf. Some 20,000 spectators, including the King, watched the events, some of them from rustic seats near the quayside. The conditions were frankly primitive. The water was very cold, between 12 and 14 degrees Celsius (53–57 degrees Fahrenheit). This dampened the enthusiasm of the crowd, though the author Pavlos Nirvanas, in one of the better descriptions of the Olympic events, put this down to the lack of visible plasticity of the virtually invisible swimmers as compared with the unparalleled grace of the discus thrower, the fine rush of the runner and the energy of the wrestler. Nirvanas, however, was able to report favourably on the naked bodies and virginal flesh of the young swimmers shivering with cold in the neat but basic changing-rooms.[5]

This was the occasion on which the American swimmer Gardner Williams was said to have jumped out of the water as fast as he jumped into it. For the 100 metres freestyle, the contestants (including Williams) were taken out to sea in boats. The starting line was set between two buoys, and the contestants swam back towards the shore between two lines of floating hollow pumpkins to a finishing line marked by a red flag. The pumpkins wobbled in the water, causing confusion. The winner was Alfred Hajos of Hungary, already the European 100 metres champion, and later to be a member of the Hungarian football team. The Hungarians present sang their own national hymn over the noise of the Austrian national anthem played by the band.

The gymnastics were the most important and long-lasting of the non-track-and-field events. They represented a different athletic tradition and it was on the combination of the two traditions that the Olympics were founded. They were held on the Thursday and Friday in the stadium. The German team, much more experienced than the Greeks, defied the threats of the German Gymnastics Association, the Deutsche Turnerschaft, to suspend them if they competed in Athens. For the first time, apart from the curious episode of the weightlifting eliminator based on 'style', the judges had to make subjective judgements based on bodily control, agility and other attributes.

The Germans won the two team events, on parallel bars and horizontal bar. On the parallel bars, the PGA took second place, beating the other Greek team from the NGA, led by Ioannis Chrysaphis. On the horizontal bar, the Germans were the only team entered. There were also individual events, on the vaulting horse, the pommelled horse, the rings, the horizontal bar and the parallel bars, won by the wrestler Schuhmann, to great acclaim, and by Swiss, Greek and German athletes. A Greek athlete won a rope-climbing event.

The tedium of the gymnastics events gave rise to some critical comments from those who did not appreciate Coubertin's principle of the equality of all Olympic sports. The Englishman G. S. Robertson commented:

> *The Germans displayed magnificent style in their squad exercises in the horizontal and parallel bars. In the former case they won without contest; indeed opposition would have been hopeless. In the latter set of exercises, they were opposed by two Greek teams, which performed what may be described as kindergarten evolutions, in perfect time. It seemed to us that any ordinary body of men could have done as well with two days' practice. The Germans, on the other hand, performed difficult exercises in beautiful style, but naturally with a few mistakes. They were at once awarded the prize. The Greek public then, perhaps on this one occasion only, forgot its good manners, and displayed its ignorance of gymnastics, by greeting the decision with yells of 'adika' (unjust).*[6]

Robertson also argued that awarding so many medals for the gymnastic events devalued the medals. But this was the price of fully incorporating the Germans and Scandinavians in the event.

The cycling events took place in the velodrome in New Phaleron, built for the Olympic Games after a Danish model at a cost of 100,000 drachmas. The velodrome held 7,000 spectators and had a modern track of one third of a kilometre with banked turns. The first event, on Wednesday 8 April, was a gruelling 100-kilometre track race of 300 laps. It was fought out between the Frenchman Léon Flameng and the Greek

22 *Léon Flameng and Paul Masson, both of France, with their cycles. (Meyer album)*

Georgios Kolettis, and was notable for one of the examples of early Olympic sportsmanship. Kolettis was forced to stop in mid-race to make repairs to his bicycle, whereupon Flameng stopped too and dismounted until his opponent was ready to remount and start again. Flameng won the event.

The well-known French cyclist Paul Masson won the one-lap (one third of a kilometre) time trial and both the 2,000-metre sprint and the 10,000 metres, the latter two on a bitterly cold day. The Greek cyclist Stamatis Nikolopoulos came second in the first two events and a Frenchman in the third. The Austrian Adolf Schmal won the twelve-hour track race from the Briton F. Keeping.

The most interesting of the cycle events was the individual road race, held on Sunday 12 April over an 87-kilometre course from Athens to Marathon and back, using the same course as for the marathon run but starting in Kiphissia Avenue and finishing in the velodrome. The pack split on the return leg, when there were a number of falls owing to exhaustion and the uneven state of the road. The leading Greek rider, Aristidis Konstantinidis, who won the event from the German August Goedrich, fell no less than three times. Both he and Goedrich had to borrow bicycles, in his case because of a puncture, in Goedrich's because of damage to his machine. Third behind these two came E. Battel, a servant at the British Embassy in Athens, who for a time held the lead. It was said that British officials tried to prevent him from taking part on the grounds that as a servant he could not be an amateur.

Returning to his hotel late on Saturday, Charles Maurras found a sheet of telegraph paper pinned up in the vestibule, bearing the words: Mr Tricoupis died at Cannes at six p.m. The following day all the Athenian press paid homage to the great leader. The nation combined in mourning, including Deliyiannis and his followers. An acquaintance gave Maurras his view:

> Yes, Tricoupis spent prodigiously. Ships, schools, railways, he ran headlong into debt in order to realise all his projects simultaneously. He should have got there bit by bit. From that came his fall, and no doubt his death. But then what have his successors done? They talked of economy when they were in opposition; their budgets are exactly the same as those of Tricoupis. Our European creditors had a moment of hope: they have lost it to such an extent that now they seek to impose a financial control commission on us.

It was the end of an era in Greek political life. Tricoupis's body was brought back to Greece on the steamer *Titan*, accompanied by his sister and helpmeet Sophia, arriving at Piraeus on 22 April, a few days after the departure of most of the athletes. For a few days it lay in state in his house. The King and the Crown Prince visited and stayed for half an hour. European statesmen and princes, including the Prince of Wales, sent telegrams of condolence. *The Times* reported that the dead man's features, which were visible through the glass lid of the coffin, seemed little altered and wore a tranquil expression.

Maurras stayed long enough to witness the obsequies. When the King stooped to kiss the glass cover of the coffin, in the traditional way, an old lady in black said, 'But he is dead. What good can all that do him?'

11

THE MARATHON

*The Athenian generals sent off a message to Sparta. The messenger
was an Athenian named Pheidippides, a professional long-distance
runner. According to the account he gave the Athenians on his
return, Pheidippides met the god Pan on Mt Parthenium, above
Tegea … He reached Sparta the day after he left Athens and
delivered his message to the Spartan government.*

Herodotus, *The Histories*, book 6: before the battle
(Penguin Books, translated by Aubrey de Sélincourt, revised by John Marincola)

*While the Persian fleet was on its way round Sunium, the
Athenians hurried back with all possible speed to save their city,
and succeeded in reaching it before the arrival of the Persians.*

Herodotus, *The Histories*, book 6: after the battle

Greek history and landscape and modern sport came together with
the Olympic Games to create in the marathon a perfect race for
the modern era.

The marathon instantly became a tradition. There was no long-
distance race of this demanding nature before 1896. Certainly not in
ancient Greece, either at Olympia or Nemea, Delphi or the Isthmus of
Corinth, the other three sites of Panhellenic Games. The longest of the

foot races at Olympia was the *dolichos*, a race of twenty-four *stades* or rather less than 5,000 metres, a *stade* being the length of a stadium, about 185 metres.

The idea of the marathon came neither from Coubertin nor from the Greeks. The longest race at the Zappas Olympic Games was a three-mile *dolichos* in the games of November 1859, and even that was too much for the subsequent Zappas games, when the foot races were of only one or two *stades*. But just as the world was ready for the Olympics, so it seems to have been ready for the marathon. Long-distance running and walking were becoming increasingly popular in Britain and the United States.

The instigator was another romantic Frenchman and educational specialist, Michel Bréal. A German-speaking Jew of French descent, born in Bavaria, Bréal moved as a young man to Alsace, where he became a devotee of ancient mythology and enthusiast for the ancient Olympic Games. An associate of Coubertin, he attended the Sorbonne congress. Before Coubertin's first visit to Athens, Bréal wrote suggesting that he should see if he could organise a 'marathon race' from Marathon to the Pnyx, the hill which faces the Acropolis. Bréal volunteered to present a silver cup for the marathon winner. It still exists, engraved in Greek:

OLYMPIC GAMES

1896

MARATHON PRIZE

PRESENTED BY MICHEL BREAL

It is to Coubertin's credit that he did not try to assume the authorship of the marathon. In fact he admitted later that he had been reluctant to create such a race, but that once the word got about it was hardly poss-ible to avoid holding it.

The word marathon entered usage as a description of a long-distance race as a result of the 1896 Olympic Games. Before that it denoted only the battle between Greeks and Persians in 490 BC, which John Stuart

Mill described as more important even as an event in English history than the Battle of Hastings, and a small village near the site of the ancient battlefield. From Byron, armchair travellers knew that the mountains look on Marathon, and Marathon looks on the sea. Today the site still has its importance not only as a battlefield, with the tumulus marking the tomb of the Greek dead, and a modest village, but for the wetlands between Marathon and the sea, inland from the beach at Schinias, where the Greek authorities have constructed a rowing and canoeing course for the 2004 games in defiance of protests by environmental and archaeological organisations. The former argue that the site is a unique wetland refuge for birdlife in an increasingly urbanised Attica; the latter that the whole area is sacred because of the battle and its resonance for human freedom and Greek identity.

The ancient authorities for a 'marathon' run (not race) are characteristically shrouded in controversy. The classic account of the battle is by Herodotus, the 'father of history', writing in the second half of the fifth century BC about events in 490, and therefore able – just – to draw on eye-witness sources.

The story starts with Athenian support for the Greek cities of the Asia Minor littoral in their resistance to the rising power of the Persian empire. The army of Darius I, the Great King of Persia, commanded by the Mede Datis, had sailed across the Aegean from Samos in 600 triremes with a fleet of horse transports, taking out the city of Eretria in Euboea, an ally of Athens, on the way to a reckoning with Athens, regarded as a thorn in the flesh of the Great King. Guided by the Athenian traitor Hippias, the Persian ships made landfall at the bay of Marathon on the east coast of Attica, where they believed there was suitable ground for cavalry operations in the narrow coastal plain. The Athenians hurried out to Marathon to confront the enemy, blocking the southern end of the Marathon plain and the exits towards Athens. They were commanded by one Kallimachos, but the most influential of their ten generals was Miltiades, former chief of the Gallipoli peninsula and son of the great Cimon, himself incidentally a three-time Olympic

winner in the chariot race: he had his team of four mares buried opposite his grave on the so called 'sunken road' outside Athens.

Facing superior forces, the Athenians explored the possibilities of
support by allies. Sparta, the dominant Peloponnesian power, renowned
for warlike skills and courage, was the obvious choice. The Athenian
generals sent off a messenger, Pheidippides – or more likely Philippides
– to Sparta. Herodotus calls him a professional long-distance runner,
and writes that he arrived in Sparta the next day, a remarkable feat of
running given the mountainous nature of the terrain, and the fact that
he claimed to have seen a vision of the god Pan in the mountains above
Tegea (though this epiphany may have occurred on his return journey).
The distance is about 150 miles. He presented to the Spartans the Athenian generals' request for support. The Spartans were moved to help, but
for religious reasons could not take the field until it was full moon,
which meant several days' delay. An ally which puts forward such a
reason for inaction is naturally suspected of inventing a pretext. But the
Spartans' reasoning was sincere. Religious inhibitions in the ancient
world were genuine and powerful. Once the moon was past full, the
Spartans marched for all they were worth, reaching Attica within three
days, another astonishing feat. Their leading squadrons reached Athens
two days after the battle: as the Greeks say today, *katopin eortis*, after the
feast. Only plucky little Plataea fought with the Athenians.

What has all this to do with a marathon race of twenty-six miles, as
instituted at the 1896 games? Very little. The Persians were defeated by a
superb and disciplined Athenian charge, and fled to their ships, many
of them being driven into the marsh at the north end of the Marathon
plain. The ships sailed south, raising the horrific possibility that they
would sail round the point of Sunium, land at Phaleron, and attack the
city of Athens. At the same time, Herodotus records, the Athenian
troops on the battlefield saw the flash of the sun on a shield high up in
the mountains, probably on Mount Pendeli (ancient Pentelikon). This
strange event, still shrouded in mystery, was assumed to be a traitorous
message to the Persians to the effect that their supporters in the city

were ready to let them in. In the face of this threat, the Athenians, hot and tired after the battle, nevertheless made for home as fast as they could. The battle had taken place in the morning. Through the hot hours of the afternoon they marched across the hills and down into the Attic plain, spending that night south of the city (so the course they covered was more than twenty-six miles). The Persians, sailing into Phaleron the next day, saw that the city was defended, and decided they had had enough. They turned for home.

This then was the original marathon course, covered by the Athenian heavy armed soldiers. Herodotus makes no reference to Philippides-Pheidippides on this occasion. But later sources reintroduce him, as having run from the battlefield to Athens, reported the news in the marketplace, and fallen dead with the word *nenikikame*, 'We have won!'

Had anyone thought of it, the route might equally have been from Athens to Sparta, following the presumed course of Philippides's run before the battle. The idea of a 150-mile race would not have occurred to late-nineteenth-century sportsmen. But in 1982 Wing-Commander John Foden of the RAF, advised and helped by John Leatham, set off from Athens with four colleagues to test Herodotus's story, and reached Sparta thirty-six hours later. The following year a 'spartathlon' race from Athens to Sparta was established. It is held in September every year over a distance of 246 kilometres, or just less than 150 miles. The record for this phenomenal achievement is 20 hours 25 minutes, by the Greek Yannis Kouros in 1984, a time which shows that Herodotus's description 'on the next day', meaning between twenty-four and forty-eight hours later, is literally possible.

Following Bréal's suggestion, the marathon race devised for the 1896 games was based on the Herodotean evidence for the march back from Marathon to Athens, following the presumed route of the Athenian troops and the probably mythical Philippides. There are two routes which Philippides may have taken from Marathon to Athens, and predictably there is no agreement among scholars which he took. One heads up the steep Vrana valley into the hills at Dionysos, and descends through pine forests to Kifissia and Maroussi and thence down into Athens. The other passes southwards along the coast for some fifteen kilometres to modern Rafina, then gradually ascends to the crest at Stavros at 240 metres, skirting Pendeli to the east and south, before a ten-kilometre descent into Athens. The former course is shorter but tougher. The 1896 organisers wisely chose the latter course, which is the more likely route of the Athenians' forced march. It remains the course of the annual Greek marathon and will be run at the 2004 games (see page xx).

The course distance was reckoned at forty kilometres/twenty-five miles, as opposed to the 42,195 metres which has become the standard modern marathon. How it was measured we do not know. The road was unpaved and dust was a potential problem. The contestants were taken out to Marathon the day before the race and lodged there overnight, some in the house of one of the members of the Crown Prince's Council. In 1906, when the same thing happened, the lodging was primitive and the runners got little sleep owing to the fleas and bedbugs.

There were seventeen starters: thirteen Greeks, including the young Spyridon (Spyros) Louis, a well-built twenty-four-year-old from Maroussi who had served in the army; Flack of Australia, Lermusiaux of France, Kellner of Hungary, and Blake of the United States. Of the foreigners only Kellner is known to have run a marathon distance before. The foreign runners were already well known to the Greek audience in the stadium, since Flack had won the 800-metre final on Thursday 9 April, and Flack, Blake and Lermusiaux had come first, second and third in the 1,500 metres on Tuesday 7 April. Each runner was allowed one helper in attendance. Flack was attended by V.W. Delves-Broughton, a member of the staff of the British Embassy with Australian connections, who bicycled alongside the lofty Australian administering aid. Three military doctors also followed the leading runners in a carriage, with their medical equipment.

At 2 p.m., in cool but sunny conditions, the starter, Colonel Papadiamantopoulos, fired his pistol in front of a few hundred spectators, and

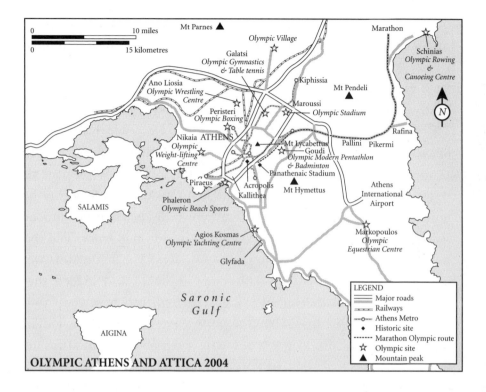

OLYMPIC ATHENS AND ATTICA 2004

the runners were off. The Frenchman Lermusiaux set a fast pace, leading Flack, Blake and Kellner all the way to Pikermi (20 kilometres). At this point the Greeks Lavrentis and Kafetzis, the former the winner of the first Greek Olympic trial, dropped out, leaving Vasilakos and Louis still in contact with the leaders and running close together. At Harvati, modern Pallini (25 kilometres), the runners were strung out in the order Lermusiaux (94 minutes), Flack (95), Blake (98), Vasilakos (101), Louis (101½), Kellner (104), Deliyiannis and Belokas (105). After proceeding through a triumphal arch erected by the villagers of Pallini in honour of the runners, Lermusiaux cracked, stopping for a rub-down from his assistant and then returning to Athens by horse-drawn carriage. Flack took the lead and Louis overtook Vasilakos and caught Flack around the 34-kilometre mark. The two men were in contact as they ran down towards the city, with Kellner of Hungary in third place ahead of Vasilakos and Belokas.

Near Ambelokipi, then a modest village in a vineyard as its name suggests, today a quarter of office blocks, cinemas and shops, Louis's sweetheart was waiting for him, offering slices of orange as refreshment. He took some and lengthened his stride downhill towards the finish. The pace was too much for Flack, who gave up the chase.

Meanwhile at the stadium, a crowd estimated at not less than 80,000 was waiting in eager tension, paying little attention to the pole vault competition in which Hoyt of Harvard and Tyler of Princeton were contesting the lead.[1] There was of course no means of real-time communication between the start at Marathon or the points on the course and the finish in the stadium. A German cyclist brought news that Flack was in the lead, to the dismay of the crowd. Later Colonel Papadiamantopoulos arrived on horseback with the news that Louis was leading.

At about 4.58 p.m., a sunburned, dark-haired man wearing a white vest with the number 17 and covered in sweat was seen to enter the stadium – 'panting, dusty, travel-stained, but still running true and strong'.[2] It was Louis. The crowd went wild. The pole-vaulters stopped in the general din and excitement. The Crown Prince and Prince George ran alongside Louis as he completed the straight and breasted the tape at the far end of the stadium. His time was 2 hours 58.50. He was followed in by Vasilakos 7 minutes 30 later, the longest gap between first and second in Olympic history. Louis proceeded to the tunnel near the end of the NE straight and is said to have drunk two cups of coffee. Presumably he drank also copious quantities of water. He was congratulated there by Queen Olga and other members of the royal family. He proceeded to the changing-rooms and was reported to have told the trainer who rubbed him down, 'Let me go, I could go on all the way to Piraeus!' Others report that the doctors measured his pulse at 112 to the minute, and found that he was neither trembling nor in pain, but with beads of sweat on his skin. Instantly he had become a hero, the man who matched the hour, and myth began to crystallise about him.[3]

Coubertin, who was watching, called this 'one of the most extraordinary sights I have ever seen'. It left him convinced that spiritual forces

23 *Arrival of Spyros Louis in the Stadium at the end of the Marathon race. He
is accompanied down the final straight by the Crown Prince and Prince
George. The famous picture is based on a photo by John Macropoulos.*
(Illustrated London News, *25 April 1896*)

play a greater role in sporting achievement than is generally believed.
Coubertin also saw, or remembered later that he saw, the beginning of
the making of the Louis legend, as a woman behind him unfastened her
watch and sent it to Louis as a present. Later Coubertin contributed to
the legend himself, remembering Louis as a 'magnificent peasant
dressed in the popular kilt' and giving currency to the story that Louis
spent the night before the race in fasting and prayer, like one of the
knights of the Round Table.[4]

The aftermath was not without controversy. The Greek teenager
Spyridon Belokas came in third after Vasilakos and before Kellner of
Hungary, who was the only foreigner to complete the course. Kellner
lodged a protest, alleging that Belokas had covered part of the course in

a horse-drawn carriage. Prince George, charged with investigating, ruled that Belokas should be disqualified, but without publishing details of his findings.

Of all the events of the games, the marathon and the discus were those in which the Greeks had an advantage. They had trained more than any others for this specific race, holding at least three eliminator trials. There is no evidence, so far as I know, for the rumour reported by Coubertin that three young Greeks actually died in training for the race.

No one on the day doubted either the magnitude or the legitimacy of Louis's victory. He won fair and square. But after the event, E.F. Benson jokily gave currency to an unpleasant rumour only to deny it in a manner that impugned Louis's honour.

So far ahead was he of all other competitors, and so phenomenal was the time in which he had covered the twenty-five miles from Marathon, that there were some ugly conjectures whispered about that he had possibly been assisted by occasionally putting his hand on the stirrup of the Greek cavalry officer who rode beside him with words of encouragement. Without doubt the suggestion was false, indeed it was refuted next year when the victor once more proved very definitely (as we shall see) his unrivalled power of speed and staying.[5]

Later that year, Benson went on – actually it was in April 1897 – the Greek armed forces advanced against the Turks in Thessaly. They were defeated and turned to retreat.

Refugees from the Greek army – they could hardly be called deserters, for the army no longer existed at all – poured into Athens, and the first to arrive, easily distancing all competitors, was Louis, the winner of the marathon race the year before. He had silenced for ever all doubts about his running.

This well-turned story was nonsense, for Louis did not take part in the war.

Louis's victory was certainly extraordinary. So far as we know it was only the second time that he had run a marathon distance. In the second trial held to select the Greek contestants for the Olympic Games, he came in, admittedly in bad conditions, in 3 hours 18.27. Technically he was lucky to be selected, since contestants in the second trial were told that they must beat the winning time in the first trial (3 hours 18, set by Vasilakos) to be selected. There is no evidence that Louis followed a systematic course of training. He was simply a naturally strong runner, said to have trained in the army and by trotting alongside his father's horse as it carted barrels of fresh water from Maroussi to Athens.

The satirist George Souris, who published a weekly sheet, *O Romios*, entirely written by Souris himself in verse, stopped the presses and when he heard the result inserted on the back page a few verses in honour of Louis, displacing the usual advertisements.

May Louis hear today the hymns of Pindar
Long live the race, the people, the crown and Maroussi.[6]

The Louis legend began to develop immediately. As Rufus Richardson wisely remarked, 'it is difficult to ascertain just what Louis has been doing since the race. A cycle of myths is already growing up about him. It is not uninteresting to be present at this genesis of myths in which the newspapers play a considerable part.'[7] Apart from Coubertin's lady with the watch, there were countless other stories of gifts to the marathon winner, ranging from free dinners for a year to free shaves for life and a lifetime's free rail travel with a place for his bicycle in the goods van; gold watches and chains, an engraved gem stone, a Singer sewing machine, a suit, a big pie and a case of brandy, a three *stremma* field in Maroussi.

The majority of these gifts were commercial promotions. It is unclear how many of them Louis accepted but it does seem that he turned down many offers. Some of the alleged gifts belong to the realm of legend. Marriage inevitably featured in the myth. A well-born young lady was said to have promised herself in marriage to the winner if he were Greek, expecting one of the aristocratic youths or officers to be the man. An American lady with a 4 million dollar dowry was reported to have arrived in Athens in quest of Louis, with two French maids and seventeen trunks full of clothes. Louis was reported to have made a request for clemency for his brother who was doing time in prison after a knife brawl. The latter story was denied by Louis. What does seem to be true is that the owners of the Maroussi water source conceded to Louis the right to sell their water in Athens, and that he took this up.

The Louis legend also obscured his background and personality. The legend was best served by the poor peasant who came from nowhere to win the race. Louis was not of a poor family. His family were solid and respectable smallholders from Maroussi. Louis lived and worked on the farm with his parents and two elder brothers. Later, after his marriage and honeymoon, spent at Averoff's invitation in his house at Alexandria, he cultivated his own market garden. Wisely, Louis was unspoiled by the fuss and unimpressed by the newspapers. He gave one interview only, to an Italian newspaper. When asked for the secret of his training, he is said to have replied, 'Tell them I used to dig in my vineyard.' Two months after his triumph, Louis was arrested for striking a young man in the street. He was acquitted, on the grounds that the young man had been harassing a lady. So even this brush with the law contributed to his aura of chivalry.

The marathon race was the main innovation of 1896 within the larger innovation of the games themselves. It sprang to life and has endured in virtually the form it took in that first year. The 1896 marathon led to an enthusiastic endorsement and diffusion of the race in Northern Europe and America. John Graham, the manager of the US Olympic team, organised the first Boston marathon in April 1897, and it has taken place annually ever since. The Paris Olympics in 1900 (notable for the bizarre fact that two of the runners were named Fast and Champion, who came in second and third respectively) and the St Louis Olympics of 1904 continued the Olympic practice. The return to Athens in 1906, when the marathon over the same course as in 1896 was won in strong style by the Canadian Billy Sherring in 2 hours 51. 23.6, confirmed the institution. The Greeks hold an annual marathon in September over the classic course. It does not have the worldwide renown and pulling power of the London, New York or Boston marathons, but as the first marathon race, over the historic course, it will remain unique.

The marathon, and Louis's victory, made the 1896 Olympic Games.

12

THE END OF THE GAMES

Greece can justly hope that the foreigners who have honoured her with their presence will point to our country as the peaceful rendezvous of the nations, as the stable and permanent seat of the Olympic Games.

King George I, from his toast at the Banquet of 12 April 1896

These games should never be removed from their native soil.

From the collective letter of the US team, April 1896

On Wednesday 15 April, in brilliant sunshine, King George took his place in the stadium and prepared to give out the prizes. The event had been postponed by one day because of rain. Now the stadium was once more full of spectators and the athletes lined up again in their national groups. The Greek national anthem was played, with its moving lines by Dionysios Solomos, 'Hail freedom, hail.' This was the moment G.S. Robertson, the 'competitor and prize winner' from Oxford, had been waiting for. Quite how he infiltrated himself into the ceremonies is not known. But at this moment he stepped forward and recited a long ode composed by himself in ancient Greek, on the model of Pindar. This was what an Oxford classical education taught you to do, and to the untutored eye the ode looks impressive. But who would have understood it? Not the King, nor any but a tiny proportion of the spectators. Even those Greeks who knew ancient Greek would have been baffled by Robertson's anglicised Erasmic pronunciation.[1]

Mounting the platform, the King distributed the prizes. One by one the athletes came to the podium. Each winner received a diploma, a silver medal, and an olive branch from the Altis at Olympia. Each taker of second place received a bronze medal and a bay wreath. Garrett received in addition a silver cup presented by the Crown Prince for the discus event. Louis received not only the Michel Bréal silver cup for the marathon, but also a fine ancient vase showing a running race, presented by the collector Ioannis Lambros. He had the good sense to pass it on to the National Archaeological Museum.

Coubertin had taken a keen interest in the prizes, even trying to get Puvis de Chavannes, whose paintings overlooked the grand hall at the Sorbonne where the Paris congress had been opened, to take on the design of the diploma. Alas, without success. Puvis looked at the photographs and drawings Coubertin had brought back from Greece and went away to ponder them, but finally refused on the grounds that he found it impossible to make the design Hellenic enough! Coubertin had more luck with the French sculptor J.C. Chaplain, who designed a medal showing on the obverse the head of Olympian Zeus and a winged Victory holding a branch of bay, on the reverse the Acropolis, with the words in Greek 'International Olympic Games in Athens 1896'. The bronze medal and the diploma were designed respectively by the well-known Greek artists Nikiphoros Lytras and Nicholas Gyzis. The diploma, in an agreeable style which Coubertin called a 'bizarre kind of modernism', showed the Parthenon with a rising phoenix, women representing Greece, a lyre and water clock or klepsydra, and Victory with an olive branch.[2]

Louis led the parade around the track, wearing for once the *fustanella* with which he is associated, and carrying the Greek flag. After him came the Americans, the Hungarians and the other national teams. For some reason Louis carried an umbrella, and a bouquet of

24 *The Victory Parade. Spyros Louis, winner of the marathon, leads it – but not*
quite: he is preceded by a man with a top hat and white gloves, Constantine
Manos, the dynamic and controversial young nationalist poet and
sportsman, who was chief steward. He later became a member of
parliament, fought in Crete and in the Balkan Wars, and was killed in an
air crash in 1913. Louis carries the Greek flag in his right hand, and clutches
his medal, olive branch and winner's diploma with his left, as do the athletes
who follow him.

flowers presented by admiring female spectators. The band played a
new march composed by the director of the Athens garrison band,
called 'We have won' the words said to have been uttered by the runner
who brought the good news of the battle of Marathon to Athens. Louis
waved his flag, the athletes processed, and the crowd cheered. The King
pronounced the closure of the games and the crowd began to disperse.
A mob of people accompanied Philemon and members of the council
to the palace to acclaim the Crown Prince and his brothers, who
appeared on the balcony. They went on to Philemon's office for more
congratulations, of Philemon and Vikelas. In all these acclamations, one

man was forgotten: Pierre de Coubertin. He was not to forget the slight.

'To those who followed closely the preliminaries to the revival of the Olympic Meeting,' wrote G.S. Robertson, 'it appeared certain that the games would be a disastrous failure.'[3] The results were certainly not impressive, compared with those at other athletics meetings in the same period. But we should bear in mind in mitigation the shape of the track, with its tight turns, and the surface prepared by Charles Perry, which was too hard underneath and too soft and loose on the surface.

The figures show that the performances at many of the Athens events were mediocre. Of the American athletes, Burke of Boston, who won the 400 metres, was an athlete of the highest class. Connolly was a competent athlete at the triple jump, Garrett at the shot put, and Clark at the high and long jump, but none of them was a world beater. Of the non-Americans, Lermusiaux, who came in third in the 1,500 metres, was good enough later to set a world record for this distance. Louis ran a strong marathon, setting a world record for what was a new event. These were the highlights.

If it was not the results and records which impressed, what was it? It was the idea of the Olympics, the setting, the charm of novelty, the beauty of the city, the sky, and the hospitality of the people. This was what the Crown Prince and Vikelas had forecast, and this is what the contemporary witnesses agreed they found. On the other hand they do not agree on the importance of the event. Although with hindsight we can see the long history of the Olympic movement curled up as it were inside the Athens stadium, set in motion by the King's proclamation of the opening of the games, ready to unroll, the contemporary witnesses did not see this. The international press, in the US, Britain and France, paid some attention, but as much because of the historic and Hellenic aspects as the sporting. This was a successful sports festival, and the most international to date. There would be another in Paris, then another in the United States. Beyond that, though Coubertin had a vision, most people could not see.

But for the time they were united in recording, often in rapturous prose, the beauty of Athens and the emotion of the moment. Robertson, having listed all the defects, spoke of 'the triumph of sentiment, of association, of distinction, of unique splendour'. The Athenian scene was unsurpassable. 'Who, who was present there, does not wish that he may once again be permitted to behold it?'

Rufus B. Richardson, the director of the American School, was equally impressed:

> *The restored Panathenaic Stadion; innumerable bands of music; concerts; illuminations at Athens and Peiraeus; torchlight processions and fireworks; the presence of the royal family of Greece in the Stadion, accompanied by the King of Servia, the Grand Duke George of Russia, whose engagement to Princess Marie, the daughter of the King of Greece, was announced on the day before the opening of the games, and the widow of the late Crown Prince Rudolf of Austria with her two daughters; and, more than all, a maximum attendance of sixty thousand people, gave something to replace Olympia, and almost persuaded one that the old times had come around again when there was nothing more serious to do than to outrun, outleap and outwrestle.*[4]

Charles Maurras also reached a positive conclusion, by a curious route. He came to Athens convinced that Coubertin's internationalism was a bad thing: 'What would Olympiads open to the whole world mean? This mélange of races threatened to lead not to an intelligent and reasonable federation of modern peoples, but to the vague disorders of cosmopolitanism.' Cosmopolitanism was a bad thing in itself. Worse, it would be to the benefit of the least cosmopolitan and the most nationalistic of races, the Anglo-Saxon. The Olympic era opening in Athens would simply offer a new element of activity and prosperity to this 'eternal rival'. 'Does not the vocabulary of the Games already help far too much to propagate a language with which the planet is infested?'[5]

As against this, the Greek reality might have a good effect on the barbarians; and the games would be a good opportunity to try to distinguish between cosmopolitanism (bad) and internationalism (good). The first diminished and destroyed nations, the second presupposed the maintenance of different nations. To his surprise, Maurras found that there was nothing to fear in cosmopolitanism, because in our days 'when several distinct races are put together and forced to frequent each other, they repel each other, distancing themselves at the very moment when they think to come together'. George Orwell wrote that 'serious sport has nothing to do with fair play … it is war minus the shooting'. Maurras would have thought that a good thing.

Maurras hated foreigners, and found good material in Athens. The most violent and noisy nationalists were the brash Americans. The Yankees seemed three times as numerous as they were; every time a victory was announced, the Union flags clacked in the breeze; the hats and berets flew in the air; the cheers shook the wooden benches. 'This America knows nothing of that rarest and most secret thing which the hellenic world has conceived, the sense of measure …' But perhaps the modern Olympiads would show the Latin peoples the numbers, the power, the influence, the insolent ambitions and even the weak or ridiculous points in these audacious Anglo-Saxon claimants to tyranny.

On balance, Maurras was encouraged. Nation states were not disintegrating. 'War is not yet dead.' In the old days contacts between peoples had been mediated by ambassadors. Now steam and electricity and easy travel meant that they could meet face to face and insult each other. For a xenophobe like Maurras this could only be for the good!

When Coubertin assessed the games, he picked out two benefits for Greece, one athletic, the other political. The games had ensured that athletics took root in Greece. He judged rightly that this benefit would take time to work through. The political benefit was the closer union of the Crown Prince with his people (a point which Coubertin no doubt picked up from Vikelas). The games themselves had been a success, of course: they had to be, for Coubertin. Yet he had reservations, beyond the personal pique he felt from being, as he saw it, neglected by the Greeks and cut out of the public congratulations which were his due. His reservations flowed from his vision of the games and of internationalism. The Athens games had been essentially a minor affair in their athletic achievements. It was the wider Olympic idea that was supreme, and that demanded more than Athens and Greece alone could give. Coubertin had created the idea, and was not going to let it be diminished.

Richardson, the director of the American School, struck a different note when he wrote that Greece had not only won the marathon, but gained a standing among the nations of the world, whose delegates would never forget their reception. 'It is a small and poor kingdom, but like ancient Hellas, great in qualities of soul.'[6]

For the Greeks, this was the point. This was why Vikelas and Constantine had taken up the challenge of the games. The radical editor of the newspaper *Acropolis* commissioned a handsome volume on the occasion of the games, with contributions from the great and the good of Greece's intellectual and political establishment.[7] It was designed to show off Greece and its achievements, to prove, in the words of the eminent scholar and National Society member Spyridon Lambros, that 'the Greece of 1896 has far outdistanced the Greece of 1862'. Paradoxically, although such propaganda should really have been addressed to a foreign audience, the audience was exclusively Greek, because it was published only in Greek. It was therefore an exercise in reinforcing the Greeks' beliefs about their inheritance of civilised values from the ancient world. Perhaps it was this conviction of the superiority of Hellenism which justified the paradox of belonging to a clandestine society outside the constitutional framework of Greek democracy.

There were chapters on Greece under King George; the royal family; the constitution; the Prime Minister's day; the administrative world; the police, the church, the parliament; the army and navy; the national university, library and academy; literature; Athens and its history (including a piece by the writer Papadiamantis); and the Olympic

Games. It contained odes to Louis and to Averoff by the poet Ephtaliotis, an essay by Palamas celebrating the ideal of the Pallikari, or young hero, and a clutch of articles about the games including one by Constantine Manos. In the section entitled 'opinions of scholars on the Olympic Games', one after another, the US Ambassador, the director of the American School, Philemon and a string of eminent men lined up to praise the contribution of the games to Greece's reputation as a civilised nation, her ability to carry through a major national project, and the rightness of the claim of Greece to be the permanent home of the games. Most also praised the role of the Crown Prince.

The foreigners stressed particularly the effective organisation of the games, and the hospitality of the Greek people. Even Robertson, who could be a severe critic, conceded that the organizational flaws were minor. The hospitality had been warm. The Americans, with their open and boisterous approach, were particularly popular. (This was reflected in the warm send-off they were given by the Greeks, the well-known cheers and all, when they left Athens by train.[8]) The niggles over the arrangements concerned the changes in programming, the difficulty in getting accurate information, the still greater difficulty in securing change when for some reason the programme did not make sense (as for runners in the 800 metres and 1,500 metres who might wish also to compete in the marathon), the tedious rhythm of some events such as the high jump and pole vault. Against the positive background, these were minor matters.

But if the games had been well organised, if the experience for the visitors and athletes had been overwhelming, if it had all done Greece no end of good, one question sprang to mind. Why should not the games stay in Greece, where they had started?

On Sunday 12 April the King gave a grand lunch for 250 guests at the palace. The guests appeared in a variety of national costumes, Louis in his *fustanella*, accompanied by his father. One American is reported to have worn bicycle shorts. The guests sat down to a feast of fillets of sole Colbert and roast beef. Virtually all the sports were over. They could relax.

In his toasts, first in French and then in Greek, the King congratulated and thanked the organisers and athletes, Greek and foreign.

> *I am sure that the champions from abroad when they leave Greece will make known the progress of our country and the great works which were carried out in a relatively short space of time so as to assure the success of the Games.*
>
> *Mother and nurse of athletic games in antiquity, having undertaken to celebrate them again today under the eyes of Europe and the new world, now that their success has exceeded all expectations, Greece can justly hope that the foreigners who have honoured her with their presence will point to our country as the peaceful rendezvous of the nations, as the stable and permanent seat of the Olympic Games.*
>
> *With this wish, Gentlemen, I drink to all those who have contributed to the success of this first Olympiad.*[9]

It is uncertain exactly when and how the King was inspired to say this. Richardson wrote that the Greeks 'early began to think of having the next meet also at Athens' and that the King was only voicing the sentiment of which the air was full. Coubertin also claimed to believe that the Greeks had been cooking up this claim for some time. There were bizarre reports that the idea originated with the Prince of Wales. The most likely originators are the Crown Prince and the King together. But even if, as Richardson says, the idea was in the air, the King's toast must have surprised many of those present. In reply Philemon gushed about the diamonds falling from the King's lips. The French correspondent of *Le Figaro* was also effusive, but only about the marathon; with Paris

25 *Picnic at Daphni after the games with athletes, most of them American. Spyros Louis in white fustanella. The three royal princes are present: Crown Prince Constantine's head stands out against the raincoat held by the right-hand standing figure. Prince Nicholas, also in uniform, sits next to Constantine against the middle standing figure, Prince George in bow tie and cap in front of the left-hand standing figure. C. Manos, the chief steward of the games, and A. Metaxas, architect of the restored stadium, are also present.*

scheduled for the 1900 games he was unlikely publicly to endorse the King's proposal. Bourchier also spoke, but we do not know what he said. Coubertin said nothing.

The King's assertion was the logical outcome of Greece's successful stewardship of the games. It was not the deal which Vikelas had signed up to in Paris in 1894. But whatever doubts they had had before the games, the Greeks had taken up the challenge and succeeded. They had also brought out the link between the games and the ancient Greek world, and it was this which, evidently, had appealed to the foreigners. For all Coubertin's modernity, he too had made this rhetorical link.

The King's words were warmly applauded, and taken seriously. Among those who backed his claim, despite the proposed allocation of the 1904 Olympics to the United States, were the American Ambassador and the director of the American School. Just as remarkably, the entire American team and their trainer John Graham lined up to support the idea that Greece should keep the games. They wrote a letter dated 14 April to Crown Prince Constantine expressing heartfelt appreciation of the great kindness and warm hospitality they had received, and acknowledging their entire satisfaction with all the arrangements for the conduct of the games:

> *The existence of the Stadium as a structure so uniquely adapted to its purpose; the proved ability of Greece to competently administer the Games, and, above all, the fact that Greece is the original home of the Olympic Games; all these considerations force upon us the conviction that these Games should never be removed from their native soil.*[10]

Nine American citizens who had been present at the games, including the artists whose sketches were published in the American press, joined them in this demarche.

The international press picked up the story. James Bourchier, who had been present at the King's lunch, associated himself with the Americans in a report to *The Times*. Other observers were also impressed. Robertson, for example, who had no axe to grind, commented that 'under the glamour of the moment' no one could have opposed the proposal and that even later, 'when the splendour has somewhat faded from the mind', it was difficult to criticise. But he recognised that there would be French opposition of the most forcible kind. Robertson defined the difficulty:

> *The opposition between the claims of utility and of taste and sentiment in this matter seems to be irreconcilable: on the one side we have the probability of a truly representative international*

meeting, conducted on purely modern lines, in a modern arena
unconnected with the memories and glories of the age which has
provided models of grace and strength for all time, on the other we
find the possibility of non-representative competitions, held in a
sport which, with every beauty of form and position, is connected
undyingly with all the magnificence of that golden age of athletics,
whose ideals it should be the object of these international
gatherings to promote. The opposition is so sharp that it would be
fair to describe it by asserting that these games, if held at Athens,
would be Olympic but, we fear, not international; if held elsewhere
than at Athens, international but not Olympic.[11]

Amid all the congratulations at the King's lunch, Coubertin was not
mentioned by name (nor at first was Vikelas, though apparently the
King was reminded and thanked him in an afterthought to his toast).[12]
Coubertin saw at once that his whole conception of the Olympics was
under threat. He was not going to take this lying down. The two pillars
of his Olympic idea were modernity and international rotation. He had
ensured that the IOC reaffirmed the principle of rotation at its meeting
in Athens during the games. He believed that Greece was incapable of
sustaining a four-yearly festival. In any case Paris was going to host the
1900 games in conjunction with the Paris world exhibition. In the
atmosphere of bonhomie and excitement of the closing lunch, however, he saw that he could not immediately confront the Greek hosts.
He therefore decided to lie low for a while. Some of his colleagues on
the IOC were ready to disband and hand over to Greece. They were
worried that the weight of international public opinion would force
them to do so. But Coubertin disregarded such defeatist talk, calculat-
ing that despite the atmosphere of exhilaration in Athens, the games
had made little impact abroad.

Coubertin wrote a polite letter of thanks to the King, informing
him that he had taken on from Vikelas the position of President of the
IOC, and noting that the King had presided over the restoration of the

Olympic Games. He made no reference to the King's design to keep the games in Athens. But a few days later Coubertin gave his public reply to the King in a sharp response to Bourchier's article in *The Times*:

An article datelined Athens, no doubt written by an enthusiastic Philhellene, informed the European press that a decision has been made to hold the Olympic Games in Greece from now on. Nothing could be further from the truth. The Olympic Games will move about the globe, as was decided at the international congress held at the Sorbonne two years ago. The 1900 Games will be in Paris. In 1904, the committee will choose between New York, Berlin and Stockholm. It is perfectly understandable that the brilliant success of our undertaking recently inspired the Greeks to desire to monopolise it to their advantage. But we cannot sanction such a plan. For my part, having wanted the Athens games even when the Athenians themselves did not believe in them and rejected them, I do not think that this is the right moment to abandon an undertaking which has just been so brilliantly begun.[13]

Coubertin had a strong case. The principle of rotation would maintain international interest and secure necessary resources for the games. As President of the IOC, Coubertin was well placed to hold the line against Greek revisionism.

Before leaving Athens, Coubertin called on the Crown Prince. They discussed the dilemma over the future site of the games. Coubertin explained his reasons for persevering with his original conception. The idea arose of a compromise, whereby what Coubertin called 'Pan-Hellenic Games' would be intercalated with the four-year Olympic cycle, taking place every four years in between the regular Olympics. It is uncertain where the idea originated. Coubertin wrote that it was his own suggestion but that the Prince had already had the idea. The question of the name was important. For Coubertin it was vital not to sully the authentic four-year Olympic cycle by giving the name Olympics to these new Athenian games.

The Athenian press meanwhile, once they realised the position, turned nasty, slating both the foreigner Coubertin, and Vikelas as a 'cosmopolite not a Greek', ignorant of athletics. Although he put the best face on things in his public comments, and claimed not to hold it against Greece, there is no doubt that Coubertin, who had a strong sense of what was due to him, was furiously aggrieved. He was particularly incensed by what he saw as the Greeks' lack of courtesy to his wife. He wrote to Vikelas on 15 May:

> *I don't care at all what the Greek newspapers say about me …*
> *Greece certainly takes first place for ingratitude. You would have to*
> *be very much in love with her to continue to love her after such a*
> *trial. You all received your olive branches, even Mr Robertson from*
> *the hands of the King in the middle of the stadium! I am the only*
> *one whose name if it was mentioned at all was mentioned under*
> *the breath! All this is shameful! My wife was ill with the*
> *impertinences which she suffered in Athens … As to the Games, I*
> *shall continue the path I have carved out as if nothing had*
> *happened …*[14]

As the former president and still a member of the IOC, who owed his position to Coubertin, Vikelas was in a difficult position, torn between his loyalty to Coubertin, his feelings as a Greek, and his respect for the Crown. He wrote a long letter to Coubertin on 19 May in which he took pride in the success of the games and reported that Averoff was disposed to complete the fine restoration of the stadium. The government was preparing a draft bill for the development of sport in Greece, which provided for four-yearly athletic games, open to all, in the restored stadium. These games would be held in the intervals of the Paris congress official series of Olympic Games. So far all this was within the bounds of what Coubertin and the Crown Prince had agreed. But now Vikelas went further. 'The Games will be called "Olympic Games" ... The Athens Games will be distinguished from the Paris Congress Games by the fact that the latter will be entitled 'International' and that they will take place in a distinct series.'

Now Vikelas became even bolder: 'However I think there would be advantage for both sides in reuniting the two series to make one, giving the Athens games the title "International Olympic Games".' He proposed that there should be a second international congress, in Paris or another future Olympic city, to consecrate the work of the first, complete the definition of amateurism, choose the host cities after Paris 1900, and consider 'the question of giving the Athens Games the name of International Olympic Games and a place in the official series'.[15]

This letter probably cost Vikelas considerable effort and even anguish. But he screwed himself up, and sent it not only to Coubertin but to all his colleagues on the IOC. Coubertin almost contemptuously brushed it aside. He regarded the idea of Olympic Games every two years, alternately in Athens and another city, as fantasy. For a time a shadow fell over the relations between the two men, since Coubertin believed that Vikelas could have done more to divert recognition to himself, but lacked the courage. When the crowds proceeded from the stadium to the offices of the committee he could have told them to go on to the Grande Bretagne Hotel and salute the true originator of the games, Baron Coubertin. At the Havre congress of the IOC in 1897 he sat on Vikelas's proposal that both the Olympics and the intercalated Athens games should be given the title Olympic Games. He continued to profess his love for Vikelas, 'the most noble creature on earth'. But it was to take years before his esteem for Greece was restored.[16]

At some point Vikelas must have recognised that Greece was on to a loser and that he was no match for Coubertin. The cataclysmic events of 1897, to be described in the next chapter, may have convinced him of this. After the war of April 1897 Olympic affairs suddenly seemed relatively unimportant. Whatever the reasons, Vikelas stepped down from the IOC, and devoted himself again to his writings and his philan-thropic pursuits.

While Greek attention focused on getting the games permanently for Greece, the need to learn the athletic lessons of the 1896 games was neglected. The task of the various committees was over and they dis-solved. Phokianos died of tuberculosis soon after the games, leaving the world of athletics without its leader. Manos's club was dissolved. The most positive results were the holding in early 1897 of the first Panhel-lenic Gymnastic Congress, at which the federation of Greek athletic clubs was established, and the spontaneous enthusiasm shown by young people throughout the country for sports.

13

GREEK EPILOGUE

In general, life resembles a journey on the railway, when we sit with our backs towards the engine. We see the mountains, the fields, the buildings, the animals and the people. Whether slowly or quickly, everything is left behind as we proceed forward. We retain more or less confused impressions of them, and we know how much of the journey we have completed in total, and how far a distance we have covered. But we do not see what is in front of us, we do not know what obstacles, what dangers the train may suddenly meet, nor whether or how we shall arrive at the terminus. And yet we are carried ever forward, with our backs turned towards this uncertain goal.

Dimitrios Vikelas, preface to his memoir, My Life

Throughout the period of the games and the immediately following months, the secret National Society, dominated by its military members, continued to be active. The main focus of the society's attention was Macedonia, where it saw a need to combat Bulgarian propaganda and the inroads of Bulgarian *komitadji* bands by similar Greek action. During the summer the society sent a fact-finding mission to Crete, dispatched a band of armed men to Macedonia, and stepped up its recruitment drive. Ioannis Metaxas, a young lieutenant serving in the Nauplion garrison, later to be dictator of Greece in the 1930s, noted in October that the trend was towards the army running everything.

In this same month the executive organ of the society, the 'Invisible Authority', decided to go public, issuing a circular message to the Greek nation in which it set out its aims as 'representative of the race'. It pronounced that it was undertaking the coordination of the necessary actions for the liberation of the unredeemed Greeks. The secular enemy Turkey was in a state of dissolution, and Greece's rivals, lacking her virtues, but united and hard-working, were ready to take advantage. The society would support any government which would support its nationalist policy and give priority to reviving Greece's military forces. Working closely with the church, the society organised a nationwide series of grandiose memorial services for those who had fallen in Macedonia.

The effect of going public in this way was probably greater than the society expected. Public opinion was carried away, seeing the society as an instrument of national liberation. The pressures building up on the government and the Crown became stronger. Only a Tricoupis might have resisted them, but he was dead. Deliyiannis, committed by his own practice and rhetoric in opposition to the sort of policies espoused by the society, tried to oppose them now but was overwhelmed. He said later that foreign policy had been snatched from his hands. The King, never one to take the path of most resistance, also gave in. On 23 November he released to the press a letter to his Prime Minister in which he endorsed the main demands of the National Society concerning the creation of a permanent camp, training, the purchase of military equipment, and annual exercises; the subtext was that there should be promotions and more established posts.[1] Among the few who kept their heads was Stephanos Dragoumis, chairman of the Olympia Committee (although, typically in the close-knit village community of Athens, his daughter Natalia was married to the National Society hero and future martyr Pavlos Melas).

The Cretan question, simmering throughout the period of the

games, came to the boil in early 1897, following outrage in western Europe over Turkish persecution of the Armenians in eastern Turkey. Following the usual pattern in Cretan crises, the government, responding to the Great Powers, tried to damp down Cretan excitement, while the opposition whipped it up, in this case egged on by the National Society. Probably both the King and the Prime Minister secretly hoped that the Powers would intervene and force the government to back down, thus incidentally enabling Deliyiannis to win credit by berating the Powers for preventing Greece from fulfilling her destiny![2] But the clamour in Athens for Greece to intervene in favour of the union of Crete with Greece carried away all sense of restraint. In February 1897 the Greek government took action. Greek warships and torpedo boats were sent to Suda Bay. While 'Big George', King George's second son, the naval captain, patrolled the waters north of Crete with a flotilla of torpedo boats, watching for signs of Turkish intervention, the firebrand Colonel Vassos with a force of 2,000 irregular volunteers landed on Crete. This was blatant interference in an area still under Ottoman sovereignty. Turkey and Greece mobilised. The Great Powers did their best to damp down the fire by pressures on both sides. Philhellene liberals in the west attacked their governments and sang the praises of the Cretans. The young Winston Churchill wrote to his mother from India deploring the 'atrocious crime' the British government was committing in blockading Crete. 'That British warships should lead the way in protecting the blood bespattered Turkish soldiery from the struggles of their victims is horrible to contemplate.' He blamed the languid, cynical Balfour and the insolent, priggish Curzon; whereas the Prime Minister, Lord Salisbury, joined the 'brains of a statesman to the delicate susceptibilities of a mule'.[3]

Not everyone was carried away by the drive to war: not even the two-thirds or more of the army's officers who had joined the National Society by April 1897, and who seem to have been taken by surprise by the success of their own propaganda. One of the doubters was Vikelas, who knew too well the likely consequences of defying the Great Powers. He strongly, but privately, criticised the society's public intervention of 16 March in which it ruled out any solution short of full union with Greece (such as a strong form of autonomy under Prince George as High Commissioner, the solution that in the end the Powers imposed).[4] Another doubter was the Crown Prince, who, the evidence suggests, was well aware of the inferiority of the Greek army to the Turkish and suspected that the enterprise was doomed from the start. Nevertheless, neither he nor his father felt strong enough to resist the growing hysteria. He was appointed Commander in Chief of the Greek armed forces and departed for Thessaly to take command, provoking paeans of praise from philhellenes in the west, including the poet Edmond Rostand, author of *Cyrano de Bergerac*.[5] Once more liberal sentiment in Europe supported the Greeks, and a foreign legion of volunteers was formed, including a substantial Italian contingent led by Ricciotti Garibaldi. On 18 April Greek forces crossed the frontier in Thessaly and attacked the Turkish army. Churchill, still in India at Bangalore, decided to go to the front as a war correspondent. He wrote to his mother, 'Of course all my sympathies are with the Greeks, but on the other hand the Turks are bound to win,' and invited his mother, who knew the King of Greece and could fix matters in that quarter, to decide which side he should attach himself to! It was too late. The war was over before he could get there.[6]

One of those who witnessed this sorry affair was Stephen Crane. *The Red Badge of Courage* is one of the great books about war, but Crane had made it up out of his head, and now wanted to find out what real war was like. On his way through London he told J.M. Barrie and Anthony Hope that if he found that *The Red Badge* was not all right he would sell out his claim on literature and take up orange-growing. Crane sent back dispatches to the *New York Journal* and wrote some more reflective pieces later for the *Westminster Gazette*. He was joined by his partner Cora Taylor.

Crane found war fever in Athens. 'This unchangeable element,' he wrote on 17 April, the day before the war started, 'is the spirit of the

Greek people.' A man told him, 'This time we shall fight. And it is better to be defeated than shamed.' Twelve days later, on his way back from Epirus through Athens to Thessaly, the people were still flocking to arms. 'In fact, this is not a King's war, not a parliament's war, but a people's war … No nation ever had a truer sense of the odds.' By contrast with the people, Crane poked fun at the assembled war correspondents, commenting that the only creature that had not been thrown off its natural balance by the invasion of war correspondents was the bold flea of Greece: 'these animals operate with drills … and afterwards one feels as if one has been attacked by a fleet of red-hot stove lids'.

The war quickly turned into a disaster of defeat and humiliation. In language which surely influenced Hemingway's dispatches from Greece and Turkey for the *Toronto Star* twenty-five years later, Crane represented the progressive disillusionment of the Greek soldiers. 'Back fell the Greek army, wrathful, sullen, fierce as any victorious army would be when commanded to retreat before the enemy it had defeated' ('The Blue Badge of Cowardice', 11 May). In Volos he saw the evacuation of refugees and the wounded in hospital ships. Stopping off at Stylida in a hospital ship with 800 wounded, he could see the dust rising in the air from Smolenski's retreating troops, wearily falling back on the historic pass of Thermopylae where Leonidas made his last stand against the Persians.

> *Still backward fall the Greek soldiers. First it was Velestino, then Domokos, next it will be Thermopylae. They have had a hard time of it. Their fiercest fighting has been rewarded, not with victory, but with orders to retreat. They have had a fierce, outnumbering enemy before them and a rear fire from the vacillating Crown Prince. They have had a campaign that has made officers cry like hysterical women with weariness and disappointment; they have marched uselessly day and night, and yet they are stout-hearted and anxious for another fight.[7]*

The ordinary soldiers wanted to fight on. The officers shrugged their shoulders and said, 'What can we do? It is better to cease.'

Crane summed up the mood of betrayal in a dispatch of 1 June from Athens recording his talk with six soldiers. One criticised the officers, the Crown Prince and the King: 'He is not a good Greek. To be sure he was not born a Greek, but he is King, and a King of the Greeks ought to be more Greek than the Greeks' – thus encapsulating the impossible dilemma of the royal family. An *evzone* said that it was the fault of the leaders: 'he [the Crown Prince] orders all these retreats. He has taught us to retreat. The men of the hills did not know how.' A wealthy, intellectual corporal added that Greece had been betrayed. A wounded *evzone* blamed the royal family for the retreats. 'They are cowards. They are not Greeks. They are foreigners.' A member of the Foreign Legion called the Crown Prince a duffer and referred to general funk at headquarters.

Crane recognised later that he had probably been unfair to the Crown Prince: 'perhaps the soldiers and also the people are beginning to understand that the blunders were the fault of everybody practically.' They were a product of the general disorganisation of the Greek army and its logistical and medical services, and the fact that they were up against an enemy far superior in numbers and equipment.

Pressure on the government by the National Society, the press, the opposition and public opinion were the factors leading to this unwinnable war. Some commentators have even suggested that by raising national morale the Olympic Games in 1896 had contributed to the sense that war with Turkey was a rational policy. Coubertin himself denied this, for obvious reasons (after all, the Olympics was a force for peace!) while referring to the 'moral mobilisation' of the Greek people occasioned by the games. It seems to me unlikely that the games played a part in the decision to go to war. That decision was the product of irrational nationalist forces which no one, neither government nor the high command nor the royal family, felt strong enough to resist.

Defeat led to a collapse in national morale and an orgy of recrimination and self-questioning. It brought the Crown to its lowest point in public esteem in the long reign of George I.[8] The politicians were happy to see blame diverted from them to others. Deliyiannis had been relieved of his post as Prime Minister during the war and was thus free to criticise. Even Vikelas, conservative as he was, blamed the King for failing to stop the rush to war; but then, he blamed the politicians and nationalists even more, and did not spare himself. Anxious to be of some use, he helped to organise a privately funded hospital ship, embarked himself, and was able to witness the sad scenes of retreat from the Thessalian front.[9]

The defeat of 1897 cancelled out the propaganda benefits for Greece of the successful conduct of the Olympic Games the year before. Even so, the dynastic connections of the royal family helped the country to extract from the Powers a favourable territorial settlement, by which Greece retained all her territory in Thessaly with the exception of one minor rectification of the frontier. In another sense, however, she suffered. The peace settlement imposed by the Powers included the payment to Turkey by Greece of an indemnity, and to guarantee its regular payment the finances of Greece were placed under the control of an International Financial Commission, dominated by Britain, with its seat in Athens. Humiliating as this was, together with the shock of defeat it ensured that the country remained prudent for the next decade and that the finances gradually recovered. Meanwhile governments began to grasp the issue of reform of the armed services, without which no future war with Turkey would be won.

On 13 June 1905 Tricoupis's long-time rival Deliyiannis was stabbed and killed while alighting from his carriage to enter the Chamber of Deputies. The murderer was an aggrieved gambler, taking reprisal for legislation closing down gambling dens. The issue of casinos is still controversial in Greece.

Vikelas's last years were spent in good works. In 1899 he founded the Society for the Distribution of Useful Books, the summation of his life's work. The society published and distributed good books to workers who had learned to read at school and who deserved better than the 'popular reading' which it was assumed was all they could cope with. The society did not patronise its readers, nor did it take sides on behalf of the extreme demotic in the debate on the language question. For this reason it earned the scorn of the leader of the demoticist movement, Yannis Psycharis. But Vikelas's judgement was proved right. The society was a success, distributing nine books in 156,650 copies in its first year. Vikelas funded its deficit and left it a handsome legacy of 92,000 drachmas, to wipe out the debt owed him by the society for the mortgage on its office building. The society still exists, and published his complete works in a handsome nine-volume edition in 1997.

Vikelas completed the second volume of his memoir *My Life* only in the year before his death, and it was published in 1908. In the preface he commented on how it was easier to describe his early memories, since 'the more recent memories come and go one after the other, and are soon forgotten. It is the same with what we see when crossing a broad plain by railway: the far off buildings and trees follow us for a long time, whereas the nearer ones as soon as we see them are violently torn away backwards.' In his last published article, in the journal *Meleti*, he proposed the strange vision of a memorial temple on the top of Mount Lycabettus, dedicated to the heroes of the war of independence and containing the statues, icons and memorials of the heroes of the war. Happily this idea was not taken up.

Vikelas died of liver cancer in 1908, a great Greek of the Victorian era in his energy, philanthropy, and not least for the determining role he played in bringing the Olympic Games to rebirth. Already before his death the poet Palamas had paid him a graceful tribute, referring to his sweetness of character, conservatism, clarity of ideas and nobility of feelings, moral concerns, and preference for the restrained and constructive over the wild and undisciplined.[10]

The fruits of this period were gathered in the Balkan Wars of 1912–13. Under the dynamic leadership of Eleftherios Venizelos, who came from Crete to become Prime Minister in 1910, Greece in alliance with Bulgaria, Serbia and Montenegro drove the Turks out of Europe. The eccentric *Times* correspondent James Bourchier, who had reported on the Olympic Games, helped Venizelos to seal the crucial alliance with Bulgaria.

Recovered from the humiliation of 1897, and restored by Venizelos to the command of the armed forces, Crown Prince Constantine led the Greek armies to victory in the Balkan Wars. The Turkish governor surrendered Salonica to the Greeks on 8 November, and Greek forces entered the city a few hours before the Bulgarians. King George took up temporary residence in the occupied city. The town was an unsettled and dangerous place as the Greeks started to impose their administration. The streets swarmed with soldiers. Besides the 60,000 Greeks, there was a division of Serbs and some thousands of Bulgarians. King George stayed in a pleasant Turkish villa near the sea. Over lunch that day with his biographer, the Danish naval Captain Walter Christmas, and Prince Nicholas, who had been appointed military governor of the city, the King revealed that he would take the opportunity of his forthcoming Jubilee later in October to abdicate in favour of his son Constantine. He reckoned he had had enough, and could allow himself a holiday. It was a good moment for Constantine, the popular victorious general, to take charge.

The King's habit was to take a walk each day. On 18 October after lunch he walked out into the city with his aide-de-camp, Colonel Frangoudis. They were followed, as usual, at a discreet distance of a few yards by two Cretan gendarmes. The two men walked as far as the White Tower, the prominent monument on the waterfront, and turned back to return to the villa. An unkempt figure rose from a bench at the corner of an alleyway, swung behind the King, drew a heavy revolver and shot him in the back from about a yard's distance. The King fell to the pavement. The shot penetrated the heart. He died almost instantly.

The shock to the Greek people was sharp. It was as if only in the time of his death did people realise how much the old king had meant to them. The Prime Minister, Venizelos, remarked to the British Minister 'It is a terrible thing to say, but it is a cause of great thankfulness that he [the assassin] is a Greek.'[11] He turned out to be an aggrieved schoolmaster. Under interrogation he jumped from a first-floor balcony and was killed. The King was laid to rest in a simple grave on his estate at Tatoi near Athens.

One of those who fought in the war of 1897 and again in the Balkan Wars was Constantine Manos, the nationalist poet and athlete who had been involved in the organisation of the Olympic Games. Manos had made of himself a figure of legendary achievements. After the games he put on Cretan clothes and went to Crete as a volunteer, leading a body of irregular soldiers. He was back in Crete in 1904, leading one of the seemingly never-ending Cretan movements of revolt against the Turks or the Great Powers. During this one he declared Crete to be united with Greece in *enosis*. Manos was then elected deputy for the Cretan city Chania. In 1909 he was elected deputy for Attico-Boeotia in the revolutionary parliament of that year. He volunteered again in the Balkan War of 1912, leading a force of Cretans, and entering Ioannina at the head of the conquering Greek army.

Besides his flamboyant acts as war hero, Manos continued to write poetry. He had composed the hymn of the Panhellenic Gymnastic Association which found its way into old primary school readers. His translation into demotic Greek of Sophocles's *Antigone*, published in 1905, was praised. He was thus a natural demoticist participant in the debates which took place in the 1909 assembly over the official language of Greece.

Manos wrote a poem foreshadowing his own death:

> *When one day my hour approaches*
> *When for me my troubles cease*
> *When I arrive at the good harbour*
> *And my soul then remains free*
> *I hope that night, the unbegotten mother,*
> *Will carry me again back here to the sky*
> *Where I shall know true light.*[12]

On 17 April 1913, in the second Balkan War, Manos took off with another hero airman in a Blériot X1-2 aircraft captured from the Turks, to reconnoitre Bulgarian positions. The two men crashed above Langada, and were killed. A man of talents who lived life at the extremes, Manos did not have the time to fulfil his potential.

Constantine – 'Tino' – ascended the throne under bright auspices. Through the successful politico-military strategy of the Balkan Wars, Greece had virtually doubled her territory and population. But neither Constantine nor any future Greek king was to repeat the long, successful reign of George I, the founder of the Glucksberg dynasty.

Constantine himself, embroiled in a bitter dispute with his Prime Minister Venizelos over the issue of war or neutrality in 1915, was forced by Greece's British and French allies to leave Athens and go into exile in

1916. In his absence Greece joined the entente and fought alongside allied troops on the Macedonian front, thus staking a claim to a share of the spoils at the post-war peace conference. The poisoned fruit of victory was a mandate to Greece to occupy Smyrna and western Asia Minor. When Venizelos fell from power in November 1920, Constantine returned to Greece after a plebiscite, only to take the road of exile once more in 1922 after the defeat of the Greek army in Asia Minor and the destruction of Smyrna. He died in exile at Palermo in 1923.[13] Thereafter republic and monarchy alternated in Greece until in December 1974 a plebiscite inaugurated the present republican regime, which shows every sign of permanence. The last King of the Hellenes, Constantine, grandson of Constantine I, one of Greece's select band of Olympic gold medal winners, lives in exile in London.

The other royal princes also died in exile. Prince Andrew's wife Alice gave birth to a son, Philip – later Duke of Edinburgh – on Corfu in 1921. Andrew left his wife and infant son to take up a command in the Greek army in Asia Minor. When the army was defeated in 1922 and the revolutionary government of Colonels Plastiras and Gonatas took power, Andrew was put on trial for high treason, on a charge of disobeying the orders of his commander in the face of the enemy. Andrew vigorously disputed this, but fully expected to suffer the same fate as the six men – five politicians and one general – who, following a revolutionary legal process known as the 'Trial of the Six', had been executed by firing squad for their alleged responsibility for the Asia Minor disaster. But British intervention saved Andrew's life and he was spirited away in a British frigate, to a less than happy life between Paris and the south of France. He returned to Greece for a time during the dictatorship of his old friend Ioannis Metaxas.

His marriage to Princess Alice ended in separation. The Princess had won respect for her efforts organising nursing facilities near the front lines in the Balkan Wars. (As in other countries, war advanced the cause of women's emancipation in Greece: it provided the occasion for Kallirrhoe Parren's Association of Greek Women to organise surgical units near the front.) But after the Great War, Alice was afflicted with religious mania, and was confined to a sanatorium for the mentally disturbed in the 1930s. She was eventually released and became a nun in her own order, living in Athens through the rigours of the Second War, and re-emerging at the marriage of her son Philip with Princess Elizabeth. She was a familiar and striking figure at Buckingham Palace when the Prince of Wales and Princess Royal were children, grey-habited, wreathed in cigarette smoke. She died there on 5 December 1969, twenty-five years after the death in Monte Carlo of her husband Prince Andrew.[14]

The fate of 'Big George', Andrew's elder and Constantine's younger brother, was no happier. He was chosen by the Powers in 1898 to be their High Commissioner in Crete, when a provisional 'solution' was required which gave some satisfaction to the Cretan people, agitating for their independence, without actually removing Crete from Turkish sovereignty. George seemed the obvious choice to preside over this diplomatic fudge. He was received rapturously by the Cretans but was soon caught in the tangle of Cretan politics, giving offence by his autocratic methods and unable to persuade the Powers to force Turkey to concede the definitive union of Crete with Greece.

In the end George had to be withdrawn by his father in the face of the revolutionary opposition of Venizelos. Thereafter he spent little time in Greece. His marriage to Princess Marie Bonaparte was a disappointment to her. Hoping for warm embraces from this tall, fair and handsome Dane, she was dismayed to find that he talked to her interminably about his experiences in Crete and the villainy of Venizelos. He did his duty by her, and two children, Peter and Eugenie, were born of the union. George's happiest hours were spent with his uncle Waldemar, and Marie came to the conclusion that he was a repressed homosexual. She herself found solace with the French Prime Minister Aristide Briand, and later was analysed by Sigmund Freud so convincingly that she herself became a psychoanalyst.

There is a tendency to patronise the past, and (on the part of the west) to patronise the Greeks, which should be resisted. The men of the late nineteenth century who staged the Olympic Games (there were no women, unlike in 2004) were solid, serious figures, wide-ranging in their political and intellectual pursuits. Their world was not fragmented. Vikelas, Philemon, Stephanos Dragoumis, Politis and Lambros were men of range and depth which would command respect in any country and any epoch. Lambros, whom we have encountered in the contexts of the Olympics and of the National Society, summed up the 1896 games in a tribute to Philemon after his death at his desk in 1898:

> *As to the Olympic Games, no one should forget that the acceptance of the responsibility for holding them and the honour for their success belong to four men out of the many who were involved. These are the Crown Prince, George Averoff, Dimitrios Vikelas and Timoleon Philemon. Of these Vikelas was in his patriotism the link which bound the West to the Greek East ... Constantine added the brilliance of the throne to the task ... Averoff poured out the blessings of his Epirot heart ... Philemon finally as general secretary of the Olympic Games was the lever who moved everything, the spirit which lit up everything, and the heart which felt everything. In his office were brought together all the threads of the complicated work ...*[15]

What bound these four men together was the Greek nation, what Lambros called 'steadfast faith in the powers of Hellenism'.

14

ATHLETIC EPILOGUE

I consider Greece to be the appropriate place for holding the Olympic Games … Choosing Greece as the permanent location of the Games is the only way to place them again on a sound basis and to restore their authentic meaning. For it is thus that the Olympic Idea shall get rid of its involvement with international political and ideological disputes, of interference by oneupmanship and professionalism, and of the commercial exploitation and economic problems created by its present form. Greece is willing to facilitate the solution of these problems by providing the appropriate area – which, it should be noted, would be at the site of Ancient Olympia – for the permanent holding of the Games.

Constantine Karamanlis, letter to Lord Killanin of 28 January 1980

Byron awoke to find himself famous after the publication of *Childe Harold*. Spyridon Louis had become famous even before he went to bed. He seems to have remained utterly unspoiled by the fuss, refusing reward for his victory other than a horse and cart which he wanted for commercial use, and the concession to sell water from the suburb of Maroussi to the thirsty people of Athens. With these he set up in trade. An observer wrote that if you started off for Maroussi on a bicycle or on foot a little before sunrise on a summer's morning, you would be sure to meet Louis and two or three of his men jogging towards the city through the violet-grey dawn, with mule-carts laden with huge red jars made of porous earth, for the Athenian kitchens.[1] The best Athens water came down from Maroussi or Kaisariani in those days, either in enormous earthenware jugs or in barrels. Maroussi is now the site of the Olympic stadium and the old Maroussi–Athens road is flanked by new glass and metal office buildings. Almost all the old pottery shops for which Maroussi, with its clay deposits, was famous have disappeared.

Louis appeared on the platform in his *fustanella*, with his winner's medal, at the Athens games in 1906. In 1913 his feet went, and he was exempted from military service in the Balkan Wars on medical grounds. He was to make one more public appearance, forty years later, in Berlin.

Of the Americans, James Connolly became a prolific writer of rousing sea stories. Robert Garrett Jnr had taken part in an archaeological expedition to Syria which fostered his interest in oriental manuscripts. The inheritor of a great fortune, derived from the Baltimore and Ohio Railroad, he became an investment banker in Baltimore and amassed over a period of four decades one of the greatest collections of oriental manuscripts in the world. In 1942 he donated the collection to Princeton University, which is still engaged in the lengthy process of cataloguing and exploring it.[2]

Garrett served as a trustee of Princeton University for forty years and continued to take an interest in the sporting education and achievements of the institution, corresponding throughout the years with Joseph Raycroft, the university's first director of sports. He presented to Princeton the discus which he threw in winning the silver medal, and a second discus which he believed to be the damaged one with which he practised in the stadium on the day before the games began.

Garrett found it a little difficult to adjust to the more informal ways of the students of the 1930s. He wrote pained letters to the President of the university and to Raycroft about the growing state of undress among tennis and soccer players on the campus – by which he meant players without shirts:

> *It seems to me that this practice is extremely unfortunate. It is bad enough to see the tendency towards nudity at the seashore and other places in the summer ... We hear a great deal nowadays about the 'Nudist Cult' as exemplified particularly in certain places in Europe. I trust we are not heading rapidly towards such extreme practices in this country and particularly among the college elements ...*[3]

A measure of crustiness was not surprising in this old-style gentleman, who was the most distinguished as well as the richest of all the 1896 athletes.

The diplomat John Gennadius, who from the London embassy had corresponded with William Penny Brookes in the 1880s, was another who amassed a great collection: of books on all aspects of Greek history and culture. He gave them to the American School of Classical Studies in Athens, where they form the core of the Gennadius Library, the best library collection in Greece. Much of the research for this book was done there, in the cool of the Gennadius reading room.

Charles Maurras, the radical conservative monarchist, went on to found Action Française and to write books of reactionary political philosophy. A strong supporter of Vichy, he was arrested in 1944 for collaboration and sentenced to life imprisonment and civic degradation. After being released on medical grounds, he lived out his life under virtual house arrest.

The later history of Coubertin, the unneglected hero, is tied up with that of the games. Having successfully seen off the Greek bid to keep the games in perpetuity, and weathered the failure of the 1900 games in Paris and the 1904 games in St Louis, he set out to nurture the Olympic movement until it was firmly rooted and capable of continuing without him. He alternated between gloom at the way in which the pressures of modern life were distorting the ideals he had fought for, and the defence of the perfection of his own creation. He resigned from the presidency of the IOC in September 1925, handing over to Count Henri de Baillet-Latour, and assumed the position of Grand Old Man of the Olympic movement.

He died of a heart attack in Geneva in September 1937, keeling over while taking his daily walk in the park. By then his life had turned to ashes in the disappointments of his family life. He was buried in Lausanne. His will prescribed that his heart was to be buried at Olympia, whither it was sent in a wooden box lined with satin. And on 26 March 1938, at a ceremony attended by Crown Prince Paul of Greece, the heart was blessed by a priest and interred in the base of a marble column beneath the hill of Kronos. His biographer John MacAloon neatly observed that 'he had finally placed his heart where his heart was'. While this is true in the sense that interment at Olympia theatrically symbolised his life's work, one cannot help reflecting on the tenuous basis – two visits in fifty years – on which Coubertin constructed his symbolic monument.[4]

Greece nearly got the games. Athens was the site of another round of games in 1906, organised once more by a Committee chaired by the Crown Prince. Coubertin refused them the title of Olympic Games, proposing the title Panathenaic Games instead, and the Olympic movement has stuck to this rather absurd position that the Athens games did not count as Olympic. Historians of the Olympic movement enjoy debating such nominal questions. It was clear to participants that they were taking part in Olympic Games, just as in 1896. The 1906 games were larger in scale than those ten years earlier, and more successful than the games of Paris and St Louis, which had flopped. There is a respectable view that the Athens games of 1906 actually saved the Olympic movement, and thus helped to ensure Coubertin's immortality. But the great man did not deign to attend. Instead he held a conference in Paris on the role of the arts in the Olympic movement.

The assumption behind the 1906 games, flowing from the compromise discussed between Coubertin and the Crown Prince, was that

Athens would serve as host city every four years, in between the regular four-yearly Olympic Games. If this had happened, the question whether these counted as Olympic Games or not might have been resolved eventually in Athens's favour. But it was not to be. 'Events' supervened before Athens could host another round of games. There was a revolution of the Young Turks in Turkey in 1908 and a *coup d'état* by a Military League in Greece in 1909. Government in Greece was paralysed until Eleftherios Venizelos was summoned from Crete as 'saviour'. This was not the time for Olympic sports. The chance was lost, and did not recur. After the Great War the Olympic four-year train resumed its course.

Of all subsequent games, the most 'Hellenic' were the Berlin games of 1936, at which the Olympic torch relay from Olympia to the host city took place for the first time. An invention of the German Hellenist Carl Diem, the relay was a triumph of invented ritual. It was calculated to satisfy a modern audience which wanted to see some connection between the Olympics and the ancient world, and to meet the claims of Germany to be the legitimate inheritor of Hellenic idealism. Through Leni Riefenstahl's lens, and through German radio broadcasters, the proceedings and the symbolism reached a mass audience in Germany.

At noon on 20 July 1936 the 'sacred' flame was lit in the Altis at Olympia by a steel reflector which focused the sun's rays on to the kindling material. Greek girls wearing short tunics played the role of virginal priestesses. A choir chanted an ode of Pindar. Someone read out a long message from Coubertin. There were speeches. A Greek athlete lit the first torch from the flame, and the relay began. It proceeded via Athens, where King George II, surrounded by maidens, received the torch in the ancient stadium and lit a flame on an altar.

The torch was carried on by runners of each host country in relays, through Greece into Bulgaria, thence to Yugoslavia, Hungary, Austria, Czechoslovakia, and Germany. At every stage it was greeted with enthusiasm. Timings were strictly kept, though once in Yugoslavia the torch flickered and died and had to be rekindled with a match. In Vienna it provoked pro-Nazi demonstrations. In Germany schoolchildren and members of the Nazi youth movement lined the route and cheered. Thus, ironically, the symbol of peaceful competition and Hellenic values came to represent Nazi nationalism. At 11.38 on 1 August the appointed German runner received the torch on the southern border of Berlin, and carried it on towards the stadium.

At the opening ceremony in the afternoon, the Greek team led the march-past. At their head was Spyridon Louis, making his last public appearance, a 'sprightly sixty-year-old' wearing traditional Greek costume and carrying the blue and white Greek flag. After the parade, a message from Coubertin was read out, conveying his well-known thought that 'the important thing at the Olympic Games is not to win, but to take part, just as the important thing in life is not to conquer, but to struggle well'. The irony of this message, delivered in front of Hitler himself, and a more competitive and nationalist bunch of athletes than ever before, needs no underlining. After Hitler had declared the games open, Richard Strauss conducted an Olympic hymn which he had specially composed for the occasion. A runner ran round the track with the Olympic torch – the 3,075th torch-bearer since the torch had left Olympia on 20 July – and lit the eternal flame. Louis was then presented to Hitler, and gave him an olive branch which had been brought from Olympia. No one knows what Louis thought of Hitler or of the games as they had developed by 1936.

King George's idea of the 'permanent and stable home' was revived in 1976. The Olympic preparations for the Montreal Olympics were in trouble, with the African countries threatening a boycott over the issue of South Africa's participation. On 29 July Prime Minister Constantine Karamanlis wrote a letter to Lord Killanin, President of the IOC, proposing that the games should return to Greece for ever.[5]

Karamanlis wrote that the boycott of the Olympics showed that politics and racism were invading the idealistic territory of the games and threatened their future. Other anomalies included the grosser forms of commercialism and advertising, and excessive costs which virtually ruled out the smaller countries as hosts. In the prevailing nationalist atmosphere not only was there no Olympic truce, the games actually sharpened international conflict.

All this led Karamanlis to propose to Killanin that 'Greece be designated as permanent seat for the holding of the Olympic Games'. Besides the symbolism, this would enable the games to be purged of all the bastard elements which had accumulated. There would be a return to a strict and pure athletic spirit, without political or national conflict. And if the compulsory truce could be established as a precondition for taking part in the games, the Olympics would be restored to the universal pedestal where its ancient creators had placed it, for the good of all humanity. The genial Killanin, who thought all this hopelessly unpractical, sent a polite holding reply from Montreal, to the effect that Karamanlis's suggestions would naturally be considered if there were any changes in the long-term policy of the IOC, which he did not foresee in the immediate future. He pointed out that the games for 1984 were due to be allocated in 1978. The Karamanlis proposal was put on the shelf.[6]

Karamanlis's proposal was both idealistic and nationalistic, attempting to take advantage of political circumstances to reclaim for the Greek nation a part of its cultural heritage. But the modern Olympics had never been conceived as a part of Greece's cultural heritage, and Karamanlis's conception was too radical to succeed. Killanin advanced as arguments against it, first, that the founder Coubertin wanted to spread the games around the world; second, that it would be unfair that some competitors would always have to compete out of their time zone; and third, that if you were going to have a permanent site then it should be in a country of absolute stability. He did not regard Greece as fulfilling that criterion, after the experience of the rule of the Colonels between

1967 and 1974, and the 'deposition of King Constantine', an IOC member and Olympic gold medallist.

Always tenacious, Karamanlis returned to his proposal in January 1980, a few days after the Soviet invasion of Afghanistan. It was clear that this would have implications for the Moscow Olympics of summer 1980. On 7 January Karamanlis inaugurated the fine sports stadium at Kalogreza which will serve as the Olympic stadium in 2004. He attributed the twenty-year delay in its construction to the Greek habit of saying a lot and doing little. He referred to the Soviet invasion and its threat both to peace and to the Olympics, and repeated his proposal that Greece should become the permanent site of the games.

Two weeks later he elaborated this in a further letter to Lord Killanin which included an intriguing new element. Karamanlis wrote that Greece offered to help solve the problems facing the Olympic movement by 'providing the appropriate area, at the site of Ancient Olympia, for the permanent holding of the games'. This area could take the form of a neutral territory by an international agreement that would guarantee the rights to the installations, establish the inviolability of the area, and recognise the decisive role of the IOC as regards athletic matters. Greece was ready to discuss the necessary arrangements with the IOC. He followed up with a personal letter complaining about Killanin's suggestion, with barbed reference to Greece, that the games must be held in neutral countries with guaranteed stability.[7]

In the context of the Soviet invasion of Afghanistan and the US decision to boycott the Moscow Olympics of 1980, some people were now prepared to take Karamanlis's proposal seriously. President Jimmy Carter was one. It was convenient for him at the time of his campaign for the boycott of the Moscow games. He told Killanin that he would gladly back such a scheme, adding inconsequentially that 'we have a large Greek community'. Karamanlis's proposal was picked up by some of the serious media, and by individuals within the Olympic movement such as the Princeton-educated Senator Bill Bradley, the American basketball Olympic champion. The US Olympic Committee resolved to boycott the games and called for them to be held at another site than Moscow, or to be postponed or cancelled. The Senate voted heavily in favour of a boycott of the Moscow games and called on the IOC to examine urgently the proposal to hold the games permanently in Greece, 'the country of their origin'. Sympathisers at the Council of Europe offered support. Governments which had no reason not to do so made polite comments about the Karamanlis proposal.

Killanin himself told Irish TV that it was not the Soviet government which would suffer from a boycott but the athletes: as to the Karamanlis proposals, 'if we can find a neutral area, which would remain neutral, with a guarantee of stability of government, then I believe there is a lot to be said for it, rather than spreading it round and running into political problems every time which has happened since 1896'. Though still sceptical, he wrote a polite reply to Karamanlis and appointed a three-man commission to investigate the proposal. Ambassador Louis Girandou N'Diaye of the Ivory Coast, an experienced IOC member and member of this commission, visited Olympia with Karamanlis in April 1980.[8]

Active support was another question. The problem was that the relentless momentum of the Olympic cycle made change so difficult to handle. At any given moment some city was already fingered to host the next Olympic Games. And at the time of one of the IOC's congresses at which the next host city would be decided, whatever political crisis had provoked interest in the idea of Greece as permanent home might well have passed. Lined up against Karamanlis's idea was the sheer inertia of the vast Olympic movement, with its dozens of IOC members accustomed to the four-year rotating cycle, and benefiting from the hospitality of potential host cities.

Karamanlis's visit to Olympia with Girandou seems to have been the last real spark of life of his proposal. By then Karamanlis had stepped down from the position of Prime Minister and become President of the Hellenic Republic, able to exert his moral authority in favour of the scheme but reliant on others to act. The moment had passed. Despite the US boycott, the Moscow Olympics took place. Los Angeles prepared for 1984. Accepting defeat, Greece decided to concentrate on the limited but attainable goal of securing the Olympic Games for Athens, and prepared to bid for the centennial games in 1996.

15

2004

Citius, Altius, Fortius (Faster, Higher, Stronger)
Motto of the Olympic Games

In 2004, the Olympic Games are returning to their ancient birthplace and the city of their revival. Athletes from all nations will unite in Greece to engage in noble competition. The Athens Olympic Games will combine history, culture and peace, with sports and Olympism. The people of Greece shall host unique Games on a human scale, inspiring the world to celebrate Olympic values.
Athens 2004 Olympic Committee, the 'Vision'

What could be more fitting than that the 1996 Olympic Games, marking the centenary of the modern Olympics, should take place, once more, in Athens? In the nationalistic climate of the times Greeks came to believe that these centennial games were theirs by right. But the Athens bid for the games was badly prepared. At the 96th IOC session in Tokyo on 18 September 1990, Athens led narrowly on the first round of voting, in a field of five cities including Atlanta and Melbourne, Manchester and Belgrade; but in the succeeding rounds of voting Atlanta took the lead, beating Athens easily in the final round by fifty-one to thirty-five votes.

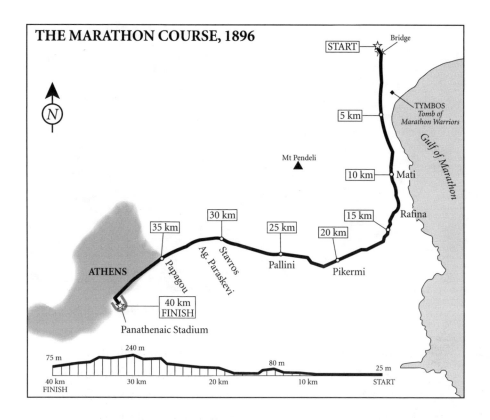

THE MARATHON COURSE, 1896

START — Bridge

TYMBOS
*Tomb of
Marathon Warriors*

5 km

Gulf of Marathon

Mt Pendeli

10 km — Mati

30 km — 15 km — Rafina

35 km — 25 km — 20 km

ATHENS — Pallini — Pikermi

Papagou — Stavros — Ag. Paraskevi

40 km
FINISH

Panathenaic Stadium

240 m

75 m — 80 m — 25 m

40 km
FINISH — 30 km — 20 km — 10 km — START

The sense of shock and humiliation in Athens was deep. The 1996 games were immediately seen as the Coca-Cola Olympics, where big business and American clout had cheated Greece of her rightful heritage. The Greek media ranted about unfairness, sinister financial and business interests, and commercialism.[1] The problems eventually encountered by Atlanta renewed the feelings of injustice. But by 1996 Athens had pulled herself together and compiled a new bid on a more professional basis.

On 5 September 1997, at Lausanne, the Greek bid team made their final presentation to the IOC, claiming the honour of hosting the XXVIII Olympiad of the modern era in 2004. The Greek bid was led by Gianna Angelopoulos-Daskalaki, a conservative lawyer and politician, supported by Athens Mayor Dimitrios Avramopoulos, a suave young diplomat who entered politics with the backing of the main

26 *Euphoria as Athens wins the bid for the 2004 Olympics: the President of the
Bid Committee, now President of the Athens 2004 Committee, Gianna
Angelopoulos-Daskalaki in the front row, with the Mayor of Athens
Dimitris Avramopoulos behind her right shoulder.*

opposition party New Democracy. Athens was in competition with
Rome, Cape Town, Stockholm and Buenos Aires. In the first round
Athens led Rome and Stockholm, with Cape Town and Buenos Aires
trailing equally in fourth place. Buenos Aires was eleminated in a run-
off. In the third round, Athens held her lead over Rome, picking up six
new votes, and Stockholm was eliminated. In the fourth round Athens
took fifty-two votes, Rome thirty-five and Cape Town twenty. At this
point it would have taken something extraordinary to lose. In the final
and fifth round of voting, Athens won comfortably with sixty-six
votes to Rome's forty-one. The joy of the Greek team at the announcement of Athens's victory is palpable in the photographs of the
moment of victory.

How did Athens bring it off at this second attempt? The sense that
complacency had spoiled the earlier bid inspired a more professional
approach. On the part of IOC members there was a willingness to see

the games return to Greece provided this could be justified by a competent bid. In Mrs Angelopoulos Greece had found a formidable salesperson. But what tipped the balance for Athens were developments in infrastructure since the earlier bid, which enabled the city to argue convincingly that it would be able to cope with the logistic problems posed by the games and the great influx of people that they would bring to Greece. For these infrastructure developments Greece had the European Union to thank, for funding provided through community support programmes. The Greek bid thus rested largely on Greece's European identity and Union membership.

The infrastructure works which made the games a feasible prospect were the new Athens airport and the Athens metro, both of which were at an advanced stage of planning at the time of the bid. The metro was opened, to great fanfares, in 2000. Though it does not extend as far as the airport, or to all the main Olympic sites, it has transformed transport in the centre of Athens. The new airport at Spata, east of Athens, between Mount Hymettus and the coast, opened in 2001, releasing the space of the old airport at Glyfada for development. In addition to these, the Greeks planned further transport links: a northern bypass connecting the national road from the Peloponnese with the national road north to Thessaloniki; a light railway linking the airport to the city; a tram from the city centre down to the coast at Phaleron, and on past the proposed new multi-sports centre and the new sailing marina at Agios Kosmas to the old airport and Glyfada.

Set against the demands of transport, accommodation and security, the sporting facilities required were not too daunting. There was already a modern stadium at Maroussi, which had been used for the European Games in the early 1980s and was well tested at international level. The Greeks commissioned the Spanish architect Santiago Calatrava to beautify it with an arching steel and glass roof. But new facilities were needed for the equestrian events, for rowing and canoeing, for basketball and other sports, as well as an Olympic village, a media centre and all the other things which the modern Olympic Games demand.

I was in Athens from 1996 to 1999 and followed the first two years of the Greek preparations for the games. In the early stages the British Embassy tried with some success to whip up interest in the commercial prospects offered by the games, with exhibitions and seminars. But it soon became evident that the Greek timetable for preparation was more relaxed than outsiders would have liked to see. This was not unexpected. The same thing had happened over the programme for Thessaloniki as the Cultural Capital of Europe in 1997. There were changes of plan and of personnel, and delays in the announcement of tenders for major Olympic contracts. The IOC started to get worried. There was even talk of taking the games away from Greece. The optimists (or realists, perhaps) said that this was the Greek way: it would all come out right on the day, at the cost of a last-minute scramble and heavy cost overruns.

No one seriously expected Greece to lose the games. But the IOC was sufficiently concerned in April 2000 for the President, Juan Antonio Samaranch, to come to Athens and wave a metaphorical yellow card at Greece, causing the Prime Minister to sound the alarm.

One answer to the problems was to replace the people running the show. In summer 2000 Prime Minister Simitis brought back Gianna Angelopoulos, who had masterminded the successful Greek bid, to run the Athens 2004 Organising Committee. Handsome, clever and rich, she was capable of standing up to difficult ministers and energising slow-moving bureaucrats. Under Gianna (pronounced Yianna), things began to move faster. But the IOC officials continued to worry about delays, and to say so loudly during their regular visits to Athens.

To host the Olympic Games in the early twenty-first century, a city must provide facilities for the range of Olympic sports; accommodation for the athletes, officials and spectators; transport to get them to the right place at the right time; and a secure environment. On top of these requirements, the city must make itself attractive; it must market itself, attract sponsors, and recruit volunteers to help things run smoothly.

The main problems facing the Athens organisers were in the areas of security, transport, accommodation and construction, and the environment.

The project which aroused the sharpest controversy was the new rowing and canoeing centre. The authorities decided to build this expensive watercourse and its associated facilities just inland from an attractive sandy beach, with pine trees and dunes, at Schinias near Marathon on the eastern coast of Attica. This decision angered two separate constituencies, the archaeologists and the environmentalists. Archaeologists resented the fact that the proposed course was only a few hundred metres away from the site of the battle of Marathon. In terms of Greek cultural nationalism, such a site is sacred. The environmentalists objected that the site chosen for the course was a rare stretch of wetland visited by a variety of wading birds. Against the attack of these two groups the government held its ground. The Schinias course is now completed.

At the time of writing it is still uncertain how much of the ambitious transport plans for the Olympics will be completed in time, and how effectively they will work in getting people from A to B. The new suburban railway scheme and the urban light railway are incomplete, whereas many of the road schemes are already in place. The Olympic village, on the slopes below Mount Parnes, is not too far from the main stadium. The saving factor will probably be the fact that the games take place in August, so that many Athenians will be away in the islands for their summer holidays. Some visitors will stay in cruise ships moored at Piraeus harbour. More modest accommodation will be available in the houses of Greeks as part of the hospitality programme, the rental for these being a further incentive to Athenians to stay away.

Security is the issue that at an earlier stage looked as if it might wreck the games. As Greece started preparations in the late 1990s, the country was still host to a small but lethal terrorist group, known as November 17 or N17 after the date of a students' occupation of the the Athens Poly-technic in 1973, in protest against the military dictatorship. N17 first appeared soon after the restoration of democracy in 1974. The assassi-nation of the Station Chief of the CIA in Athens on 23 December 1975 was the first of a long series of bombings, rocket attacks and murders, of Americans, Turks and, most of all, Greek businessmen, politicians and judicial officials.[2] The group, assumed to be a small group of Marx-ist-nationalist fanatics formed out of resistance elements in exile in the Junta years, propagated its bombastic message through long statements issued after each attack. A favoured method was to shoot the victim through the window of his car at traffic lights on the long and crowded road from the northern suburbs into Athens.

N17's apparent invulnerability – for after twenty-five years the police appeared to have made no progress towards apprehending the crimi-nals – and the fact that there were American victims, caused Greece to feature prominently on the American list of countries rife with terror-ism. Senior American officials speculated that the group had some pro-tection from within government circles. The Americans used the forthcoming Olympics to press for more effective action. A terrorist incident, or series of incidents, shortly before the Olympics would seri-ously damage Greece and could prejudice the games. At the back of Greek minds was the spectre of a boycott by some national teams.

On 8 June 2000, N17 struck again. The British Defence Attaché, Brigadier Stephen Saunders, travelling to work from the northern sub-urbs in the early morning rush hour, was shot in his car at traffic lights on Kifissia Avenue. The two assassins escaped on a motorcycle. This murder can be seen in retrospect as a turning point in the attitude of the Greeks to terrorism as well as in the pursuit of N17. The widow of the victim, Heather Saunders, impressed all in Greece with her demeanour, at the same time dignified and impassioned. Many people watching her on television seem to have grasped for the first time the personal tragedies involved in terrorist murders. Scotland Yard sent a team of detectives to work with the Greeks. The Greeks found that they did so with more discretion than the sometimes overbearing FBI. A young Minister of Public Order, Michalis Chrysochoides, attacked the problem with a new sense of urgency and efficiency.

In June 2002, very suddenly, the threat of N17 was removed. A young man named Savvas Xiros was seriously injured in Piraeus in the course of preparing an attack with explosives on the office of the Flying Dolphins hydrofoil company. His accomplice, Dimitrios Kouphodinas, a bee-keeper, fled. Taken to hospital, Xiros talked. He named a number of accomplices. The Greek police swooped and arrested the apparent ringleader, the white-haired Alexandros Yiotopoulos (alias Michalis Oikonomou), and others. Under interrogation the picture emerged of a small group of which Yiotopoulos was the mastermind. He had learned his revolutionary politics as a student in Paris in the 1960s. The image of ruthless efficiency which had been built up around the group was dissolved. They turned out to have escaped detection for so long by a combination of luck, mistakes by the Greek police, and the too often enabling environment of Greek public opinion. They were brought to trial in conditions of the highest security, at Korydallos prison, over the spring and summer of 2003. The trial concluded in December 2003 with the conviction and sentence of the leading members of the organisation to life imprisonment.

With the threat of N17 removed, the Greek authorities could concentrate on the still substantial issue of security at the Olympics. Chrysochoides established an Olympic Advisory group of senior law enforcement officers from seven countries – the US, Britain, Australia, Spain, France, Germany and Israel – which between them had unrivalled experience in counter-terrorism and recent and relevant experience of the Olympics. A major contract for supplying security services to the games was won by a consortium led by Science Applications International, after the usual delays. At the time of writing, while no one can be sure that there will be no security incident, it can at least be said that the Greeks have taken strenuous and apparently effective measures to ensure the security of athletes and the public. In fact there is a danger of overkill. The European summit held in April 2003 at the Zappeion, at which the prospective member states signed their Treaties of Accession to the Union, was taken by the Greek authorities as a dress-rehearsal for managing a large-scale event. The centre of Athens was closed, public servants were given the day off, and the public was caused considerable inconvenience.

Throughout 2003 and early 2004 Athens was in a fever of Olympic preparation, not so much because of the construction of Olympic sports facilities, the effects of which were local, as from the associated transport infrastructure works, and the architectural project which the Greeks call the 'Unification of the Archaeological Spaces'. The Greek government seized on the Olympics as a pretext for pushing through as much as possible of this ambitious plan for beautifying the city. In essence this is a scheme, first canvassed many years ago, for linking the main ancient sites with pedestrian ways and greenery in a broad band running from near the ancient Panathenaic stadium in the east through the precinct of the temple of Olympian Zeus and the arch of Hadrian, the Acropolis and its environs, and the Agora, to the Kerameikos, the area of the ancient cemetery. The responsible body for this 'Unification' project, known as EAHA, has widened its brief to include the remodelling of Syntagma, Omonia and two other squares, and the cleaning and restoring of the façades of many buildings in the centre of Athens.

This fever of construction has boosted employment, especially of immigrant men, and property prices. Economic migrants have been buying small apartments in downtown areas such as Kypseli and Patissia. The press in its gloomy way has started to write of the inevitability of a slump as men are laid off after the games.

The largest cultural projects connected with the Olympics are the development of the Phaleron delta area and the construction of a new Acropolis Museum. The Phaleron delta, south of the Stadium of Peace and Friendship, taking in the mouth of the Ilissos river, is being comprehensively developed and improved, to include beach sports, leisure areas and a park. The Acropolis Museum, which is not yet built, is designed to house not only the contents of the existing museum, which crouches discreetly on the sacred rock, but also the Parthenon sculptures, otherwise known as the Elgin Marbles. The Acropolis and the Parthenon sculptures have no connection with the Olympic Games; but the Minister of Culture set himself the deadline of 2004 and argued with the British government and the British Museum that the sculptures should be repatriated by the time of the games. To no avail. The new director of the British Museum, Neil MacGregor, has confirmed the refusal of his predecessor to return the marbles. It remains to be seen how the Greeks will dispose of the museum spaces without the Parthenon sculptures. There are plenty of fine things to put on display. Nevertheless, it seems likely that the museum will be seen, depending on your point of view, as a reproach to the British for not returning this crucial and symbolic part of Greece's heritage, or to the Greek ministry for spending so much money on a project the main point of which has not been realised.

Not all of the planned 'unification' will take place on time. But it has already much improved the city, from the viewpoint of the tourist and visitor. The façades of many buildings in central Athens have been cleaned up and advertising removed. It is now possible to stroll along the southern side of the Acropolis on a well-designed, broad pedestrian street, without being assailed by the roar and fumes of coach and car traffic. That is a major gain in itself.

Of course most of the changes are contested. EAHA set out with high hopes in 1998 by holding open competitions for the remodelling of four of the great squares of Athens: Omonia, Syntagma (Constitution), Monastiraki and Koumoundourou (or Eleftherias). When the plans of the young winners were revealed they aroused controversy and were quickly altered by the interventions of the Municipality and the Archaeological Service. The modernist Omonia Square scheme is an architects' folly of concrete modernism (though the architects blame the bureaucrats for not implementing their scheme in all its purity!). Thus a promising scheme was compromised because the competitions were held under time pressure and with an inadequate brief. The Chairman of EAHA wearily commented that the city of Athens was paying for the opportunity given to youth. Other plans also have aroused controversy. Local residents have protested against the plans for 'improving' Philopappou Hill.

It will not be possible until after the games are over to draw up a balance sheet of long-term advantages and disadvantages from the various Olympic works. But I believe that the balance will be positive. On the plus side are the beautification of the city, the improvements in infrastructure, and the acquisition of a number of top-quality sporting sites. On the minus side is the further incrustation of the Athens basin with objects and buildings, some of which will prove to be ugly and underused.

What is the connection between 2004 and 1896, apart from the fact that both games are in Athens?

The *Illustrated London News* for March and April 1896 records the outward signs of late-nineteenth-century European culture. Comparing them with the present day, one finds rather surprising continuities in the world of consumer products. Many brand names have survived from that time: Bovril; Hovis bread, 'cheapest and best'; Beecham's Pills at 1s 1 ¼d.; Elliman's Universal Embrocation; Lipton's tea at 1s.7d. per lb; Player's Navy Cut cigarettes.

In April 1896 Kitchener was advancing on Dongola in the Sudan, gathering forces to assemble at Wadi Haifa with the aim of reconquering Khartoum. There were reports of Turkish massacres of Armenians in eastern Anatolia. Oxford beat Cambridge in bad weather in the boat race. A new National Portrait Gallery opened in St Martin's Lane. There were reports of the Matabele rising; a shocking railway accident on Mount Snowdon; the training of carrier pigeons as 'naval war messengers' on battleships. The Hereditary Prince of Hohenlohe-Langeburg married Princess Alexandra of Saxe-Coburg-Gotha (several pages of pictures). Rudyard Kipling refused an American commission to write an article on the question 'Why America did not conquer England'. Into this collage of imperialism, social news of European minor royalty, sports and oddities, the Athens Olympics found its place with an article, none too accurate, on 'The Olympic Festival at Athens' by John Gennadius, the Greek Minister at the Court of St James, with the well-known picture of Louis winning the marathon, spread over two pages, based on a photo by John Macropoulos.

Compared with the modern world some of these particulars seem quaint, but the general picture is recognisable. Royal weddings still fascinate. Dolphins rather than carrier pigeons are now recruited for military purposes. There are still massacres and cruelties. We still drink Lipton's tea. It is the games which have changed more than the context.

They have become gigantic. Some time ago the Olympics became a genuinely global event, reaching through television into homes in every country. In Athens there will be thirty-seven Olympic sports and disciplines ranging from archery in the ancient stadium to wrestling (ten sports in 1896). The number gives a misleading impression because all the track and field events are bundled together under the single discipline Athletics. The organisers expect more than 10,000 athletes, more than 20,000 media representatives, and more than

4 million ticketed spectators, not to speak of the thousands of officials, delegations, sponsors and corporate guests. Athletes from virtually every country in the world will live in a specially constructed Olympic village, competing in stadia and halls and sites spread east, north, south and west of the city, from Marathon and Markopoulos in the northeast to the marina at Agios Kosmas on the coast below Phaleron. The Greek and international media will require a Media Centre of their own. The budget, which was 2.5 billion euros will be much exceeded. The security will be ubiquitous and, possibly, oppressive. A large volunteer programme will help keep the wheels of this giant enterprise running.

The core of sport remains, and in some quarters there remains a core of idealism which Coubertin would recognise. But the IOC themselves are conscious that the sheer size of the festival, along with the drugs and doping, and the commercialism against which Constantine Karamanlis complained, risk changing its nature. Many Athenians are equally concerned by these, as well as by the more immediate impact of the games on their city. Archbishop Christodoulos of Athens, a popular and populist figure, has associated himself with Karamanlis's charges, and the lost cause of bringing the games back to Greece permanently.

For the Archbishop, the answer is clear: 'We experience the Olympic Games bathed in the light of the Gospel, which teaches brotherhood, peace and love between people regardless of their race or religion.'

The official Greek answer to the problem of gigantism, commerce and exploitation is that these Olympics will be returned to a 'human scale'. This phrase, which features in the Organising Committee's 'Vision', has been picked up and repeated by organisers and ministers. Superficially it seems to be denied by the relentless concentration on numbers in the committee's publicity, which is intended not just to respond to the appetite of the media for factoids, but to prove the magnitude of the organisational task. These Olympics will still be giant, just as were those at Sydney. But the phrase, which is consistent with the

IOC President's wish to reduce the number of events (easier said than done), reflects what Coubertin saw as the ancient Greek ideal of a balance of mind and body, a harmony of living. It is also connected with the relative simplicity, freshness and idealism of the 1896 games.

The problem is that so much conspires to undermine freshness, harmony and human scale. 'Maybe the Gods had the same view from their rooms,' announces an advertisement for a major hotel; 'But, on the other hand, THEY were missing Air Conditioning, Direct Dial Phone, Internet, Swimming Pool, Satellite TV, Mini Bar, Room Service ...' Well, yes. Perhaps the effort to redeem the games, however well-intentioned, is misconceived. Perhaps they should be celebrated as a triumph of modernity, capitalism, commerce, sporting prowess and celebrity culture. Gestures in the direction of balance and human scale are gestures of respect to the mythical origins which the games have escaped.

Ultimately, for Greece these Olympic Games, like those of 1896, are a national and a nationalist enterprise. They are designed to assert Greece's place in the community of civilised, progressive nations, to meet the organisational challenge, and to assert a connection between these games and the ancient games in the continuum of Greece's history. I remember Mr Theodore Pangalos, the former Foreign Minister, telling his audience at an Olympic Conference in 2000 that the aim was not to show off the cradle of democracy but to show that a small country could handle a large project. But actually it is both. It is impossible to put a price on such ambitions. That is why the debates over cost overruns and procurement scandals, while interesting in the context of domestic politics, are beside the point. The Greeks must meet a challenge for the sake of their own national self-esteem, and to impress the outside world, and the cost of this will be met.

It is also an opportunity for Greece to show the world her own sporting talent: Greek athletes such as the sprinters Katerina Thanou and Kostas Kenteris and the weightlifter Pyrros Dimas, all Olympic gold medal winners. The Greek weightlifters, led by Dimas, are as good as any in the world, and a tribute to the openness of Greek society, because most of them come from Albania (though from the Greek minority in southern Albania, the area which the Greeks once claimed as Northern Epirus). Two of them, George Tzelilis and Victor Mitrou, were part of the wave of illegal immigrants who trekked across the mountains from Albania into Greece in 1991, moving by night to avoid frontier controls and police patrols.

The Greeks also want to show that the Olympic Games are essentially Greek. There are Greek links, which will never be lost, in the name, the memory of competitive striving at Olympia, the universality of the ancient games within the Greek world, and even in some of the events, in particular the discus, where Myron's discobolus remains a wonderful image of the greatness and beauty of the human body. But other alleged links of modern with ancient – torch rituals, the Olympic truce and such like – are constructed rituals and traditions. We shall hear much of them in 2004. It is the necessary price of holding the games in Greece that they should be presented as set within a 'cradle of democracy'.

The Olympic truce is a case in point. It was an essential feature of the ancient Olympic Games, guaranteeing the safety of athletes and spectators travelling to the games at Olympia in a Hellenic world that was constantly at war with itself. The truce was a guarantee of the universality of the ancient games, allowing them to take on a Panhellenic character. In the modern world the 'truce' which the IOC has tried to construct, with United Nations endorsement and with enthusiastic support from the Greek Foreign Minister, has no such constitutive function. It is a pleasing conceit which would not survive the harsh realities of modern interstate relations.

Two symbolic images within the Greeks' control are the Olympic torch, and the official Olympic mascots. The torch, elegantly designed by Andreas Varotsos in olive wood and magnesium, will travel a longer journey then ever before in its relay from Olympia to Athens, passing through all five continents. The mascots chosen by Athens 2004, however, caused surprise. They are a pair of pin-headed children inspired by ancient Greek dolls. These two cheeky little creatures, brother and sister, were named Phevos and Athena, after Phoebus Apollo the sun god, and Athena the goddess of wisdom and guardian of Athens. With their triangular form, pin heads and big flapping feet, and garish colours, Phevos and Athena will I suppose impose themselves on the imagination of millions of viewers at the time of the Games. The designer, Spyros Gogos, who won an open competition for the best mascot, says that he was inspired by the department of childhood, toys and games at the Benaki Museum in Athens: 'Dolls have been a favourite children's toy since ancient times. Our thinking was that we could combine ancient Greek elements with the modern concept of play. Phevos and Athena were directly inspired by the bell-shaped terracotta doll known as "daidala", which had moving limbs attached to the body with wire.'

The idea of drawing on ancient sources for some of the imagery and emblems of the Olympics is very natural, but the actual model is an unfamiliar and surprising one, which usefully escapes the clichés of ancient Greek heritage. The problem is that the mascots look to most people awkward and ugly. They will crop up in every context, from souvenir pins and T-shirts to animated cartoons. The organisers' hope will be that their playful animation will overcome the severe initial reactions to them.

Before the 1896 Olympic Games, Crown Prince Constantine spoke of the challenge for Greece:

I am also firmly convinced that, despite the insufficient resources at our disposal to give a brilliant reception to the foreign athletes, they will carry home with them on their return excellent memories of our country. We are in a position to show them real progress in all the branches of human activity … Those who visit Greece on this occasion will receive cordial and irreproachable hospitality, which together with the beauty of our sky, will easily make up for any defects. That is why the celebration of the Olympic Games at Athens will have an undoubted moral utility for us.

This time the resources should not be insufficient. In other respects, the words still apply. For reasons of national self-esteem, the challenge that Constantine and Vikelas identified for Greece must still be met.

SELECTED READING

The best book about the modern Olympic revival is David C. Young, *The Modern Olympics: a Struggle for Revival*, an exciting intellectual exploration based on a usually meticulous reading of the relevant texts including Greek. Some of his judgements are skewed by his hero-worship for William Penny Brookes and his eagerness to find a causal progression from the ancient Olympics, through Soutsos, Brookes and Zappas, to Coubertin and the modern games.

Coubertin's own voluminous works are essential sources, but the history of their publication is confusing and he gave different versions of events. The most convenient collection of his writings is *Pierre de Coubertin, 1863–1937, Olympism, Selected Writings*, ed. Norbert Müller. The liveliest book about Coubertin is John C. MacAloon's biography, *This Great Symbol*.

There is no outstanding book in English about Vikelas, though Young writes well about him. In Greek, the essential works are Alexandros A. Oikonomou, *Three Men: a Contribution to the History of the Greek People 1780–1935*, vol. 2, *Dimitrios M. Vikelas 1835–1908*; and *D. Vikelas, Complete Works*, 5 vols., ed. Alkis Angelou, which contains his memoir *My Life* (which does not cover the Olympic Games), his address 'The International Olympic Games', and his important memoir 'The War of 1897'.

There is a vast Olympic bibliography covering chronology, results, ceremony, Olympic politics, and every aspect of the subject. I have found most useful Bill Mallon and Ture Widlund, *The 1896 Olympic Games: Results for All Competitors in All Events, with Commentary*.

The prospect of the 2004 Games in Athens has given rise to a quantity of publications and exhibitions in Greece, including two good books about the history and restoration of the Panathenaic Stadium by Maria Beneki and Aristea Papanicolaou-Christensen; there is an English as well as a Greek edition of the latter, *The Panathenaic Stadium: its History over the Centuries*.

These books and many others are listed below, with details of publication; but not all the books and articles mentioned in the footnotes are listed in this select reading list. The main archival sources are those of the IOC at Lausanne, which have been well used by Young (not least Coubertin's correspondence with Vikelas); the Gennadius Library at Athens (for the papers of Stephanos Dragoumis); the Vikelas archive in the National Library, Athens; the Brookes papers at the Wenlock Olympian Society; and papers in the Mudd Library, Princeton University, on the Princeton team, especially Garrett.

I have found useful the websites of Athens 2004 (*www.athens2004. com*) and of the International Olympic Committee (*www.olympic. org*).

About, Edmond: *La Grèce Contemporaine*, Paris, 1854; published in translation as *Greece and the Greeks of the Present Day*, Edinburgh, 1855.

Acropolis: *I Ellada kata tous Olympiakous Agones tou 1896: Panellinion Eikonographimenon Lefkoma* (*Greece at the 1896 Olympic Games: Panhellenic Illustrated Album*), Estia, Athens, 1896.

Alpha Bank and ELIA: *Olympiaka Enthymimata 1896–1956 Olympic Memorabilia*, Athens, 2003

Anninos, Haralambos, and others: *The Olympic Games BC 776–AD 1896*, 2 vols., Charles Beck, Athens, 1896 (referred to as Beck); vol. 1

by Sp. Lambros and N.G. Politis with a prologue by T. Philemon; vol. 2 by Coubertin, Philemon, Politis and H. Anninos.

Arvin-Bérod, Alvin: *Les Enfants d'Olympie, 1796–1896*, Paris, 1996.

Baedeker, Karl: *Greece: Handbook for Travellers*, 2nd revised edn, Leipzig, London, New York, 1894.

Bastea, Eleni, *The Creation of Modern Athens*, Cambridge, 2000.

Benaki Museum: *Athens 1839–1900: a Photographic Record*, Athens, 1985.

Beneki, Eleni: *Stadion Panathinaikon kai Kallimarmaron: Stigmiotypa Athlitikou kai Dimosiou Viou* (*The Panathenaic Stadium: Incidents of Athletic and Public Life*), Athens, Greek Literary and Historical Archive (ELIA), 2002 (but publication has been delayed).

Benson, E.F.: *As We Were: a Victorian Peep-Show*, London, 1930.

Birley, Derek: *Land of Sport and Glory: Sport and British Society 1887–1910*, Manchester, 1995.

Bolitho, Gordon, and Bower, Leonard: *Otho I: King of Greece*, London, 1939.

Buruma, Ian: *Voltaire's Coconuts, or Anglomania in Europe*, London, 1999.

Christmas, Walter: *The Life of King George of Greece*, London, 1914.

Chrysaphis, I.E.: *Oi Synchronoi Diethneis Olympiakoi Agones* (*The Modern International Olympic Games*), Athens, 1930.

Clark, Ellery: *Reminiscences of an Athlete: Twenty Years on Track and Field*, Boston and New York, 1911.

Clogg, Richard: *A Concise History of Greece*, 2nd edn, Cambridge, 2002.

Coubertin, Pierre de: *Olympism, Selected Writings*, ed. Norbert Müller, IOC, Lausanne, 2000.

—— *L'Education en Angleterre*, Paris, 1888.

—— *Une Campagne de 21 Ans*, Paris, 1908.

—— *Mémoires Olympiques*, Lausanne, 1931.

Crane, Stephen: *Reports of War: War Despatches*, vol. 9 of *The Works of Stephen Crane*, University of Virginia Press, 1971.

Curtis, Thomas P.: 'High Hurdles and White Gloves', *The Sportsman*, no. 12, 1 July 1932, reprinted in Bill Mallon and Ture Widlund, *The 1896 Olympic Games: Results for All Competitors in All Events, with Commentary*, Jefferson and London, 1998, pp. 41–5.

Drosinis, Georgios: *Skorpia Phylla tis Zois Mou* (*Scattered Leaves from My Life*), ed. Yiannis Papakostas, Athens, 1982, 1983, 1985.

Furbank, Muriel, Cromarty, Helen and McDonald, Glyn: *William Penny Brookes and the Olympic Connection*, Wenlock Olympian Society, 1996.

Grande Bretagne Hotel: *Athens 1896 – a Remembrance: the Revival of the Olympic Games and the Historic Involvement of Hotel Grande Bretagne*, 3rd edn, Athens, 2000.

Hart-Davis, Duff: *Hitler's Games*, London, 1976.

Holmes, Burton: *The Olympian Games in Athens, 1896: the First Modern Olympics*, facsimile edn, New York, 1984.

Holt, Richard: *Sport and Society in Modern France*, London, 1981.

Horton, George: *Modern Athens*, London, 1902.

Kardasis, Vassilis: *Oi Olympiakoi Agones stin Athina 1896–1906; The Olympic Games in Athens 1896–1906* (text in both Greek and English), Athens, 2002.

Killanin, Lord: *My Olympic Years*, London, 1983.

Koliopoulos, John S., and Veremis, Thanos M.: *Greece: the Modern Sequel, from 1831 to the Present*, London, 2002.

Koulouri, Christina: *Athlitismos kai Opseis tis Astikis Koinonikotitas: Gymnastika kai Athlitika Somateia 1870–1922* (*Sport and Views of Bourgeois Society: Gymnastic and Athletic Bodies 1870–1922*), Athens, 1997.

Koulouri, Christina (ed.): *Athina 1896 kai A' Diethneis Olympiakoi Agones* (*Athens 1896 and the 1st International Olympic Games*), Athens (forthcoming).

Lambros, Spyridon: *Logoi kai Arthra 1878–1902* (*Speeches and Articles 1878–1902*), Athens, 1902.

Linardos, P.N.: *Apo to Orama stin Praxi: D Vikelas* (*From Vision to Reality: D Vikelas*), Athens, 1996.

Llewellyn Smith, M.: *Ionian Vision: Greece in Asia Minor 1919–1922*, London, 2nd edn, 1998.

—— *Athens*, Signal Books, Oxford (forthcoming).

—— *The British Embassy, Athens*, Athens, 1998.

MacAloon, John J.: *This Great Symbol: Pierre de Coubertin and the Origins of the Modern Olympic Games*, Chicago, 1981.

Mahaffy, J.P.: *Rambles and Studies in Greece*, 5th edn, London, 1907.

Mallon, Bill, and Widlund, Ture: *The 1896 Olympic Games: Results for All Competitors in All Events, with Commentary*, Jefferson and London, 1998.

Mandell, Richard D.: *Sport: a Cultural History*, New York, 1984.

—— *The First Modern Olympics*, Berkeley, 1976.

Marchand, Suzanne L.: *Down from Olympus: Archaeology and Philhellenism in Germany, 1750–1970*, Princeton, 1996.

Martin, David E., and Gynn, Roger W.H.: *The Olympic Marathon*, Human Kinetics, 2000.

Maurras, Charles: *Anthinea: d'Athènes à Florence*, Paris, 1913.

Miller, William: *Greek Life in Town and Country*, London, 1905.

—— 'The Early Days of Modern Athens', Anglo-Hellenic League, London, 1926.

Murray: *Handbook for Travellers in Greece*, 6th edn, John Murray, London, 1896.

Newsome, David: *Godliness and Good Learning: Four Studies on a Victorian Ideal*, London, 1961.

Oikonomou, Alexandros A.: *Treis Anthropoi: Symvoli eis tin Istorian tou Ellinikou Laou 1780–1935, vol. 2, Dimitrios M Vikelas 1835–1908* (*Three Men: a Contribution to the History of the Greek People 1780–1935, vol. 2, Dimitrios M. Vikelas 1835–1908*), Athens, 1953.

Papanicolaou-Christensen, Aristea: *The Panathenaic Stadium: its History over the Centuries*, Athens, Historical and Ethnological Society of Greece, 2003 (There is also a Greek edition).

Politis, Nikos E.: *Oi Olympiakoi Agones tou 1896* (*The 1896 Olympic Games*), Patras, 1996.

Richardson, Rufus B.: 'The Revival of the Olympic Games: Restoring the Stadion of Athens', *Scribner's Magazine*, January–June 1896, vol. 9, pp. 453–9.

—— 'The New Olympian Games', with illustrations by Corwin Knapp Linson, *Scribner's Magazine*, September 1896, vol. 20, no. 3, pp. 267–82.

Rizos-Rangavis, A.: *Apomnimonevmata* (*Memoirs*), Athens, 1894, new facsimile edition, Athens, 1999.

Robertson, G.S.: 'The Olympic Games, by a Competitor and Prizewinner', *Fortnightly Review*, no. 354, June 1896.

Roides, Emmanuel: 'Athinaikoi Peripatoi' (Athenian Walks), in Roides, *Complete Works*, ed. Alkis Angelou, vol. 5, 1894–1904, nos. 100, 102, 103.

Sullivan, J.E.: *The Olympic Games of 1906 at Athens*, Spalding's Athletic Library, vol. 23, no. 273, 1906.

Svolopoulos, K.: *Konstantinos Karamanlis: Archeio, Gegonota kai Keimena* (*Constantine Karamanlis: Archive, Events, Texts*), 12 vols., Athens, 1996, vols. 9 and 11.

Tarassouleas, Thanassis: *The Annals of the Pre-Olympic Games Period: Athens 1895–1896*, Athens, 1997.

Tsaousis, D.G. (ed.): *Opseis tis Ellinikis Koinonias tou 19ou Aiona* (*Aspects of Greek Society in the 19th Century*), Athens, 1984.

Tuckerman, Charles: *The Greeks of Today*, New York, 1878.

Vickers, Hugo: *Alice: Princess Andrew of Greece*, London, 2000.

Vikelas, Dimitrios: *Apanta* (*Complete Works*), ed. Alkis Angelou, Athens, 1997.

—— 'L'Athènes d'Aujourd'hui', in *Complete Works*, vol. 5, ed. Alkis Angelou.

—— 'Oi Diethneis Olympiakoi Agones' (The International Olympic Games), in *Complete Works*, vol. 5, pp. 124–39.

—— *I Zoi Mou* (*My Life*), in *Complete Works*, vol. 1.

—— 'O Polemos tou 1897' (The War of 1897), in *Complete Works*, vol. 1.

Xiradaki, Koula: *I Athina prin 100 Chronia: Philologikos Peripatos* (*Athens 100 Years Ago: a Literary Stroll*), Athens, 1982.

Yiannoulopoulos, Yiannis: *I Evgeni mas Typhlosis: Exoteriki Politiki kai 'Ethnika Themata' apo tin Itta tou 1897 eos ti Mikrasiatiki Katastrophi* (*Our Noble Blindness: Foreign Policy and 'National Issues' from the Defeat of 1897 to the Asia Minor Catastrophe*), Athens, 2001.

Young, David C.: *The Modern Olympics: a Struggle for Revival*, Baltimore, 1996.

NOTES

Introduction

1. 'Sport was one of the ways that perpetuated childhood ... Sport was also a result of a new relationship between work and leisure' (Theodore Zeldin, *France 1848–1945*, Oxford, 1977, vol. 2, pp. 681–2).

Chapter 1: A Little Kingdom

1. C. Wordsworth, *Athens and Attica*, 2nd edn, London, 1837, p. 51; contemporary accounts by the German archaeologist Ludwig Ross and others are quoted in William Miller's pamphlet, 'The Early Years of Modern Athens', Anglo-Hellenic League, 1926.

2. David C. Young, *The Modern Olympics: A Struggle for Revival*, Baltimore, 1996, pp. 1–12, traces in detail the story of Soutsos and early attempts at Olympic revivalism.

3. E. Prevelakis, *British Policy towards the Change of Dynasty in Greece*, Athens, 1953, p. 117.

4. *Leaves from the Diary of Henry Greville*, ed. Countess of Strafford, vol 4, London, 1905, pp. 151–2, 27 October 1863.

5. William Miller, *Greek Life in Town and Country*, London, 1905, p. 51.

6. E.F. Benson, *As We Were*, London, 1930, p. 161. Benson reworked his Athens experiences in *Our Family Affairs 1867–1896*, London, 1920, esp. pp. 286–97.

7. E.F. Benson, *Final Edition,* London, 1930, p. 218. Benson was an unreliable witness, but there are corroborative accounts.

8. Benson, *As We Were,* p. 162.

9. George Horton, *Modern Athens,* London 1902, p. 71.

10. Benson, *As We Were,* pp. 159–60.

11. Hugo Vickers, *Alice, Princess Andrew of Greece,* London, 2000, p. 66, quoting a note on the death of Prince Christopher of 25 January 1940 by the US Ambassador to Greece, Lincoln MacVeagh.

12. A. Syngros, *Apomnimonevmata* (*Memoirs*), vol. 2, Athens, 1908, p. 141, an important source.

13. Byron, Notes on Greece in the preface to *Childe Harold.*

14. Richard Clogg, *A Concise History of Greece,* Cambridge, 2002, p. 57.

15. Hansard, 24–27 June 1850: Palmerston's speech at the close of the second night of the debate at cols. 380–444 (the *civis Romanus* quotation at col. 444); Gladstone's speech on 27 June at cols 543–90.

16. The story is told in Romilly Jenkins, *The Dilessi Murders,* Prion Books, London, 1998.

17. Miller, *Greek Life in Town and Country,* p. 23.

18. The phrase ('*dystychos ephtochefsame*') does not appear in the proceedings of the Greek parliament. But Syngros thought he heard it, and all Greeks now assume that Tricoupis said it.

19. Edmond About, *Greece and the Greeks of the Present Day,* Edinburgh, 1855, pp. 2–3.

20. *The Journals and Letters of George Finlay,* ed. J.M. Hussey, 2 vols., Camberley, 1995, *Journals,* p. 410.

21. Charles Tuckerman, *The Greeks of Today,* New York, 1878, p. 352.

22. E.A. Freeman, 'Mediaeval and Modern Greece', in *Historical Essays,* vol. 3, London, 2nd edn, 1892, pp. 308–9.

23. In the large literature on nation-building and Hellenic identity, see e.g. John Koliopoulos and Thanos Veremis, *Greece, the Modern Sequel, From 1831 to the Present,* London, 2002, esp. part 5 on Ideology.

Chapter 2: The Rise of Sport

1. J.K. Rühl lists thirteen 'Olympic' festivals, from Robert Dover's Cotswold Games to a plethora of games in the nineteenth century, ranging from Dessau in Germany, Grenoble in France and Ramlosa in Sweden to Montreal and New York, and of course Athens: 'The Olympic Games in Athens in the Year 1877', *Journal of Olympic History*, vol. v, no. 3, 1997, p. 27.

2. Dover's life in the *Dictionary of National Biography*; also Richard Mandell, *The First Modern Olympics*, Berkeley/Los Angeles/London, 1976, to which I am indebted for the quotation at the head of the chapter.

3. Alvin Arvin-Bérod, *Les Enfants d'Olympie, 1796–1896*, Paris, 1996. This interesting book illustrates the tendency of authors to 'nationalise' Olympism. The author attributes the Olympic revival to three factors: the French Revolution and the *lumières*; the liberal reformist Catholic tendency in education, led by the Dominicans; and the creation of modern sport. The hero is the Dominican priest Henri Didon. Anglo-Saxon authors dwell on the importance of British sports, 'fair play', etc.

4. J. Astley Cooper, 'An Anglo-Saxon Olympiad', *The Nineteenth Century*, vol. 32, September 1892, pp. 381–8; 'The Pan Britannic Gathering', vol. 34, July 1893, pp. 81–93; 'The Americans and the Pan-Britannic Movement', vol. 38, Sept 1895, pp. 427–41; and 'Olympic Games: What Has been Done and What Remains to be Done', vol. 63, June 1908, pp. 1011–21.

5. Richard Holt, *Sport and Society in Modern France*, London, 1981.

6. Christina Koulouri, *Athlitismos kai Opseis tis Astikis Koinonikotitas: Gymnastika kai Athlitika Somateia 1870–1922* (*Sport and Views of Bourgeois Society: Gymnastic and Athletic Bodies 1870–1922*), Athens, 1997.

7. The rise of Greek sport and the development of its institutions are described in Christina Koulouri, op cit.

8. Yiannis Yiannoulopoulos, *I Evgeni mas Typhlosis* (*Our Noble*

Blindness: Foreign Policy and 'National Issues' from the Defeat of 1897 to the Asia Minor Catastrophe), Athens, 2001, pp. 3–9.

9. There are gaps in our knowledge about the Society, largely owing to the secrecy of its proceedings, reflected in the oath: 'I swear on the holy Gospel and on my honour that I will not reveal to anyone what I have seen, nor what will be revealed to me, nor any part of it, nor the name of any of those present here'; General P.G. Danglis, *Anamniseis, Engrapha, Allilographia* (*Memoirs, Documents, Correspondence*), vol. 1, Athens, 1965, p. 137.

Chapter 3: Forerunners: Brookes and Zappas

1. A.E. Housman, *A Shropshire Lad*, No. XIX. A.D. Stallings, '"The Time You Won Your Town the Race": A Shropshire Lad and the Modern Olympics', *The Classical Outlook*, vol. 73, no. 4, summer 1996, pp. 113–16, looks for connections and concludes 'There is no way to know if Housman witnessed the events of the Olympic games at Wenlock. But it is almost impossible that he did not *know* of them.'

2. The charter is among the papers at the Much Wenlock Olympian Society archive, the basis of which is Brookes's own archive. He was a compulsive recorder. This account is drawn mainly from the exhaustive researches of Young, *The Modern Olympics*, in these archives. The Wenlock Games have been 'adopted' by the IOC as a part of Olympic history. The Princess Royal, Princess Anne, visited Wenlock in 1990, and Juan Antonio Samaranch as President of the IOC in 1994, the centenary of the Paris congress. Wenlock today has an 'Olympian Trail' starting at the Much Wenlock Museum. Muriel Furbank, Helen Cromarty and Glyn McDonald, *William Penny Brookes and the Olympic Connection*, Wenlock Olympian Society, 1996.

3. A. Rizos-Rangavis, *Apomnimonevmata* (*Memoirs*), Athens, 1999, p. 378.

4. The Olympic Committee's published circulars can be found in

bound volumes which start with the Royal Decree of 19 August 1859 and the text of Zappas's will, in the Greek Literary and Historical Archive (ELIA).

5. J.P. Mahaffy, 'The Olympic Games at Athens in 1875', *Macmillan's Magazine*, no. 32, 1875, pp. 324–7.

6. It is impossible to be more precise about what Brookes proposed since his letter is lost; its terms must be deduced from the subsequent correspondence: Young, *The Modern Olympics*, pp. 58–60.

Chapter 4: Pierre de Coubertin

1. Coubertin, *L'Education Anglaise en France*, Paris, 1889, quoted in *Pierre de Coubertin 1863–1937, Olympism, Selected Writings*, ed. Norbert Müller, Lausanne, 2000, p. 71 (hereafter cited as *Olympism*).

2. Coubertin, *Une Campagne de 21 Ans*, Paris, 1908, p. 5. J. MacAloon, *This Great Symbol: Pierre de Coubertin and the Origins of the Modern Olympic Games*, Chicago, 1981, makes too much of this so-called 'Vision in Rugby Chapel'.

3. 'L'Education Anglaise', in *La Réforme Sociale*, vol. 7, series 2, no. 3, June 1887, pp. 633–48, quoted in Coubertin, *Olympism*, p. 115.

4. David Newsome, *Godliness and Good Learning: Four Studies on a Victorian Ideal*, London, 1961, a masterly study by a more recent Master of Wellington.

5. Pierre de Coubertin, *L'Education en Angleterre*, Paris, 1888, p. 302.

6. Newsome, op. cit., pp. 44–5.

7. This and subsequent quotations from Coubertin, *Universités Transatlantiques*, Paris, 1890, quoted in *Olympism*, pp. 78–103.

8. Coubertin, 'Les Jeux Olympiques à Much Wenlock', *La Revue Athlétique*, vol. 1, 25 December 1890, no. 12, quoted in *Olympism*, pp. 281–6.

9. Coubertin, *Olympism*, p. 297; speech at the USFSA Jubilee, 25 November 1892.

10. Coubertin, *Olympic Memoirs*, Lausanne, 1997, quoted in *Olympism*, p. 315.

11. Ibid., p. 318.

Chapter 5: The Paris Congress

1. D. Vikelas, *I Zoi Mou* (*My Life*), Athens, 1908, reprinted in Vikelas, *Apanta* (*Complete Works*), ed. Alkis Angelou, Athens, 1997, vol. 1.

2. The English edition was translated by J. Gennadius, Minister at the Greek Embassy in London, who wrote a preface: D. Vikelas, *Loukis Laras: Reminiscences of a Chiote Merchante during the War of Independence*, London, 1881. The story about the early printing history of the book is from Georgios Drosinis, *Skorpia Phylla tis Zois Mou* (*Scattered Leaves from My Life*), Athens, 1985, vol. 1, pp. 184–5.

3. D. Vikelas, 'Oi Diethneis Olympiakoi Agones (The International Olympic Games)', address to the Greek students of Paris of 5 April 1895, in Vikelas, *Complete Works*, vol. 5, pp. 124–39.

4. On Waldstein, see Mary Beard, *The Invention of Jane Harrison*, Cambridge, Mass. and London, 2000.

5. David Young confuses Alexis Rangavis with his father Alexandros, the former minister. Apart from this, his reconstruction of what happened at Paris, in *The Modern Olympics*, pp. 96–105, is a masterpiece of speculative detective work. The key sources used by Young are Vikelas's correspondence with Coubertin, in the IOC Library, Lausanne; Vikelas's correspondence with Rangavis and Phokianos, now published in P. Linardos, *Apo to Orama stin Praxi: D. Vikelas* (*From Vision to Reality: D. Vikelas*), Athens, 1996. Chrysaphis, *Oi Synchronoi Diethneis Olympiakoi Agones* (*The Modern International Olympic Games*), Athens, 1930, publishes in full Phokianos's memorandum to the Paris congress, which Vikelas thought laboured, too long and off the point.

6. Vikelas's account is in his address to the Greek students of Paris, see note 3 above. Coubertin's accounts are in *Bulletin du Comité International des Jeux Olympiques*, no. 1 of July, 1894; *Une Campagne de 21 Ans*, Paris, 1909; and *Mémoires Olympiques*, Lausanne, 1932, quoted in *Olympism*, p. 320.

7. The full text of Vikelas's important note, of which Coubertin quoted the beginning in his *Campagne de 21 Ans*, is in the book of Coubertin–Vikelas correspondence in the IOC Library, Lausanne.

8. Text from Coubertin, *Bulletin*, quoted and analysed by Young, *The Modern Olympics*, pp. 102–3.

9. Linardos, *Apo to Orama Stin Praxi*, pp. 35, 49, letters of Vikelas to Phokianos of 25 June, 6 July, 1894.

10. Stephanos Dragoumis archive, Gennadius Library; File 235.1, no. 98, Vikelas to Dragoumis, 22 October 1894: 'Your Committee on the Olympia both from its name and its destined function is as if it had been formed expressly and prophetically for this circumstance.'

11. Vikelas to Dragoumis, 15 October 1894, written in haste before his departure for Paris; Dragoumis archive, File 235.1, Gennadius Library.

12. Coubertin's account of his visit to Greece is in *Olympic Memoirs*, Lausanne, 1997, reprinted in *Olympism*, pp. 321–5. Vikelas wrote to Dragoumis on 22 October 1894 telling him of his discussions with Coubertin and preparing him for Coubertin's arrival. He hoped, and probably expected, that Coubertin's powers of persuasion would be too much for Dragoumis and Prime Minister Tricoupis to resist; and he continued to argue the case for holding the games in Athens on grounds of national morale and because this was a 'unique opportunity for Greece in the midst of the present miseries': Vikelas to Dragoumis, 22 October 1894, and 10 November 1894, Dragoumis Archive, File 235.1, Gennadius Library.

13. Full text of Dragoumis's letter of 1 November 1894 in Bill Mallon and Ture Widlund, *The 1896 Olympic Games; Results for All Competitors in All Events, with Commentary*, Jefferson and London, 1998, pp. 8–9.

14. Young, *The Modern Olympics*, p. 113, suggests, unconvincingly in my view, that Coubertin was politically naïve in consulting an ally of Tricoupis about the relationship of potential committee members with the royal family.

Chapter 6: Olympia Rediscovered

1. Judith Swaddling, *The Ancient Olympic Games*, London, 1980, new edition 1999, gives the best short account of the games; M.I. Finley and H.W. Pleket, *The Olympic Games: the First Thousand Years*, London, 1976, a good longer account.

2. Richard Chandler, *Travels in Asia Minor and Greece*, 3rd edn, London, 1817, vol. 1, preface; subsequent quotations from his description of Olympia, vol. 2, pp. 323–35.

3. For Curtius see Suzanne L. Marchand, *Down from Olympus: Archaeology and Philhellenism in Germany, 1750–1970*, Princeton, 1996.

4. J.P. Mahaffy, *Rambles and Studies in Greece*, 5th edn, London, 1907, p. 252.

5. e.g. Victor Duruy, who brought out in 1887 an expanded edition of his *Histoire de Grèce*, including several pages on the Olympic Games and Curtius's plan of the site: MacAloon, *This Great Symbol*, pp. 138–43.

6. Coubertin, *Une Campagne de 21 Ans*, p. 89.

7. Coubertin, *Olympic Memoirs*, p. 33, quoted in *Olympism*, p. 325.

8. The quotation is from a lecture which Coubertin gave in Paris on Olympia on 6 March 1927: *Olympism*, p. 564.

Chapter 7: Preparations

1. The parliamentary debate, in the *Journal of Parliamentary Debates* (*Ephimeris ton syzitiseon tis Voulis*), session 17, November 24 (o.s.), 1894, pp. 176–83, not only illustrates the arguments for and against holding the games, but also helps to establish what happened during Coubertin's visit to Athens. Skouloudis gave an account of the Zappeion meeting and the second thoughts of the committee. Dragoumis, on the back foot, defended the Zappas Olympia committee's inability to give financial support on the grounds that they had no money, analysing the provisions of the Zappas bequests.

2. The article by Timoleon Philemon in the official book of the games,

The Olympic Games 776 BC to 1896 AD, Charles Beck, Athens, 1896, vol. 2, pp. 8–28, gives a detailed account of the organisational structures with the names of committee members, who included a clutch of ministers and notables. There are a number of different language editions of this rare and beautiful book (henceforth referred to as Beck), which was 'published with the sanction and under the patronage of the central Committee in Athens, presided over by HRH The Crown Prince Constantine': one in Greek and French, one in Greek and English, one in Greek and German. Part 1 has articles by Lambros and Politis, with a preface by Philemon. Part 2 has articles by Coubertin, Philemon, Politis and Anninos.

3. Spyridon Lambros, 'The Crown Prince's Speech', *Estia* 15 January (o.s.) 1895, reprinted in Lambros, *Logoi kai Arthra 1878–1902* (*Speeches and Articles 1878–1902*), Athens, 1902, pp. 397–9.

4. Young, *The Modern Olympics*, pp. 118–26, argues that Coubertin, preoccupied with his marriage and the history book he was writing, virtually abandoned Vikelas and the Greeks in 1895. He cites Vikelas's agitated letters from Athens in January and February asking for guidance, and suggests that at one point Coubertin may actually have resigned from the IOC.

5. T. Tarassouleas, *The Annals of the Pre-Olympic Games Period, Athens 1895–1896*, Athens, 1997, provides useful summaries of the minutes of the twelve-member council and of the specialist committees.

6. Metaxas, who studied in Germany, later designed the Ionian Bank, the Benaki house, which became the Benaki Museum, and the Venizelos house in Loukianou Street, which became the British Embassy. The latter was commissioned by Helena, Venizelos's second wife, as a suitably imposing house for the great Cretan statesman. When he died in 1936, she sold it to the British government. It is still the British Ambassador's residence. Michael Llewellyn Smith, *The British Embassy Athens*, published by the British Embassy Athens, 1998.

7. By the time of the 1896 games the stadium had been restored in Pen-

telic marble up to the corridor separating the lower tiers of seats from the upper. The work continued after the games, Averoff donating further funds and leaving money in his will for the purpose. The project was completed in time for the 1906 games. The total costs were of the order of 4 million drachmas, or about £102,600 (gold £ = 39,31 fr): Oikonomou, *Vikelas*, p. 481.

8. Ibid., p. 481.

9. Kostis Palamas, 'Eis to Stadion (In the Stadium)', *Apanta* (*Complete Works*), vol. xv, p. 323.

10. Tarassouleas, *The Annals of the Pre-Olympic Games Period*, pp. 57–68, records the details of the debate, which is interesting both for the workings of the committees and for the state of the outlying suburbs of Athens at this period.

11. Chrysaphis, *Oi Synchronoi Diethneis Olympiakoi Agones*, p. 295.

12. Vikelas letter to *Estia* of 22 March o.s., cited in Oikonomou, *Vikelas*, pp. 489–90: 'It was a great honour for Greece to be the first to crown the first victors at these worldwide games. This is a new recognition of the special position which Hellas, through her name, holds in the civilised world. Those who come here from all over the world come not as strangers to a strange land, but as spiritual children of ancient Greece, paying a tribute of gratitude to the common mother and nurse of their civilisation. This is why the victory of every athlete whether Greek or not equally honours Greece and should be hailed with equal enthusiasm.'

13. Vikelas, 'Oi Diethneis Olympiakoi Agones', pp. 138–9.

14. G.S. Robertson, 'The Olympic Games, by a Competitor and Prize Winner', *Fortnightly Review*, no. 354, June 1896, pp. 944–57.

15. Young, *The Modern Olympics*, p. 124. Jebb, an early proponent of a British School for classical studies at Athens, had earlier been involved in a titanic scholarly dispute with Mahaffy.

16. Ellery Clark, *Reminiscences of an Athlete*, Boston, 1911, pp. 123–5.

17. Ibid., p. 68.

18. Ibid., p. 130, which dates the arrival to 5 April, the eve of the games.

19. The *Daily Princetonian*, 17 March 1896, reported that the games were to be held in Athens from 5–15 April inclusive, 'or by the Greek calendar from the 24th March to the 3rd April'. It is very hard to credit that the team really did not know when they were supposed to arrive when the press did. The NBC television film about the Olympics makes much of the alleged calendar error, blaming it on the American team's travel agent, and claiming that they only discovered the mistake on arrival at Naples. From there onwards it was a rush!

20. William Miller, *A History of the Greek People, 1821–1921*, London, 1922, p. 174.

21. Coubertin, *Olympism*, p. 329.

22. File 863, Vikelas archive, National Library of Greece. Chrysaphis, *Oi Synchronoi Diethneis Olympiakoi Agones*, pp. 297–308, gives a full description of these trials, with a list of those selected for the games (for most events, two athletes only), and numerous criticisms of the organisation, principally aimed at Manos, the *alytarchis*, or director of the games. The Greek press took offence at its treatment by the organisers, and temporarily broke off relations with the Olympic Committee.

23. The row is well described by Chrysaphis, *Oi Synchronoi Diethneis Olympiakoi Agones*, pp. 262–79, who as director of the NGA gym and a teacher of gymnastics was, with Phokianos, President of the PGA and director of the central gymnasium, one of those directly affected. Chrysaphis publishes the successive letters to the Greek press, and the correspondence with the IOC, and Coubertin's views, all of which he was given by Vikelas. The papers of the Olympic Committee on the 1896 games were lost when the Melas house was destroyed by fire.

24. Thanassis Tarassouleas, *Olympic Happenings III: Medical Care during the First Modern Olympic Games of 1896*, Athens, 2002, pp. 24–9.

25. For Manos's views on sports, see his article 'After the Games' in the handsome special publication of the *Acropolis* newspaper on the

games, *I Ellada kata tous Olympiakous Agones tou 1896: Panellinion Eikonographimenon Leukoma* (*Greece and the Olympic Games of 1896: Panhellenic Illustrated Edition*), Athens, Estia, 1896, pp. 125–6.

26. Christina Koulouri, *Athlitismos kai Opseis*, p. 108. Chrysaphis, *Oi Synchronoi Diethneis Olympiakoi Agones*, pp. 282–4, describes the Manos trials, at which the Greek spectators spoke French with Kolonaki accents.

27. Haris Yiakoumis and Isabelle Roy, *La Grèce: La Croisière des Savants*, Paris and Athens, 1998, an account of these cruises illustrated with photographs taken during them.

Chapter 8: Athens revived

1. Growth in population, according to William Miller, *Greece*, London, 1928 (figures rounded to nearest thousand): 1813: 12,000; 1836: 15,000; 1840: 26,000; 1896: 129,000; 1921: 293,000; 1928: estimated 642,000. These figures exclude Piraeus, which also grew rapidly, and from the even lower base of only one house in 1834! Vikelas, 'L'Athènes d'Aujourd'hui', *Complete Works*, vol. v, Athens, 1997, adds figures as follows: 1863: 45,000; 1879: 64,000; 1889: 114,000, and points out that the number 129,000 for the 1896 census is probably an underestimate even before the numbers of refugees from Crete and Thessaly are added in.

2. Benson, *As We Were*, p. 157.

3. Burton Holmes, *The Olympian Games in Athens, 1896: the First Modern Olympics*, New York, 1984, p. 23.

4. Charles Tuckerman, *The Greeks of Today*, p. 42; Eleni Bastea, *The Creation of Modern Athens*, Cambridge, 2000, pp. 193–4.

5. *Olympic Memorabilia 1896–1956*, Alpha Bank and ELIA, 2003, p. 34.

6. Drosinis, *Skorpia Phylla tis Zois Mou*, vol. 2, pp. 126–8. Drosinis was an editor of *Estia*. Among the Saturday night group, besides him and Vikelas, Phokianos and Palamas, were the sculptor Georgios Vroutos, who made the statue of Averoff outside the stadium, and the artist Nikiphoros Lytras, who designed the diploma for Olympic winners. Quite an Olympic galaxy.

7. Emmanuel Roides, 'Athenian Walks (Athinaikoi Peripatoi)', *Apanta* (*Complete Works*), vol. 5, 1894–1904, ed. Alkis Angelou. Bastea, *The Creation of Modern Athens*, ch. 7, gives a good account of Athenian society in the 1890s.

8. Horton, *Modern Athens*, p. 39.

9. A. Papadiamantis, 'Athens as an Eastern City', in *I Ellas kata tous Olympiakous Agones* (*Greece at the Olympic Games of 1896*), Athens, 1896.

10. Holmes, *The Olympic Games in Athens*, pp. 32–3.

11. J.E. Sandys, *An Easter Vacation in Greece*, London, 1887, pp. 26–7.

12. Eleni Beneki, 'To Mega Panorama pros to Stadion (The Great Panorama by the Stadium)', *Ta Nea tou ELIA* (*Greek Literary and Historical Archive News*), winter 2001, no. 59. Panoramas were introduced first in Edinburgh, then London, by the British artist Robert Baker in the late eighteenth century, spread to France, and became popular. This one, created by Henri-Emmanuel-Félix Philippoteaux, was entitled 'La Défence de Paris contre les armées allemandes' and consisted of panoramic views on canvas measuring 50 feet in height and 400 feet in circumference. Another panorama, showing the siege of Missolonghi, was set up in the downtown area. The cinema put an end to the growth period of panoramas and dioramas, but superb examples can still be seen in the US and Europe, from Waterloo to Sevastopol.

13. Alkis X. Xanthakis, *I Ellada tou 19ou aiona me ton phako tou Petrou Moraiti* (*19th century Greece through the lens of Petros Moraitis*), Athens, 2001; see also the Benaki Museum catalogue, *Athens 1839–1900: a Photographic Record*; Athens, 1985.

14. Charles Maurras, *Anthinea: d'Athènes à Florence*, 9th edn, Paris, 1913, pp. 275–6.

15. Yiannoulopoulos, *I. Evgeni mas Typhlosis*, p. 38. For Politis, see the entry by Neni Panourgia in Graham Speake, *Encyclopedia of Greece and the Hellenic Tradition,* London and Chicago, 2000, vol. 2, pp. 1379–80 (but referring to 1909 she writes Tricoupis when she means Venizelos).

16. Vikelas, *Complete Works,* vol 1, 'O Polemos tou 1897 (The War of 1897)', esp. pp. 269–85.

17. Rufus B. Richardson, 'The Revival of the Olympic Games: Restoring the Stadion at Athens', *Scribner's Magazine,* vol. 9, January–June 1896, pp. 453–9. Richardson had succeeded Waldstein as Director of the American School at Athens.

18. Text of Coubertin letter in Mallon and Widlund, *The 1896 Olympic Games,* pp. 12–13. This was the first of a series of dispatches which Coubertin wrote for *Le Journal des Débats.* A slightly different text (e.g. in the list of participants at the end) is printed in *Olympism,* pp. 334–6.

Chapter 9: The Games Begin

1. The report is by Haralambos Anninos, in *The Olympic Games BC 776 – AD 1896,* Charles Beck, Athens, 1896, vol. 2, pp. 47–109 (hereafter cited as Beck). Anninos, a member of Athenian literary society, was one of two brothers who owned the newspaper *Asty.* My account of the games draws on Anninos and on a selection of other eye-witness accounts including those of Coubertin, Richardson, Robertson, Curtis, Holmes and Clark. I have given health warnings when an account is doubtful, as (unfortunately) in the case of some of Curtis's best stories. Estimated numbers of spectators vary between sources, as do many of the details of competitors and results, but the best source for the latter is Mallon and Widlund, *The 1896 Olympic Games.*

2. Coubertin, *Olympism,* p. 353.

3. Anninos in Beck. Coubertin wrote that the ladies used large paper fans because parasols, which would have obstructed the view, were prohibited. He contrasted the skirts and braided jackets of the *palikars* with the sombre and ugly European garments: *Olympism,* p. 353.

4. Coubertin, *Olympism,* p. 328. On ritual, which excites Olympic historians and psychologists of mass sport, see *Olympic Ceremonies:*

Historical Continuity and Cultural Exchange, International symposium of Olympic Ceremonies, Barcelona-Lausanne, November 1995.

5. The Palamas-Samaras Olympic hymn, which was criticised by one
or two reactionary orthodox theologians because it was pagan, was
played again at the Athens Games of 1906, but the British played
their own national anthem in London in 1908 and others followed
suit. In 1936 the Berlin Olympics were inaugurated with an Olympic
hymn specially composed by Richard Strauss. The Samaras-Palamas
hymn was accepted as the official anthem of the Olympic movement
only at Melbourne in 1956.

6. Maurras, *Anthinea,* p. 259.

7. Gustave Larroumet, *La Grèce: La Croisière des Savants 1896–1912,*
Paris/Athens, 1998, p. 142. File 863 of the Vikelas archive, National
Library of Greece, contains a selection of programmes and booklets
of rules.

8. J.E. Sullivan, *The Olympic Games of 1906 at Athens,* Spalding's Athletic Library, vol, 23, no. 273, 1906.

9. Clark has Curtis winning the first heat, Lane the second: *Reminiscences of an Athlete,* p. 132.

10. Thomas P. Curtis, 'High Hurdles and White Gloves', *The Sportsman,*
July 1932, reprinted in Mallon and Widlund, *The 1896 Olympic
Games,* pp. 41–5.

11. Holmes, *The Olympian Games,* p. 79: 'Much amusement was caused
at the king's luncheon when his majesty sent his chamberlain to the
American table with a request that our boys should kindly repeat
their strange "war cries". "The King," he said, "had listened at a distance to these incomprehensible shouts, and was curious to give
them a critical hearing at close quarters." All arose and gave a rousing, "Rah, rah, rah – Ellas, Ellas, Ellas, Zito! Hurrah for Greece!" and
his majesty expressed himself as satisfied. The papers alluded to
these war cries as "Onomatopeia", considering them frenetic shouts
difficult to comprehend.'

12. Joseph E. Raycroft papers, Mudd Library, Princeton University;

folder of correspondence with Robert Garrett, 1912–50; letter from Garrett to Raycroft, 24 April 1948. Garrett here makes no reference to the story, which features in a number of 1896 accounts, that he had commissioned a discus at Princeton following what he thought was an ancient Greek model, but found it too heavy to throw and abandoned the idea of entering the discus event at Athens. The light and easily handled discus he found in the stadium then changed his mind. Tyler was evidently unaware of such a story, which is probably another legend.

Chapter 10: The Games Continue
1. Curtis, 'High Hurdles and White Gloves', reprinted in Mallon and Widlund, *The 1896 Olympic Games*, pp. 41–5. As Mallon argues, the story is unlikely to be true, though Williams may well have complained of the cold during practice.
2. Clark, *Reminiscences of an Athlete*, p. 136.
3. Full results in Mallon and Widlund, *The 1896 Olympic Games*, pp. 17ff.
4. According to Curtis, Goulding was boastful and strutted around Athens with a clutch of medals on his chest: Curtis in *Reminiscences of an Athlete*, ibid., pp. 42–3.
5. P. Nirvanas, 'The Swimming', in *I Ellas kata tous Olympiakous Agones tou 1896 (Greece at the 1896 Olympic Games)*, Estia, Athens, 1896.
6. Robertson, 'The Olympic Games', pp. 946–7.

Chapter 11: The Marathon
1. Oikonomou, *Vikelas*, p. 492, drawing on the Vikelas archive, writes that 71,800 tickets were issued for this day, at 2 drachmas for the lower ranks of seats and 1 drachma for the upper. In addition, 4,000 received complimentary invitations. Adding in the spectators congregated on the hillside above the stadium, he reckons there were 100,000, not counting the large numbers who lined the streets and the entrance to the stadium.

2. Clark, *Reminiscences of an Athlete*, p. 138.

3. Oikonomou, *Vikelas*, p. 492.

4. Coubertin, *Olympism*, p. 333.

5. Benson, *As We Were*, pp. 166–8.

6. Nikos E. Politis, *Oi Olympiakoi Agones tou 1896* (*The Olympic Games of 1896*), Patras, 1996, pp. 105–6; ibid., pp. 93–101, is good on the Louis legend.

7. Richardson, 'The New Olympian Games', *Scribner's Magazine*, September 1896, no. 3, p. 281.

Chapter 12: The End of the Games

1. Robertson's ode, in translation by E.D.A. Morshead, is printed as an appendix to Mallon and Widlund, *The 1896 Olympic Games*, pp. 143–4: sample:

    I too, who sing hereof,
    I too in strenuous sport, with sons of Hellas strove.
    'All hail!' we cry, 'All hail!'
    Fair mother of the Arts! O violet-crowned
    Home of Athena! Glory's sacred ground!
    Onward, in love of thee, we spread our eager sail!

2. Details of prizes from Politis, *Oi Olympiakoi Agones tou 1896*, pp. 111–12.

3. Robertson, 'The Olympic Games', p. 944.

4. Richardson, 'The New Olympian Games', p. 268.

5. Maurras, *Anthinea*, pp. 263–8.

6. Richardson, 'The New Olympian Games', p. 282.

7. *I Ellas kata tous Olympiakous Agones tou 1896: Panellinion Eikonographimenon Lefkoma* (*Greece and the Olympic Games of 1896: Panhellenic Illustrated Edition*), Hestia, Athens, 1896. This fine book was published in instalments, each with a cover picture by a different distinguished artist. Publication of the later parts seems to have been aborted by the Greco-Turkish war which broke out in April 1897, so that there is very little of vol. 2 as compared with vol. 1.

8. The Americans' departure is described in *Asty*, 6 April 1896 (o.s.), quoted by Eleana Yalouri, 'When the New World meets the Ancient. American and Greek experiences of the 1896 "revival" of the Olympic Games', in *Athina 1896 kai A' Diethneis Olympiakoi Agones*, Ministry of Culture and Historical and Ethnological Society of Greece (forthcoming).

9. Anninos in Beck, p. 100.

10. *New York Times*, 3 May 1896.

11. Robertson, 'The Olympic Games', p. 957.

12. Oikonomou, *Vikelas*, p. 493, quotes the King's words of thanks, 'I thank you, Vikelas, for your initiative. At first I was terrified by your idea, but the successful results show that you were right …', suggesting that it was not the King who put up Vikelas to propose Athens as host city.

13. *The Times*, 30 April 1896, reprinted in *Olympism*, p. 363, which wrongly attributes it to the *New York Times*. The original is in French and is dated 23 April. I have modified the translation.

14. Oikonomou, *Vikelas*, pp. 496–7.

15. Vikelas letter to Coubertin, 19 May 1896, in French: copies in File 791, Vikelas archive, National Library of Greece.

16. Oikonomou, *Vikelas*, pp. 497–8.

Chapter 13: Greek Epilogue

1. Yiannoulopoulos, *I Evgeni mas Typhlosis*, p. 163, quoting Metaxas's enthusiastic reaction from Nauplion.

2. Yiannoulopoulos, ibid., argues in this sense.

3. Churchill's letter of 25 February 1897, in Randolph Churchill, *Winston Spencer Churchill*, vol. 1, *Youth*, p. 315.

4. Vikelas, 'O Polemos tou 1897 (The War of 1897)', *Complete Works*, vol. 1, pp. 270–73, a long and important memoir which was found among his papers at his death.

5. Rostand, 'Pour la Grèce', *Le Cantique de l'aile*, Paris, 1922, pp. 29–30, quoted by Sophie Basch, *Le Mirage Grec*, Athens, 1995, pp. 298–9: for example:

Et c'est pourquoi mandons le salut le plus ample
A celui qui fouetta nos langueurs d'un exemple
A Georges de Holstein-Glucksbourg, prince danois,
Prince Hamlet qui devient le plus actif des rois,
Qui semble nous crier: 'Les routes sont faciles
Des pâles Elseneurs aux rouges Thermopyles!'
Prince qui, s'il pouvait, hier encore, parfois,
Garder peut-être un peu de l'accent de sa mère,
Parle aujourd'hui le grec avec l'accent d'Homère.

'And so let us render the most ample greeting / To him who whipped us out of our inertia by his example / To George of Holstein-Glucksberg, prince of Denmark, / Prince Hamlet who has become the most active of kings, / Who seems to cry out to us: "The ways are easy / From pale Elsinores to blood-red Thermopylaes!" / Prince who, if sometimes in the past / He still kept perhaps a little of the accent of his mother, / Today speaks Greek with the accent of Homer.'

6. Randolph Churchill, *Winston Spencer Churchill*, p. 341; Winston Churchill's letter to his mother of 21 April 1897.

7. Stephen Crane, *Reports of War: War Dispatches*, vol. 9 of the *Works of Stephen Crane*, University of Virginia Press, 1971, p. 57; all other quotations are from the same. Crane acquired a puppy behind the Greek lines and called it Velestino after one of the engagements of the war.

8. Yiannoulopoulos, *I Evgeni mas Typhlosis*, pp. 162–3, describes the breakdown of order in Athens on 28 and 29 April, with quotations from the British Ambassador's reports.

9. Vikelas, 'The War of 1897', pp. 251–346.

10. Article by Palamas, first published in *Estia*, 1892, reprinted in Vikelas, *Apanta* (*Complete Works*), ed. Angelou, vol. i, pp. 353–8.

11. Letter of 1 April 1913 from Sir Francis Elliot, British Minister, to Sir Edward Grey, quoted in Hugo Vickers, *Alice: Princess Andrew of Greece*, London, 2000, p. 105.

12. Koula Xiradaki, *I Athina prin ekato Chronia* (*Athens One Hundred Years Ago: a Literary Stroll*), Athens, 1982, p. 157.

13. Constantine is a figure somewhat neglected by modern historians, and caricatured by contemporaries as either a saint or a devil (the obverse of the treatment accorded to Venizelos). There is no modern biography. There is a good section on the cult of Venizelos and Constantine in George Th. Mavrogordatos, *Stillborn Republic: Social Coalitions and Party Strategies in Greece, 1922–1936*, Berkeley/London, 1983, pp. 55–64.

14. Vickers, *Alice: Princess Andrew of Greece*, describes the strange course of Alice's life and marriage.

15. Lambros, 'Timoleon Philemon,' in *Logoi kai Arthra (Speeches and Articles) 1878–1902*, pp. 597–606.

Chapter 14: Athletic Epilogue

1. Horton, *Modern Athens*, pp. 18–19.

2. Don C. Skemer, 'The Garrett Collection Revisited', *Princeton Library Chronicle*, vol. 56, no. 3, spring 1995. The collection includes the largest collection in the western hemisphere of Islamic and Ethiopian mss., a fine collection of European medieval and renaissance mss., and Coptic, Syriac, Samaritan, Byzantine, Old Church Slavonic, Armenian, Georgian and Hebrew mss.; Babylonian clay tablets and Egyptian papyri; Indic, East Asian and South East Asian mss.; mss. in Maya and other indigenous languages of the Americas.

3. Garrett to President John Grier Hibben, 26 October 1931, copied to Joseph E. Raycroft, in Raycroft papers, Mudd Library, Princeton University, folder of Raycroft's correspondence with Garrett, 1912–50.

4. MacAloon, *This Great Symbol*, p. 6. MacAloon extracts as much significance as he possibly can from the occasion – too much in some respects (e.g. Prince Paul's military uniform).

5. K. Svolopoulos, *K. Karamanlis: Archeio, Gegonota, Keimena (C. Karamanlis: Archive, Events and Texts)*, 12 vols., Athens, 1996, vol. 9, pp. 269–70; Karamanlis to Lord Killanin, 29 July 1976 (text in Greek: English translations of the correspondence with Killanin are in the

Karamanlis archive at the Constantinos G. Karamanlis Foundation, Athens).

6. Lord Killanin, *My Olympic Years,* London, 1983, pp. 147–9.
7. Svolopoulos, *K. Karamanlis,* vol. 11, pp. 375–7; Karamanlis letters of 28 and 29 January 1980 to Killanin.
8. Killanin's replies of 4 February to Karamanlis's two letters: ibid., pp. 377–8.

Chapter 15: 2004

1. Eleana Yalouri, *The Acropolis: Global Fame, Local Claim,* Oxford/New York, 2001, pp. 86–7, for the complex of feelings of Greeks about what was perceived as a slight on the nation.
2. For the history and ideology of November 17, see George Kassimeris, *Europe's Last Red Terrorists: the Revolutionary Organization 17 November,* London, 2001, written before the murder of Brigadier Saunders and the 'endgame'; Alexis Papachelas and Tasos Telloglou, *17: Phakelos 17 Noemvri (17: the 17 November File),* Athens, 2002.

INDEX

(Entries in bold type refer to illustrations.)

Finally, a gift that challenges the status quo

2014 2015 2016 2017 2018 2019

We hope you enjoy this unconventionally romantic gift of a Guardian Weekly subscription, bought for you by the special person in your life. Handpicked from that week's The Guardian and The Observer, we collect the best news and stories from all over the world, and present them in one beautifully designed package you can really take your time over.

Dear